S. Middiman sc.

TRAVELLING

Recent Reviews of other Odyssey Guides...

"Thorough and beautifully illustrated, this book is a comprehensive—and fun—window into Afghan history, culture, and traditions. A must have for travel readers and a gripping read for anyone with even a passing interest in Afghanistan."
—Khaled Hosseini, author of *The Kite Runner*—

"...for coverage of Chongqing and the Gorges, and of the more placid and historically notable sites below Yichang and downriver to Shanghai, it is unrivalled..."
—*Simon Winchester*—

"It is one of those rare travel guides that is a joy to read whether or not you are planning a trip..."
—*The New York Times*—

"...Essential traveling equipment for anyone planning a journey of this kind..."
—*Asian Wall Street Journal*—

"If travel books came with warnings, the one for AFGHANISTAN: A COMPANION AND GUIDE would read, 'Caution: may inspire actual voyage.' But then, this lavishly produced guide couldn't help do otherwise—especially if you're partial to adventure."
—*TIME*, August 22nd 2005—

"Above all, it is authoritative and as well-informed as only extensive travels inside the country can make it. It is strong on the history. In particular the synopsis at the beginning is a masterly piece of compression."
—*The Spectator* (UK)—

"A gem of a book"
—*The Literary Review* (UK)—

"...Quite excellent. No one should visit Samarkand, Bukhara or Khiva without this meticulously researched guide..."
—*Peter Hopkirk, author of* The Great Game—

"The Yangzi guide is terrific"
—*Longitude Books*—

"...The bible of Bhutan guidebooks..."
—*Travel & Leisure*—

"...It's a superb book, superbly produced, that makes me long to go back to China..."
—*John Julius Norwich*—

"...Odyssey fans tend to be adventurous travelers with a literary bent. If you're lucky enough to find an Odyssey Guide to where you're going, grab it..."
—*National Geographic Traveler*—

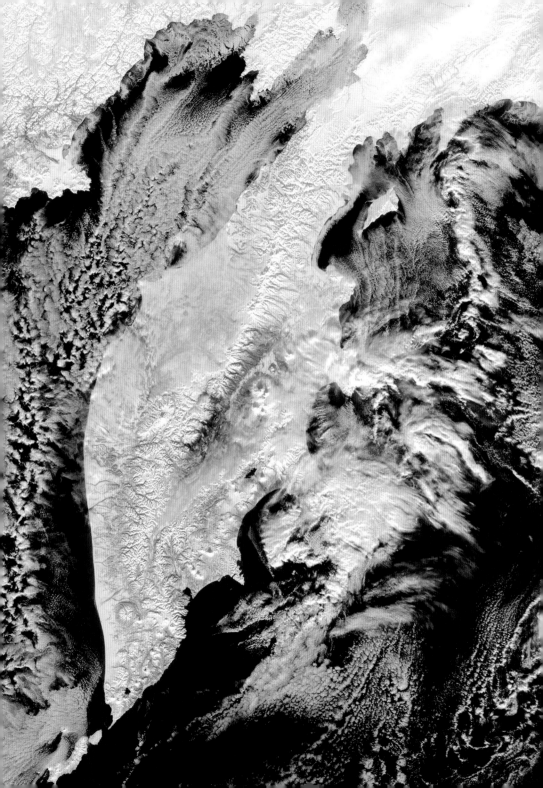

ODYSSEY BOOKS & GUIDES

Odyssey Books & Guides is a division of Airphoto International Ltd.
903 Seaview Commercial Building, 21–24 Connaught Road West, Sheung Wan, Hong Kong
Tel: (852) 2856-3896; Fax: (852) 2565-8004
E-mail: sales@odysseypublications.com; www.odysseypublications.com

Distribution in the USA by W.W. Norton & Company, Inc., 500 Fifth Avenue, New York, NY 10110, USA
Tel: 800-233-4830; Fax: 800-458-6515; www.wwnorton.com

Distribution in the UK and Europe by Cordee Books and Maps, 3a De Montfort St., Leicester, LE1 7HD, UK Tel: 0116-254-3579; Fax: 0116-247-1176; www.cordee.co.uk

Kamchatka, First Edition

ISBN-13: 978-962-217-780-2   Library of Congress Catalog Card Number has been requested.

Copyright © 2007 Airphoto International Ltd.
Maps Copyright © 2007 Airphoto International Ltd.

Front cover photography: Daisy Gilardini
Photography/illustrations courtesy of Tina Billeter 217; Central Navy Museum, St Petersburg 88; Jacques Descloitres, MODIS Land Rapid Response Team, NASA/GSFC 1; Fergus Crystal 223, 224, 225, 226; Daisy Gilardini 11, 30, 58, 63, 82, 96, 99, 101, 104, 106, 120, 127, 132, 134, 135, 137, 138, 143, 149, 187, 208-209, 212-213, 243, 298; Diana Gleadhill 50, 51, 53, 54, 55, 56, 61, 66, 70, 71, 73, 78, 79, 80, 81, 109, 110, 111 (top), 121, 140, 141, 142, 156, 161, 194, 201, 204, 205, 207, 215, 218, 221, 231, 233, 235, 259, 264, 265, 266, 267, 270; Paul Harris 4-5, 6, 14-15, 114-115, 130-131, 145, 147, 150, 153, 154, 170, 188, 228, 237, 238, 240, 249, 275; Zhenya Krasnokutsky 85, 196, 197; NASA Blue Marble 36; NASA/JPL 87; NASA/JPL/NIMA 33, 125; NASA Landsat Program and the Global Land Cover Facility (www.landcover.org) 52, 190; Andrei Nechayev 256, 262; Sergei Polushin 18, 21, 22, 25, 29, 39, 65, 67, 68, 69, 72, 75, 77, 92-93, 95, 103, 111 (bottom), 118, 122, 123, 159, 199, 260, 269, 272-273, 282, 284, 289, 295; State Library of Victoria 45, 48-49, 164-165, 171 (and inside front cover), 177, 181 (and inside back cover), 185, 251, 255, 303.

Archive maps on pages 41, 89 and 91 photographed from the *Atlas of Kamchatka Region History* issued by the Far Eastern Aero Geodesic Enterprise and Kamchatka Mapping Center. Illustrations on pages 35, 128, 183 and 306 scanned from postcards issued by the Museum of Archeology and Ethnology of the Institute of History of Peoples of the Far East. The publisher has made every effort to obtain express permission of all copyright holders and to give proper attribution wherever possible; any omission of credit in whole or in part is unintentional.

Managing Editor: Jeremy Tredinnick
Design: Sarah Lock
Cover design: Sarah Lock and Au Yeung Chui Kwai
Maps: On The Road Cartography

Production and printing by Twin Age Ltd, Hong Kong
E-mail: twinage@netvigator.com
Manufactured in China

(Preceding page) A true colour satellite image of Kamchatka in the grip of winter.
(Following pages) A close bond exists between Kamchatka's northern ethnic groups and their reindeer; the rivers and surrounding ocean of this fertile volcanic land teem with fish.

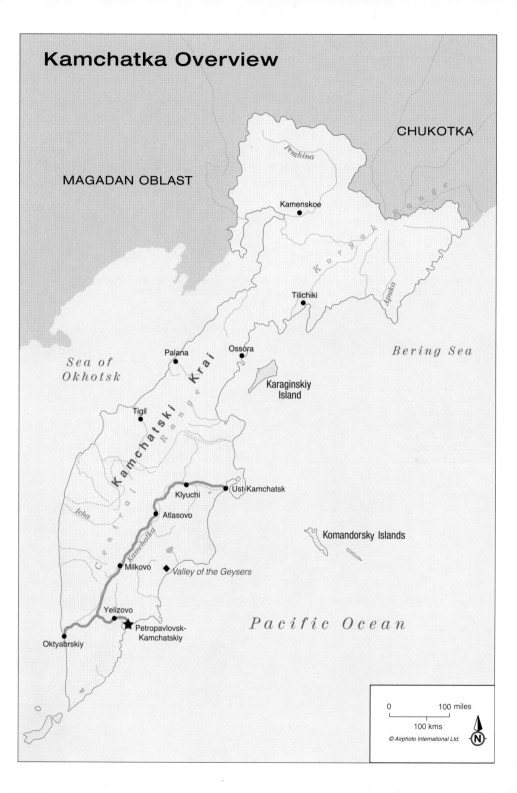

Kamchatka Overview

CHUKOTKA

MAGADAN OBLAST

Penzhina

● Kamenskoe

Koryak Range

Apuka

● Tilichiki

Bering Sea

Palana ●

Sea of Okhotsk

● Ossora

Kamchatski Krai

Range

Karaginskiy
Island

Tigil ●

Kamchatski Range

Icha

● Klyuchi

Ust-Kamchatsk ●

Central

● Atlasovo

Kamchatka

Komandorsky Islands

● Milkovo

◆ *Valley of the Geysers*

Yelizovo ●

Pacific Ocean

★ Petropavlovsk-
Kamchatskiy

Oktyabrskiy ●

0	100 miles

100 kms

© *Airphoto International Ltd.*

N

Kamchatka

A Journal & Guide to
Russia's Land of Ice and Fire

Diana Gleadhill

DEDICATION

For Joal and Eve in Kenya, Erin in Ireland and Pasha in Kamchatka.

ACKNOWLEDGEMENTS

Here is the most satisfactory part of writing this book – showing my appreciation of all the people who have helped in its production, and without whom it simply couldn't have been possible. If there are any omissions, please forgive me. Thank you.

Elise Coburn: I never cease to appreciate how lucky I am to have such a great travelling companion! We have laughed and cried together at so many shared experiences. Thanks also for your photographs and constant support throughout the writing of the book.

Chris Stillman: For reading my original sketchy diary of Kamchatka and encouraging me to try and get it published – *it's all your fault Chris!* Also for writing the Foreword/Geology section.

Magnus Bartlett: My publisher, who also read the original diary and somehow saw enough in it to encourage me to find out *a lot* more about Kamchatka. Your constant enthusiasm and encouragement during the first tentative stages have resulted in sending me on this amazing literary learning curve.

Jeremy Tredinnick: My editor, who in the later stages kept my nose to the grindstone – the "carrot and stick" approach.

Sarah Lock: For having such a great affinity with me, and doing such a wonderful job designing the book.

David Jeffrey: Who, although very unwell and with little or no eyesight, managed, with the help of his wife and daughter to write his expert piece about the Vegetation of Kamchatka.

Josh Newell: For your academic knowledge of and interest in a Foreseeable Sustainable Future for Kamchatka, thank you for writing this piece.

Fergus Crystal: For your lovely piece and photographs about the Birds of Kamchatka.

Daisy Gilardini: For your beautiful photographs. It was a lucky meeting and an incredible experience for us both in 2000 at the Even reindeer herders' camp.

Paul Harris: For your lovely photographs.

Andrei Nechayev: For the amazing photographs of the "Eruption of the Century".

Billy Chittick: For your zany good humour when asked on countless occasions to print and enhance our photographs.

Valentina Zukovskaya: For being such a brilliant guide, cook and translator on our first trip to Kamchatka.

Lisa Strecher, ethnography student at University of Hamburg: For your enormous help with ethnographic advice and contacting Lydia Chechoolina.

Lydia Chechoolina: For your fascinating, touching story about Life Among the Koryak.

Michael McCracken: For translating Lydia's text.

Paul Craven from Steppes Travel: For advice in Facts for the Traveller.

Robert from Avacha Bay Co: For advice and contacts in Kamchatka (www.avachabay.com).

To my family, friends and Sam for putting up with my mumbling on for the past year and a half about "The Book".

And last but not least, my thanks to three young Russian friends who became so intrigued with the idea of an Irishwoman writing a book about Kamchatka, that they gave freely and unstintingly of their time.

Tatiana Boyko: For being our guide in Petropavlovsk in 2006, and for almost single-handedly writing Facts for the Traveller (kamboiko@mail.ru).

Zhenya Krasnokutsky: For spending your leave running round Petropavlovsk looking for "permissions" for old maps and books – you now know about copyright! Also for your photos, translating and general enthusiasm. Good luck with your new travel business "Kamchatka Sun" (www.kamchatka-sun.ru, info@kamchatka-sun.ru, kaa10@list.ru).

Sergei Polushin: It was hard to choose from the dozens of beautiful photos you so generously gave me. Sergei now runs a service for visitors. He has a reliable 4WD vehicle, has a profound knowledge of the geology and flora of Kamchatka and will take you to dizzying heights to get "just the right camera shot" (sphoto@mail.kamchatka.ru).

And finally to the people of Kamchatka, forgive me for any inconsistencies or omissions – they are totally unintentional.

Contents

In today's post-perestroika world, old traditions still survive thanks to young people who
are fascinated by the dances and songs of their ancestors.

(Following pages) Local dance company Mengo used to travel around the winter camps providing entertainment in remote parts of Kamchatka. Since the fall of the Soviet Union they have also begun travelling both nationally and internationally to carry on the tradition of Kamchatka's tribal and traditional song and dance.

INTRODUCTION

At the tender age of 11 I was sent to boarding school in the south of England, in those days a ship's voyage and two train journeys away from Northern Ireland and home. It might just as well have been the end of the world as far as I was concerned, and paradoxically, in view of this story, I was pathetically homesick.

There were, however, two bright extenuating circumstances in my sad and tearful little life – one was athletics training, and the other was Miss Margaret Gifford from Dublin, my housemistress and geography teacher. She was a strict disciplinarian and did not suffer fools gladly, but she had a great sense of humour and was a wonderful teacher, whose enthusiasm for her subject made the world seem a magical and exciting place. It was, without doubt, under her tutelage that the seeds were sown for my wanderlust and curiosity about other peoples and places.

On leaving school – with good grades in Geography – I did indeed work in Belgium and the United States, the latter leading me on into Mexico. However, marriage beckoned and children followed with the inevitable years of upbringing, and travel became an odd dash to the sun for a "toes-up" fortnight of relaxation. So it wasn't until my children became more or less independent that travel became, again, a possibility.

I had been going skiing with my childhood friend, Elise, for some years, when one year, on the flight to Geneva, I voiced the throwaway line, "this year the Alps, next year the Himalayas".

"You're on," was the inevitable reply. And so it was that in 1984 we had a wonderful time trekking and river rafting in Nepal.

There followed very successful jaunts, twice to South America, several times to Africa where my son lives, and an incredible trip in Papua New Guinea, until in 1991 with "perestroika" and more relaxed conditions, the way became clear to visit the erstwhile Soviet bloc countries.

I had, for a long time, wanted to visit Mongolia and could just picture myself riding heroically across the endless steppe on one of the hardy little Mongolian horses, and so a trip was organized to go on the Trans Mongolian Express, from Irkutsk, through Mongolia to China in 1996. Then, in 1998, we experienced a magical journey from Peshawar in northern Pakistan, over the Kunjerab Pass into China, and on over the Torugart Pass into the gerrymandered area loosely known as Central Asia. We explored Kyrgyzstan, then travelled west into Uzbekistan and the Fergana Valley, Samarkand and Bukhara. This last adventure was probably the most politically and ethnically interesting of our journeys.

By 2000 we had now become really involved with the former Soviet Union; I was particularly interested in the politics and people, and wanted to find out more about how country people – or as they say, the "grass roots" folk – were coping, so with very little knowledge of the country . . . Kamchatka beckoned.

ICE & FIRE: AN INTRODUCTION TO
THE GEOLOGY AND NATURAL HISTORY OF THE KAMCHATKA PENINSULA

By Chris Stillman, Professor and Fellow Emeritus, Trinity College Dublin

A huge sulphurous fumerole draws visitors on the slopes of Mutnovsky Volcano.

A land of spectacular wild beauty – of mountains raising their gleaming white heads into a cerulean blue sky, of hillsides covered in a profusion of wildflowers, of stretches of Siberian "taiga", of rivers fringed by reeds and woodlands, of forests of birch and conifer, this is the Kamchatka Peninsula in summer. A projection of land 800 miles (1,280 kilometres) long and 250 miles (400 kilometres) wide at its broadest, shaped

like a leaf-bladed spear from ancient times, shafted northward into the Koryak Mountains of eastern Siberia and southward plunging into the cold waters of the Seas of Okhotsk and Bering, while further south, like drops of blood dripping from the tip of the blade, the string of volcanic islands called the Kurils dot the icy ocean.

What a place to visit for the nature lover who has seen the world and seeks a piquant difference. Reindeer, herded and hunted by tribesmen, browse through a land alive with the heartbeat of active volcanoes and geysers, steaming springs and bubbling mud pools, mountains which erupt with uncertain frequency, throwing ash into the air and pouring red fire, quickly congealing to black lava, down the mountainsides. Brown bears and wolves hunt through the woodland, and sea eagles circle the heights. Rare grey whales and enormous numbers of seals and sea lions inhabit the coastal waters, and wild salmon and otters the rivers. But beware: come to visit only during the few brief months of summer – from June to September – for the winter here is long, hard and unforgiving, and the mountains are lost in the snows and blizzards which every year replenish their ice caps and power their glaciers. Though lying at a similar latitude to Great Britain, cold arctic winds from the Siberian Anticyclone combined with the cold Oya-Shio sea current result in a far colder and longer winter, the peninsula being snow-covered from October to late May. Consequently the tops of the mountains are covered with permanent ice caps, and glaciers flow down their upper slopes.

Perhaps it provides a special attraction for those who seek the lonely places, but it must be admitted, Kamchatka is hard to reach; it is as far east as one can go in the Russian Federation, and is incredibly remote from Russia's main population centres with their road and rail networks. It lies east of the Kolyma mountain chain that marks the eastern edge of Siberia, and is accessible only by air or sea. But for intrepid travellers such as Diana and Elise, it is well worth the effort.

A peninsula comparable in size to Japan, which lies 600 miles (960 kilometres) to the south, it has only a tiny fraction of that nation's population. It does possess considerable potential for mineral, oil and gas wealth, but this is barely exploited, due to the lack of roads, and severe winter conditions. During the 20th century, most of the urban activity was centred on the large military and naval establishment of the Soviet Eastern Command, and today most of the sparse population live near this in the regional capital, Petropavlovsk, situated on its southeastern shore. The rest of the people, many still living a traditional way of life, live in scattered villages and very small towns, few of which can be reached by paved roads. Sadly the larger centres are disfigured by the drab concrete structures – tenements, shops and public buildings – typical of the Soviet period, but efforts are being made, since the political changes that brought about the formation of the Russian Federation, to provide a vestigial tourist infrastructure and to encourage the local people to welcome visitors into their homes. The rewards are great for visitors who love the open country, grandiloquent volcanic scenery, and are attracted by the traditional lives of hunters, herders and fishermen.

Kamchatka is undoubtedly a mecca for earth scientists. Geologically it is extremely active, dominated by earthquakes and volcanic activity. Part of the Pacific "Ring of Fire" – a volcanic girdle around the ocean caused by the Pacific Ocean plate being pushed under the surrounding continents – the Kamchatka mountains are but part of a chain of volcanoes that continue southward along the Pacific margin through the Kuril Islands and on through Japan. Northwestwards the volcanoes continue along

Richly hued rocks augment the already impressive view from Avachinsky Volcano.

the line of the Aleutian Islands and on to Alaska.

All the hills of Kamchatka are volcanic in origin, associated with the subduction zones. The line of western hills are extinct volcanoes and markedly older. The eastern hills are active volcanoes. All these are being studied and monitored by the Russian Academy of Science Institute for Volcanology in Petropavlovsk. One of their projects is to record the seismic activity from a series of active sites. When seismic activity is plotted for location and depth the resultant printout is a textbook illustration of the subduction zone.

To explain this, I must write a little of the geological structure of the Earth's crust. The solid ground on which we live is far from stable and unchanging; the crust is not a continuous skin like the rind of an orange, but is actually composed of a jigsaw of gigantic "plates", slabs of crust of various sizes, up to 60 kilometres thick and more or less rigid, which slowly move over a plastic underlay of partially melted rock known as the "mantle". Over millions of years the great crustal plates have moved relative to

A brave soul goes for an impromptu swim in the frigid glacier lake of Mutnovsky Volcano's crater.

one another, splitting apart in some places, colliding in others and sliding past one another elsewhere. These are separated from one another by fault lines, along which earthquakes and volcanoes are concentrated. The Pacific Ocean is one of the largest plates, and the Eurasian plate is another. The Pacific plate here in Kamchatka is moving northwest at about eight centimetres per year, pushing against the northeastern Russian section of the Eurasian continental plate. Where ocean plates collide with continental ones, a phenomenon known as subduction occurs. What happens is that the ocean floor, made almost entirely of a dense, dark-coloured volcanic rock called basalt, sinks below the lighter rocks of the continental crust, and is pushed down below the continent margin along a slope known as a subduction zone.

Kamchatka, along with the Kurils and Japan is located above one of the world's great examples of large-scale subduction, and the ocean plate pushing under the Eurasian continental plate causes stresses which repeatedly buckle and crack the crust, producing earthquakes and generating great heat which melts the lower crust and the rocks beneath – a melt which bursts through to the surface in volcanic eruptions along the length of this convergent plate boundary. The result is a chain of volcanoes, over 300 of them in Kamchatka alone, many of which are little over 20,000 years old. Twenty-nine are active today, and several small ash cones have appeared with little fuss in the last few years. Occasionally activity is more explosive, as was the case in 2000 on Mutnovsky Volcano, when a 500-metre-wide crater appeared in the middle of the glacier that occupies the caldera.

Though geologically active, the Kamchatka volcanoes have never imposed any serious danger on the inhabitants – they keep their explosive products within themselves. For example, Kluchevskoy Volcano, one of a group with Kamen, Bezymyany and Plosky Tolbachik, erupts on average every five years, though sometimes the eruptions take place annually, and occasionally last for a number of years. The more powerful explosions throw ash and gas to considerable heights, ash that does fall back on the surrounding countryside, but this has never posed a severe threat to the nearest town of Klyuchi, which is only 30 kilometres away. Sometimes they produce glowing rivers of lava, which flow down the slopes but congeal over quite short distances.

I once met a Russian volcanologist who had actually walked on one of these lava flows. What's more he had the photos taken by a colleague to prove it. He was attempting to measure both the speed of the lava flow, and its temperature – somewhere around 1,000 degrees – using a thermocouple on the end of a long pole. Finding he could not keep up with the speed of the flow by running over the rough ground alongside it, he jumped onto a cooling black congealed patch on its surface and was rafted along at the same speed as the flow. When I exclaimed that he must have burned his boots, he explained that he stood on one leg until the pain was too great then danced onto the other, and let the first foot cool before putting it down again! Eventually the raft came to the side of the flow and he was able to jump off. Devotion to science beyond the call of duty, I reckoned.

Because the volcanic heat persists in the ground for centuries, in many places ground water is heated to a high degree, bubbling up in hot springs, mud pools and geysers. Such a place is the Eurasian continent's only "Valley of the Geysers", which is found in the Kronotsky Reserve. Kronotsky Volcano is central to this great nature reserve in which almost all of Kamchatka's natural attractions can be found, and one of the most beautiful views of its geometrically regular white-capped cone can be seen reflected in the still waters of the peninsula's largest lake.

Farther north is Kluchevskoy Volcano, the largest active volcano in Eurasia. Along with its group of smaller volcanoes, they mark the meeting point of the Kuril-Kamchatsky volcanic chain (which stretches from Japan up along the Kuril Islands and southern Kamchatka) and the Aleutian volcanic chain (which is traced by the sweeping arc of the Aleutian Islands).

Another site calling out for eco-tourists is the Uzon Caldera, a huge hollow about 10 kilometres in diameter, which was created 40,000 years ago by a series of explosive eruptions and collapses, the last of which took place 8,500 years ago. The following centuries of intensive hydrothermal activity have developed a unique symbiosis of volcanic products and wildlife, a collection of everything that Kamchatka is famous for: hot springs and cold rivers, poisonous mud cauldrons and pure lakes full of fish, a tundra rich in arctic berries, birch forests, bogs and animals – including enormous bears, bighorn sheep and of course birds. It is a wonderland that draws scientists of almost every persuasion: geologists, botanists, geochemists, microbiologists . . .

In the hot springs natural minerals crystallise, and incredible algae and bacteria live in the scalding, sulphur-rich water. For the artist, the few short days of early autumn are the time to be here; the tundra is a bright scarlet in colour, the birches golden, the fumarolic steam rises in pillars to the blue sky . . . but with the first gusts of autumn storms the leaves fall, the tundra fades and only the mud cauldrons keep boiling a colourful paste.

One could go on for pages listing the fabulous volcanic features to be seen, but this would be wearisome for the eco-tourist reader, unless she or he had a single-minded devotion to such things. Diana and Elise had other amazing experiences to fuel their interest, and it will be for Diana to tell of them in this book.

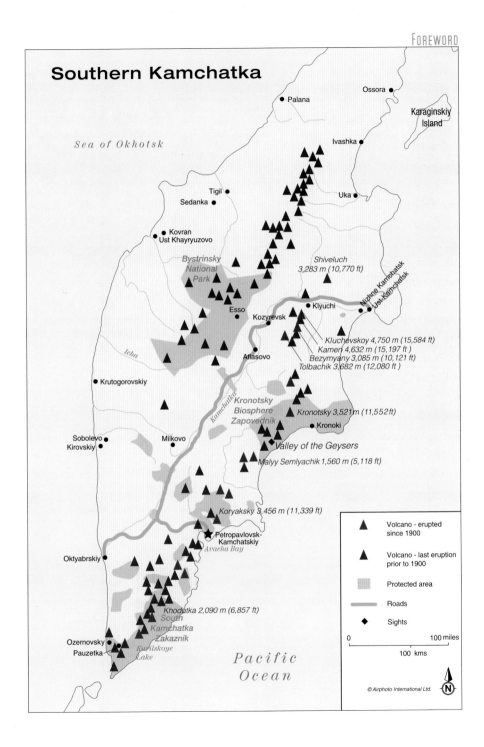

Southern Kamchatka

Ossora

Palana

Karaginskiy
Island

Sea of Okhotsk

Ivashka

Tigil

Sedanka

Uka

Kovran

Ust Khayryuzovo

*Bystrinsky
National
Park*

*Shiveluch
3,283 m (10,770 ft)*

Nizhne Kamchatsk
Ust-Kamchatsk

Esso

Klyuchi

Kozyrevsk

*Kluchevskoy 4,750 m (15,584 ft)
Kamen 4,632 m (15,197 ft)
Bezymyany 3,085 m (10,121 ft)
Tolbachik 3,682 m (12,080 ft)*

Atlasovo

Icha

Krutogorovskiy

*Kronotsky
Biosphere
Zapovednik*

Kamchatka

Kronotsky 3,521m (11,552ft)

Kronoki

Sobolevo
Kirovskiy

Milkovo

Valley of the Geysers

Malyy Semlyachik 1,560 m (5,118 ft)

Koryaksky 3,456 m (11,339 ft)

Petropavlovsk-
Kamchatskiy
Avacha Bay

Oktyabrskiy

Khodutka 2,090 m (6,857 ft)

*South
Kamchatka
Zakaznik*

Ozernovsky
Pauzetka

*Kurilskoye
Lake*

*Pacific
Ocean*

▲	Volcano - erupted since 1900
▲	Volcano - last eruption prior to 1900
	Protected area
	Roads
◆	Sights

0   100 miles

100 kms

© Airphoto International Ltd.

N

KAMCHATKA'S ACTIVE VOLCANOES

Volcano	Last erupted	Height	
Avachinsky	1991	2,751m	9,026ft
Bezymyany	2006	2,869m	9,413ft
Bolshoy Semyachik	Unknown	1,739m	5,706ft
Dzenzur	Unknown	1,262m	4,141ft
Gamchen	Unknown	2,576m	8,451ft
Gorely	1986	1,829m	6,001ft
Ichinsky	Unknown	3,607m	11,835ft
Ilinsky	1901	1,577m	5,174ft
Kambalny	Unknown	2,161m	7,090ft
Karimsky	2003	1,468m	4,817ft
Kikhpinych	Unknown	1,552m	5,092ft
Kizimen	1928	2,375m	7,792ft
Kluchevskoy	2004	4,750m	15,585ft
Komarova	Unknown	2,050m	6,726ft
Koryaksky	1957	3,456m	11,339ft
Kosheleva	End of 17th century	1,853m	6,079ft
Krasheninikov	Unknown	1,856m	6,090ft
Kronotsky	1923	3,521m	11,552ft
Ksudach	1907	1,079m	3,540ft
Maly Semyachik	1854	1,563m	5,128ft
Mutnovsky	2001	2,323m	7,618ft
Novy Tolbachik	1976	Series of volcanic cones	
Opala	1894	2,460m	8,071ft
Plosky Tolbachik	1976	3,085m	10,122ft
Shiveluch	2003	2,800m	9,187ft
Ushkovsky	1890	3,943m	12,937ft
Uzon Geyser	1986	n/a	
Zheltovsky	1923	1,956m	6,421ft
Zhupanovsky	1957	2,923m	9,590ft

Sulphur rocks on Avachinsky Volcano add fantastic colour to the landscape.

Northern Kuril Island's Active Volcanoes

Volcano	Last erupted	Height	
Alaid	1986	2,339m	7,674ft
Ehbeko	1991	1,156m	3,793ft
Chikurachki	2002	1,816m	5,958ft
Fuss	1854	1,772m	5,814ft
Karpinskovo	1952	1,345m,	4,413ft
Tatarinova	17th century	1,530m	5,020ft

Touching Kamchatka

We arrive in Kamchatka. Paratunka. Avacha Bay

Why on Earth did we choose to go to Kamchatka? Not only did Elise and I ask ourselves this question, but so did everyone else. Having had one very successful and interesting trip to Russia, Mongolia and China via the Trans Siberian Railway, and another to Central Asia, I wanted to see more of post-Soviet Russia. Kamchatka, being so far east of Moscow and European Russia, seemed an interesting place where we might try and discover how people were coping with "perestroika". I had had a bit of a dodgy back in the past year or so, and Elise admitted to having sore knees from time to time! We had sworn in 1984, after camping in Nepal, that although the walking was fine, hard nights in a tent were perhaps not for us. Yet, here we were, 16 years older, attempting to do a great deal of camping, and in Russia for-bye, where we knew not what the food and general conditions would be like.

I had read an article in *National Geographic* magazine in 1994 about Kamchatka's volcanoes, its pristine wilderness, its bears and the indigenous reindeer herders of the country. It had been totally closed to foreigners, and indeed to the Russian people for many years of Soviet rule, the country being turned into a Cold War fortress of tracking stations, and it is only since perestroika that the outside world has discovered its existence.

Kamchatka is a 1,000-kilometre-long peninsula in Russia's Far East, attached to mainland Russia at about 62 degrees north at Penzhino Bay, separated from the mainland by the Sea of Okhotsk, nine time zones east of Moscow, and part of the Pacific's "Ring of Fire". It was the southern half of Kamchatka that we intended to visit. Apart from an

The remains of a bear's breakfast at the foot of Kronotsky Volcano.

amazing 160 volcanoes, about 30 of which are active, the country is covered by mixed forests, grassland and tundra, and home to a great assortment of wildlife, including brown bear, reindeer, snow sheep, sable, beaver, otter, ermine and marmot. The rivers teem with salmon and trout and here is where the wonderful Steller's sea eagle makes its home. The population is only about 380,000, at least two-thirds of whom live in the capital, Petropavlovsk-Kamchatskiy, more commonly known as "PK" or Petropavlovsk.

The person credited with "discovering" Kamchatka, travelling overland in 1696 from Anadyr, was Vladimir Atlasov, who brought with him a group of 65 Cossacks and 60 Yukaghir natives to fully explore the country. However, the existence of the Kamchatka Peninsula was already known to Russia with explorers such as Ivan Kamchatiy and Ivan Rubetz having brought back stories of a land rich in fish and fur. There is also some evidence that other Russians had arrived in Kamchatka by boat and who lived peaceably among the local people until jealousies arose over these strangers sleeping with the local girls. According to the story, the inhabitants agreed with one another to murder the Russians while they slept, and so temporarily rid themselves of their invaders.

Atlasov, like almost all explorers of the time, was hopeful of finding a new land that he could exploit, and thus he established two bases on the Kamchatka River from where the Russian traders who followed him were able to extract tithes of furs from the local people. It wasn't long before the doubtful peace between the Cossacks and the "Itelmen" came to an end when the Cossacks went into the nearest villages, and with brute force robbed and plundered everything they found. They took the sons of the houses as servants, and stole sable and fox pelts.

During the ensuing years uprisings were common between the native Koryak, Chukchi and Itelmen and their self-appointed Russian overlords, and in the rebellion of 1731 the Cossacks regrouped and with cannon and firearms totally overwhelmed the native people. Their numbers were greatly diminished, from approximately 20,000 at the beginning of the 18th century to an estimated – and shocking – 8,000 by the 1750s.

Today, the remnants of the Koryak people mostly live in the Koryaki Autonomous Okrug, or region on the northwest coast of the peninsula around their capital, Palana, while the Chukchi inhabit the desolate north of the country. The Itelmen, or Kamchadals, are greatly integrated with the Russians and mostly inhabit the south of the peninsula. The fourth indigenous group are the Even people, who live around Esso in the Bystrinsky area in the middle of the peninsula, descendants of the Evenki who arrived here around 150 years ago from the Sakha Republic to the northeast of Kamchatka. It is quite evident

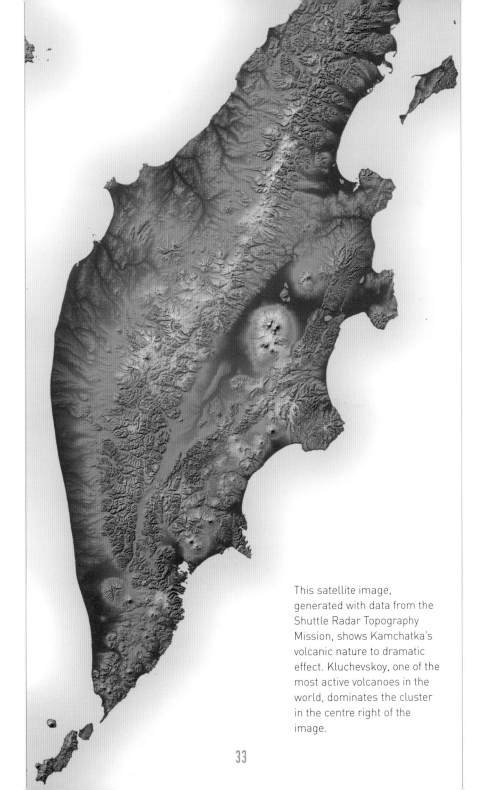

This satellite image, generated with data from the Shuttle Radar Topography Mission, shows Kamchatka's volcanic nature to dramatic effect. Kluchevskoy, one of the most active volcanoes in the world, dominates the cluster in the centre right of the image.

that these reindeer herding peoples from the north still have much more in common, culturally, visually and geographically with the Inuit people across the Bering Strait in Alaska, than with a Russian administration emanating from Moscow.

Kamchatka, being so far away from European Russia, and indeed even from eastern Siberia, was considered the most inhospitable part of the Russian Empire and when Russia sold Alaska to the Americans in 1867 the country might well have been on the market if the Americans had shown any interest. There was one American named Washington Baker Vanderlip who did show some interest and was offered a 60-year concession by Lenin, but the two men couldn't agree on the minutiae of the deal and it never went through. During the Cold War, Kamchatka became an important strategic base and was consequently off-limits to any foreign interest.

Nobody we knew had heard of Kamchatka, and the travel company we used admittedly knew very little about it. We couldn't find any contemporary information on the country except for Christina Dodwell's fascinating, post-perestroika book *Beyond Siberia*, published in 1993, which described her journeys in northern Kamchatka staying with the Koryak people and which we read several times; the seven pages in the Lonely Planet guidebook dedicated to Kamchatka; and of course the original piece in *National Geographic*. (I still had not quite come to terms with the celebrated Internet). As luck would have it, a good friend, the professor emeritus of geology at Trinity College Dublin showed us a wonderful video of the "Valley of the Geysers" taken by a colleague, Professor Adrian Phillips, who had done some research a few years previously in Kamchatka. We were advised not to leave it too late in the year as the country is completely snow-bound from October until about May.

Apart from this information, we knew very little about where we were going or what it would be like in present-day Kamchatka. We just knew that it seemed remote and untouched by tourists. Elise and I were both very keen to see the infamous bears which seemed so plentiful, and I was particularly interested to meet, and possibly stay with some of the local people as well as the reindeer herders. If we were ever going to go there, it had better be sooner rather than later.

And as for you, my reader, why not come with us on our adventure. Give me your hand and I will take you to touch on an extraordinary country; a place where bears and reindeer roam; where indigenous people live in harmony with nature; a wild and fiery land – Kamchatka – at the far eastern extreme of Russia.

A beautiful postcard illustration of Even women and children
– with their treasured reindeer in the background.

Sticking out into the North Pacific, the Kamchatka Peninsula, along with the Aleutian Islands that sweep west from Alaska and the Kuril Islands that march south to Japan, mark the northern border of the Pacific Ring of Fire.

MOSCOW. MOSKVA HOTEL. 22 AUGUST 2000

It is pouring tonight in Moscow – thunder, lightning and torrential rain. We watched it from our hotel window having eaten deliciously at an outdoor café, with good Russian beer, *blinis*, all the while listening to an excellent saxophonist. What was more, the girls serving us were smiling and friendly. Now that was an improvement on the last time we were here. The girl who collected us at the airport gave us directions to a different restaurant, but somehow we got them wrong, and wandered around for a while looking for the place. In fact, at that time it was a gorgeous evening, and it was exciting to be in Red Square with St Basil's floodlit, so we rather enjoyed our little perambulation.

As usual, the wait going through passport control had been dreadful, terribly slow with everyone seeming grumpy and unhelpful. Our hotel is huge and soulless – really pretty horrible, but again we think the staff are just slightly more tourist-friendly than when we were here four years ago – and as we won't be here for long it does us OK. We think Moscow itself also seems a little different than the last time, maybe a bit more cosmopolitan, or maybe it's just that we have had a beer and are on holiday. We'll see tomorrow as we have half a day to ourselves to take a look around.

PARATUNKA. HOTEL HELIOS. 24 AUGUST

We've lost a day somewhere! We are now 12 hours ahead of the UK. And here we are safe and sound in Kamchatka – hurray!

Our flight from Moscow was from the domestic airport Sherematova 1 and was delayed by two hours. We had no idea what was being announced on the tannoy so I can only imagine we must have appeared rather "pale and sadly loitering", but a young priest who told us he was collecting alms for "the oldest church in Russia" befriended us and told us in quite good English when to go through to security (if you want to call it that!). Here we sat for some time until there was another announcement and many of our companions jumped up and started pushing towards the door. Nothing daunted we joined in and on producing our boarding passes were told in a scathing, guttural voice, "You are not for Minsk!" A lucky escape; thank goodness they do actually look at your boarding pass.

By this time we had lost our precious hard wooden seats so decided to have an ice cream. We stood and waited until eventually the girl at the kiosk took some notice of us. Unsmiling and without a word she took our money while we pointed to the ice cream we wanted and waited for our change. She went into reams of abuse at our money. We assumed, of course, that it was too large a denomination, but we had nothing smaller. We tried smiling and doing our best to look cringing and apologetic, Elise grinning inanely and pulling her mouth with her fingers into a grotesque grin, but the salesgirl was not to be won over and went off to get change from another vendor – a metre away! I guess the average Russian doesn't have much to smile about, but I hope someday they will find it costs nothing, and may well gain a great deal. Our flight eventually left and was surprisingly good – being that we were now travelling Business Class – oh, the luxury of space, good food and vodka until it was coming out of our ears! I slept fairly well as is my wont, with poor Elise wide awake, flying the plane every mile of the journey.

As we approached Petropavlovsk we flew over Avacha Bay and a seemingly endless theatre of volcanoes. Taxiing in to the airport building we passed literally dozens of ancient propeller-driven aircraft, which looked like remnants of the last war. We disembarked and were met by a very pretty girl in a pale-blue mini skirt and high heels who introduced herself as Valentina, our guide and interpreter. She was accompanied by her father Nikolai, who would be our driver. Our luggage duly arrived on an ancient conveyor belt into a tin shed, just about big enough to hold the occupants of our flight! All the Russians' luggage was well protected, wrapped in cling-film or heavily taped with wide sticky tape; we knew nothing of these precautions and there was ours looking pristine and rather naked, but safe enough.

It had been raining but was by then clear and warm and we made our way outside, skipping over large, muddy puddles and piling into the car to drive the 35 kilometres here to our hotel in Paratunka, an area of geothermal springs. Our room is basic, even Spartan. Two narrow beds, two chairs and some hooks on the wall. The bathroom has no basin but the toilet and shower work. The corridors are painted bright pink and our room is papered. But there is no cupboard, mirror, pictures or mats. Why are we still surprised? The hotel is a two-storey concrete block. It is unbelievable to any uninitiated Westerner how this could possibly be a top-class tourist hotel – and the chosen one for us. However, Valentina is young, pretty and very cheerful, and the hotel staff appears to be also. The girl in the bar/canteen/dining room is drop-dead gorgeous. Tall and slim with peroxide blond hair, long clinging black dress slashed to the crotch showing gorgeous legs in high-heeled red shoes! She is all smiles, helpful and a total anachronism. She looks as though she is about to start work as a croupier in a high-class casino.

We were very tired, and after discussing what we would like for dinner – we jokingly suggested roast duck and garden peas, and for pudding we thought strawberries would be a good idea – we repaired to bed for a snooze. About an hour later, Valentina arrived back in our room with an enormous bucket of strawberries from her father's *dacha* (a Russian country house). We were quite embarrassed, having inadvertently said how much we liked strawberries, but how we will eat all of these I don't know. We'll probably both get spots and make ourselves sick, but my goodness, what a lovely gesture, bothering to go off into the garden and picking pounds of strawberries. I think we are going to like these people.

We had our sleep and dinner (which did not include roast duck) and then spent an hour in a warm, outdoor mineral pool. The pool and surroundings were very basic, none of your glamorous basket chairs, colourful umbrellas and patio bar, oh dear me no, just a couple of wooden school-type benches and grey, cracked concrete. However, the pool was divine and we floated about under a navy-blue, starry evening sky feeling it was all rather surreal.

The flight into Petropavlovsk provides spectacular views over Avacha Bay and Viljuchinsky Volcano – if the weather permits.

ABOUT THE FIRST OCCUPATION OF KAMCHATKA

Excerpts from *Steller's History of Kamchatka*
By Georg Wilhelm Steller, 1709–1746

Translated by Margritt Engel and Karen Wilmore
With permission University of Alaska Press

It is regrettable that the Kamchatka Government archives make no mention whatsoever of this country's occupation, ie the manner in which this large population was conquered; any record of what happened; how one place after another was taken; or what rebellions or skirmishes occurred from time to time is lacking...

...This much is certain, that Kamchatka was discovered by Yakutsk and Anadyrsk Cossacks travelling overland. However two different remarkable incidents, which could make this theory of overland discovery debatable, catch the eye. First, during the occupation of the country by Cossacks, it was learned from the Kamchadals that once before, strangers had come to them on a vessel from the ocean, had settled down with them, intermarried, and lived very peaceably with them. Among them was one Theodurus but known by the name of Fetka: to this day a small tributary flowing into the Kamchatka River has kept its name. The question remains where had this Fetka come from. Perhaps a ship coming from the Kolyma River had passed by Cape Chutotskiy and arrived here. This is somewhat confirmed by another piece of information. The Chukchi tell of a people on the mainland to the east across from

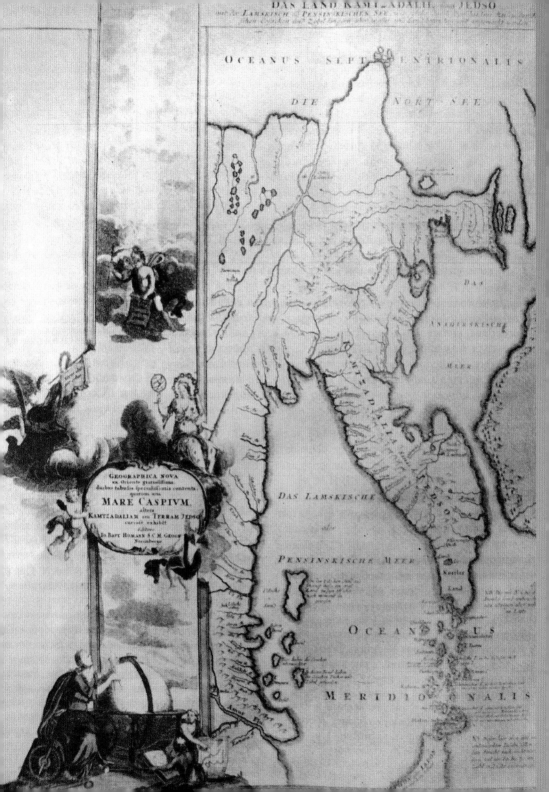

the Chukchi headland who look exactly like the Russians, who also all have Russian manners as well as Russian kutoks, or violins, which they play and to which they dance just as the Russians do. These people were said to be big-bodied, with big beards. After much questioning, I received from a Chukchi one of these people's bowls, which I am sending to the natural science collection. This bowl is inlaid with bone and for decoration studded with iron nails that resemble Russian handiwork. And this struck me as very thought provoking, since the Chukchi do not know anything of iron ore or smelting. Nor did the rest of the Americans have iron, and I myself saw at Cape Elias and on Shumagin Island, and it is quite possible that some of the ships that were thought to be lost and wrecked at sea were driven to America by contrary winds, where the sailors looked for iron, smelted it and used it as necessary. It is quite possible that some of them were lucky enough to get to Kamchatka.

Second, there are clues and accounts that, prior to the Russian's overland arrival on the Tigil River, Russians had already been there. It is said that, approximately ten years before the occupation, a vessel with Russians had sailed up the Tigil River, the Russians had stayed with the inhabitants a year, killed all kinds of animals with "five barrels", thereby gaining the natives' awe and respect, and were not considered bad people.

But because these strangers slept with the natives' daughters, who had only too happily obliged, they had become jealous of each other and in a quarrel one had stabbed another to death with a knife. When the inhabitants saw this, the story went, they agreed with one another to murder them – a sinister scheme they carried out at night while the Russians were asleep.

One must not believe, however, that this vessel sailed out of the Kolyma River, but from the Penzhina River instead. Twenty to 25 years ago, the Cossacks often paddled from Anardysk to the Bolshaya River in baidaras in this way. From Anardysk they went by dogsled as far as the upper reaches of the Penzhina River, where they built large baidaras and went down the Penzhina River and then along the coast as far as the Bolshaya River. It is my opinion that the Russians travelled in exactly this way from Anadyrsk to reconnoitre the west side of Kamchatka, having had news of its eastern side from the Koryaks long before the occupation. I shall try extremely hard to supplement this report in Nizhnoi and Anadyrsk in order to verify its truth.

Nizhnoi Village on the Kamchatka River was the first to be occupied and inhabited by the Cossacks, who had previously received good information and also interpreters from the Koryaks. From the Kamchatka River, the Cossacks went by baidara to Kronoki and from there overland to where Verkhnoi Village is now, with a total strength of only seventeen men. At the time, a powerful Itelmen called Iwar-Asidam lived there. All the area as far as the Bolshaya River stood under his command. To my great regret, this man, to whom I had very much wanted to speak, died in 1741. Iwar Asidam sent messages to the Bolshaya River and had some of the seafaring Cossacks come before him, and through a Koryak woman interpreter, asked them what they wanted and from where and why they had come. The Cossacks answered that they came from the great and powerful ruler under whose command the whole land stood, and the Itelmen were to give him an annual iasak (tribute) for living on his land. Even though it struck the Itelmen as very strange that they were said to live not in their country but in another's, about whom they had never heard anything, this Iwar, nevertheless called a council and proposed that, because these four strong, big and plucky men had had the nerve to come among such a mass of people and so freely to demand iasak for their lord, it appeared to him that they had to be mighty people and very smart to boot, which one could see from their clothing and iron instruments. Besides, since they brought with them all sorts of useful iron wares, taking only fox and sable pelts in return, he was of the opinion that no harm should be done them. Since they, the Itelmen, had so many animals, they should agree to the visitors' request, and, for such a little thing as pelts, not antagonize these people, because if they killed them, others might come in larger numbers to avenge their brothers. He also took into consideration the Kamchadals' courage and strength versus the Russians'. When the Russians were allowed back into the council, the Itelmen threw more sables among them than the Russians had anticipated. In return, the Russians made the people gifts of knives, and Iwar used his souvenir knife almost to his death. Then, under strict orders not to harm them, the Itelmen escorted the Russians with their sables to the Bolshaya River with a parting admonition: they would do well not to return in the future.

Bolsheretsk Village was built in the last century and already fairly well established when the windbag Vladimir Atlasov arrived from Yakutsk (in 1697). He was only the first of a long line of people who returned from there to Yakutsk and Moscow with a lot of plundered goods and ill-gotten wealth. Only their children are left behind in Yakutsk, eking out a scanty living or going begging. I have diligently gathered a register of these thieving, unchristian overseers who, in a short time, unlawfully acquired a large capital, and upon enquiry, I did not find a single one whose descendents could enjoy it. While a Christian in these parts might not need this warning, it should certainly keep half a fool, with the help of his other, sensible half of a brain, from being blinded by a false sense of security due to the distance, urging him to be content with his pay and inflict force and pain on no one.

But the peace between Cossacks and Itelmen lasted only until the Russian Village was finished. Then the Cossacks went into the nearest native villages with brute force robbing and plundering everything they found. They robbed the men of their wives and daughters, pressed the sons into servitude, took the sleds and dogs for their own use, and stole sable and fox pelts as well as provisions from the balagans. As a result, the inhabitants in the vicinity conspired to attack and destroy the Russian village, and not to leave a single soul alive. But because the Cossacks had always employed the ruse of maintaining friendship with some deceitful Itelmen, they always learned from these and from the girls, whom they used en masse for fornication, the news of all the undertakings of the Itelmen and defended themselves against them. One cannot marvel enough at the bravery shown and the cunning plots carried out by the Cossacks, who were just a handful of mostly misfits, who had either run away from justice, or had been sent here from Russia because of all sorts of knavery. But these are the best people for such dubious enterprises. In their first attempt to overrun Bolsheretsk, so many Itelmen arrived overland that they could not be overlooked, bragging about how they were going to slay the Cossacks with their hats and eat them alive. The Cossacks, altogether about seventy men, rushed at them from the village and immediately chased them away, in the process massacring as many as possible. The second time, so many Itelmen arrived by boat on the Bolshaya River that even the Cossacks lost heart; nevertheless the Cossacks dispersed their forces in the river channels and kept the Itelmen from being able to help one another. Thus, the largest number of Itelmen who escaped the bullets and spears ignominiously drowned, and this was the Cossacks' second victory.

Some Itelmen who were captured at that time were mercilessly whipped or clubbed to death; others, young and old, were stripped naked, smeared with stinking fish and thrown, alive, before hungry dogs to be torn to death.

On the whole, since the Cossacks saw that these people were so numerous that they could not possibly get the better of them, nor secure lasting possession of the

An early depiction of the settlement that would eventually become Petropavlovsk, created by a member of French explorer Le Comte de La Pérouse's expedition in 1787.

country, the Cossacks insulted them in a way that could not possibly be ignored, providing the Itelmen with the opportunity to start something. Then the Cossacks killed all the grown men they got hold of, even the old, and made the women and children their slaves and the possessions their booty. Within 40 years they reduced the inhabitants to a twelfth or fifteenth of what they had been. On top of that, the inhabitants themselves were at each others' throats, from which the Cossacks profited, helping one party against the other, and finally, having weakened them, subjected all of them to their will...

...But since the occupation of the country, not even a third of all the Cossacks who have died on Kamchatka died a natural death, most of them having been killed somewhere or other, according to my research in the church register where the slain are listed separately. As a result of this chaos in these desolate regions, the Russian nation suffers as much damage as do the Itelmen.

GEORG WILHELM STELLER, 1709-1746

Excerpts from the Preface to *Steller's History of Kamchatka*

Translated by Margritt Engel and Karen Wilmore
With permission University of Alaska Press

Georg Wilhelm Steller died November 12th, 1746, in Tiumen in western Siberia while returning to St. Petersburg after ten years of scientific discovery and research as a member of the Second Kamchatka Expedition (1733–1743). He was born thirty-seven years earlier in Bad Windsheim in Germany where he grew up in a middle-class family. He studied theology at Luther's Wittenberg before pursuing his real interests in medicine and natural sciences at the University of Halle, an institute committed to pietistic ideals. Even though he passed his botany exams with honours in Berlin, he did not get the teaching position he hoped for. In the face of dismal job prospects in Germany, and perhaps more importantly, with a passionate longing to explore foreign territory, Steller, as other German scholars at that time, turned towards Russia. In Danzig, he obtained a position as a military doctor with Russian troops, accompanying the wounded to St. Petersburg where he became acquainted with scientists at the St Petersburg Academy and was accepted as a botanist on the Second Kamchatka Expedition, later termed the Great Northern Expedition...

...In September 1740 Steller arrived in Bolsheretsk, at the mouth of the Bolshaya River on the west coast of Kamchatka. Steller and Krasheninnikov travelled to Avacha Bay on the east coast of Kamchatka during the first part of the winter of 1740-41.

Shortly after the New Year Steller organized a dog-sled expedition to the southern part of Kamchatka. His Kamchatka research was then interrupted by Bering's invitation to join his expedition to America. Fourteen months of incredible hardships later, Steller was back on Kamchatka, where he devoted the winter of 1742-43 to preparing his manuscripts of his journey to America and his "Beschreibung des Landes Kamchatka" (Description of the Land of Kamchatka). That spring he travelled to the Kamchatka River and then on to the vicinity of Karaga Island in northeastern Kamchatka, where he remained until the spring of 1744...

...Today Steller is credited with contributing knowledge about Kamchatka primarily in his research on fish and birds, and his ethnographic observations. For example, on Kamchatka alone, Steller discovered more than thirty new species and two new genera of fish. He devoted a great deal of time and effort to studying fish, partly out of his own interest, partly because he had been instructed to gather information on fish as an economic resource. He mentions almost half of all the species known today on Kamchatka and adjoining areas of the Pacific Rim. He was the first scholar to describe the peculiarities of the life-cycle of the Pacific salmon, eg that the king salmon is found in the Kamchatka River but not in the river systems emptying into the Sea of Okhotsk, and that silver and red salmon prefer spawning on lake/river systems. He suspected that the Kamchatkan steelhead trout returned to its birth river. The exactness of Steller's descriptions still forms the definition of some fish species today, eg the Pacific herring shark and the marbled eelput. Steller's ichthyological data allow researchers today to determine changes in the distribution of fish due to natural and human causes. In this sense, Steller's data contribute to contemporary ecological and evolutionary research.

Steller's known ornithological works list about 100 bird species from Soberi, Kamchatka, Bering Island and the islands between Kamchatka and America, some of which he was the first to discover and describe. His best-known discovery was the now extinct cormorant *Phalacrocorax perspecillatus*. In Steller's honour, Pallas names a Siberian eider Steller's Eider, (*Polysticta Stelleri*) and Gmelin named the black crested jay Steller's Jay (*Cyanocitta Stelleri*)...

...Steller's comprehensive and detailed description of the native people and their way of life on Kamchatka was for that time extraordinary and would have been impossible without his flexibility and courage in adapting to living in a harsh land, his willingness to disregard his own physical comforts, and his ability to relate to the native people as a sympathetic observer so that they allowed him access to their way of life. Equally unusual for that time was the respect Steller had for these indigenous people, recognizing that their culture was based on adaptations to their natural surroundings. For the some 1,400 Itelmen remaining today on the west coast of Kamchatka, Steller's detailed ethnographic descriptions are their most important sources of knowledge of their ancestors' way of life as they begin to re-establish connections with their own traditions. Steller also fills a gaping hole in the official Soviet version of the history of Kamchatka – that of a brutal exploitation by the Russians...

...The "Description of Kamchatka" also provides intriguing glimpses of Steller the man in all his human ambiguities. Steller the moralist consistently condemns the

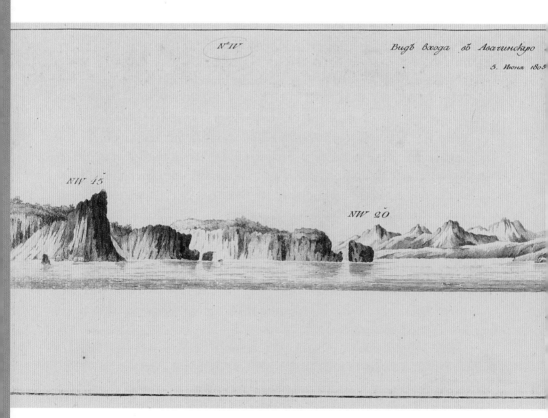

Russians' mistreatment and corruption of the native peoples as well as denounces the native people's religious beliefs and voracious sexual appetites. At the same time he marvels at how much the Itelmen manage to enjoy life, Steller the scientist describes with scientific thoroughness the sexual and other exploits of the remarkably stupid Kutka, the Itelmen's god, homosexual practices among the Itelmen, and the native women's genitalia. But the complaint that a man could not get any woman to do his sewing unless he were willing to pay for the service with sexual favours does not sound like a dispassionate scientific observation. Finally, there is Steller's sense of humour, dark though it may be, which allowed him to appreciate the same in the Itelmen. [Also named for Steller were: the Steller sea lion, the now extinct Steller's sea cow, and Steller's sea eagle.]

"View of the Coast of Kamchatka from Cape Lopatka" from an expedition by Captain Von Krusenstern in the years 1803-1806.

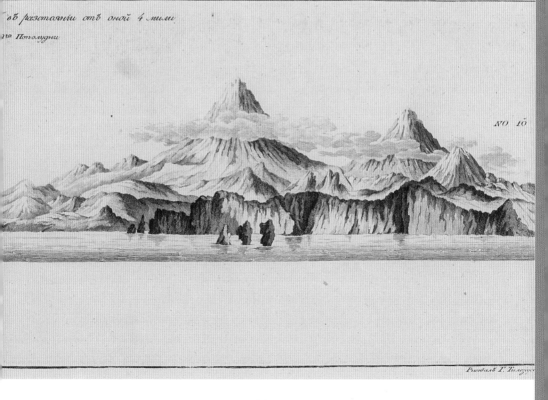

PARATUNKA. HOTEL HELIOS. 25 AUGUST

Avacha Bay is stunningly beautiful, a huge natural harbour surrounded by volcanoes. We spent a gorgeous day after a rather sleepless night. It was sunny, warm and calm, so off we went for a day at sea. The visibility was perfect and we could see the two great cones of the volcanoes, Koryaksky and Avachinsky, which last erupted in 1991. These two volcanoes tower over Petropavlovsk only about 30 kilometres distant. The town itself, as far as we could see, didn't have one redeeming feature. No one seems to notice, or care about the pot-holed streets filled with rubbish and rusty iron bits. Half finished – or started – buildings augment the appalling drab, crumbling housing blocks the residents of which fear earthquakes much more than the threat of nearby volcanic eruptions. It is, to our eyes, a most unattractive town in the most fabulous setting.

We went on down to the harbour where there was a boat waiting to take us off for the day. Some Japanese had joined us; unfortunately, they thought they had the boat to themselves and had brought along three young, rather pathetic prostitutes! We fairly mucked up their plans, and boy they let us know it by being downright rude. Nothing daunted we set off in the neat little fishing boat with a lovely, very friendly captain, bringing far more helpers than we could really have needed, all obviously taking the opportunity for a sunny day's free outing. We picked our way past two small yachts and an assortment of rusted hulks. Old holed rowing boats on the beach and piles of chain, scrap iron and sundry abandoned items were the remains of what passed for Petropavlovsk's yacht club.

We made our way out to the open sea drinking Russian cognac with our bus driver and exchanging stories. The coastline here is rocky and wild with some extraordinary high rock formations standing up out of the sea, given names such as "The Three Brothers", "The Devils Finger" and "Three Grannie's Stone". Trawling up and down the coast, we started fishing with Elise and me both managing to catch fish, as did some of the crew. Needless to say the grumpy Japanese had their thoughts on other pastimes. We saw large numbers of cormorants, puffins, gulls and masses of grey and bearded seals, then, to our huge delight, on top of a high rocky stack we spied a pair of

sea eagles with, as far as we could see, at least one chick in their nest.

When the captain decided we had enough fish we motored off, and proceeded to a little beach of black sand at Tikhaje Bay where, the water being so deep, we were able to get close enough in to go ashore along a gangplank from the stern of the boat to the beach. A fire was built and on it we cooked a delicious Russian bouillabaisse. Everyone mucked in and helped, with the little local girls giggling and chattering to everyone. By this time even the Japanese had become resigned to our being around and were being a little bit friendlier, even exchanging the odd bit of chat with us.

What a lovely day we had. On the way back to harbour we both had a go at steering the boat, letting our imaginations run wild as we watched the Japanese gents take it in turns to go below with the girls. I understand that nowadays the Japanese make a habit of taking group holidays to eastern Russia, Vladivostok in particular, in order to enjoy the pleasures of the local prostitutes!

On returning to the hotel, Valentina sat us down and we went over our itinerary. Well, her itinerary and that of Steppes East, our tour operator, have very little in common. To begin with we are not now going to Palana! This was a big blow as we are very keen to visit the Koryak reindeer herders who inhabit that area, but Valentina said there is not always enough fuel to return, and often the locals try and blackmail you into paying a lot of money with the threat of not being able to get back. She has promised us that we will see reindeer herders much further south than Palana, somewhere near the enigmatically named town of Esso, which we can reach by 4WD and helicopter. We really have no choice;

it's just a case of a slight lack of communication that we didn't know of this problem. But never mind, we will just have to get on with it and I'm sure all will be well – after all, what is adventure about?

Having digested this bad news, we were treated to our most hated meal – dumplings. Yuck! We extricated the stuffing and managed to force down a little, but they are the same as in Central Asia, pale, slippery gobs of greasy dough. We just couldn't manage them. Instead we were brought salmon caviar, in fact salmon roe, which was definitely off. Nevertheless, we finished up with the remains of the strawberries and some yoghurt that was delicious. Then, even though it was late, we poured ourselves a vodka each and repaired once more to the hot pool for a half-hour or so.

On returning to our room we couldn't get the key in the door. Amazingly, and totally illogically, the keys are kept on unnumbered hooks in the lobby, so it's happy-go-lucky-dip time when you go to get your key. The local handyman was called to try and open the door using the same key, unsurprisingly to no avail. Eventually we had one handyman, the girl from the dining room and the manageress all standing round giving advice. I vacillated from total irritation to finding the whole pantomime hysterically funny. Finally someone had the brilliant idea of trying some of the other keys until we found one that fitted and put a blue elastic band on it. Maybe it will be there tomorrow and maybe it won't!

Paratunka. Hotel Helios. 26 August

We should be in the "Valley of the Geysers" tonight but the chopper didn't fly as it was unable to land due to the terrible weather conditions in the valley. It was very disappointing but not unusual, so we hope to go tomorrow. Instead we went with Valya (Valentina's shortened name) and Sergei, our driver for the volcanoes, to the heliport to organize things for the following day, then on to Sergei's parents' dacha to see their garden.

The garden was wonderful. Immaculate patches of strawberries, raspberries, beetroot, carrots, cabbages, herbs and black and red currants, all interspersed with flowers, and

A Landsat image clearly shows the expanse of Avacha Bay and Petropavlovsk's sprawl.

barely a weed in sight. Two greenhouses bulged with growing tomatoes and cucumbers – and they also had a sauna.

The house, like most round about, was wooden and tiny, cobbled together in a rather Heath Robinson fashion with extra bits added on here and there as the need arose. Everyone here has a dacha for the summer, where they all work like mad, growing, harvesting and preserving their produce, but in winter they live in the horrible apartments in Petropavlovsk. It's too cold in the country with no central heating, and anyway, the ground is covered with deep snow.

As Sergei is separated from his wife, his son lives here with his granny. She and her husband work all hours in the garden. Both of them look very well but poverty stricken – what savings they have are locked away in her several gold teeth! We ate loads of fruit in the garden and then to our embarrassment were asked to stay for lunch. The kitchen had so little in it and no hot water; the cold water came in a pipe straight into the kitchen, with no sink unit at all, just a bucket. What did we have for lunch? Surprise, surprise, salmon caviar! I got mine down with difficulty after last night.

After lunch we drove off to the countryside round Avacha Bay. After exploring a disused defence area with a hundred or more tanks camouflaged with brambles and weeds, ancient reminders of the Cold War and guardians of Avacha Bay from the rest of the world, we drove on to the beach. Cold, grey waves curled in to break on the long, bleak, deserted stretch of black volcanic sand bordering this part of the North Pacific. But people were in the dunes gathering small, black berries – some sort of bilberry – for preserving, in the

same way people back home pick blackberries for jam-making. We found lots of late blooming wildflowers, including low-growing, dark-red dog roses.

We walked through birch forests that looked absolutely pristine, as though no one had ever been there before us. But then we came across a group of people gathering mushrooms, the like of which I had never seen before. We joined in and got separated from each other as we wandered through the woods. The birch trees looked so pretty with their silvery bark and an undergrowth of light indigenous wild plants. I gathered loads of mushrooms, which I joyfully produced for Sergei, who disparagingly discarded

most of them as being poisonous. Among them was the very attractive, scarlet and white-spotted hallucinogenic *Amanita Muscari*, or fly agaric, which is used extensively by the Koryak people to induce a trance. Sergei also told us about some of Kamchatka's wild flowers, including the sarana (*Fritillaria Kamchatcensis*), a purple lily, the bulb of which the Kamchadals used as a substitute for bread; another bright orange lily, locally called Tsar Locks, and the large-flowered slipper orchid, both quite rare.

On the way back to Paratunka, we went to the market in Petropavlovsk to buy vodka and all our provisions for our volcano trek. The outdoor market mainly comprises fish stalls, but also many selling garden produce including preserves of all kinds. Two ladies selling all sorts of strange-looking fungi were very shy about talking to us of their wares, and hid their faces with embarrassment when I tried to take their picture. A large indoor market was full of Western goods, both everyday and luxury, there for anyone to buy if they could afford it.

Then it was back to Sergei's dacha for an evening meal. His mother, who is simply delightful, warm-hearted and friendly, is called Maria and his stepfather, who is much more reserved, is named Fyodor Haritonavitch.

What a wonderful evening! The rather dull, grey afternoon had turned into a beautiful, warm sunny evening. We laid a table in the garden and Valya picked flowers for a centrepiece. Sergei, who is a keen fly fisherman, had caught some very rare fish in the river, a bit like a white salmon, about the same size and very firm – probably char. Floured and fried it was absolutely delicious. Potatoes, tomatoes, cucumber and raspberries – all from the garden – made a feast fit for a king. We toasted each other with straight vodkas

and another Russian drink we had bought on Sergei's recommendation as a present for Maria and Fyodor, who visibly softened with a drink or two and ended up laughing and enjoying it all. They have so very little; Elise and I were the only ones with cutlery (a fork each) and Elise ate off a saucer while I sat on a stool borrowed from next door. They didn't have any glasses until Maria suddenly remembered some new ones that she had been saving for a special occasion, in a plastic bag in an outhouse, and went rushing off excitedly to find them. They had never been used and had to be well wiped to get rid of all the spiders. Our hosts were so generous and kind, and it was a privilege to share their hospitality. We have been invited back before we leave Kamchatka.

We are still having trouble getting the key into our door – I don't know if it's the same one that we put the rubber band on, because naturally enough it's missing. This is getting beyond a joke!

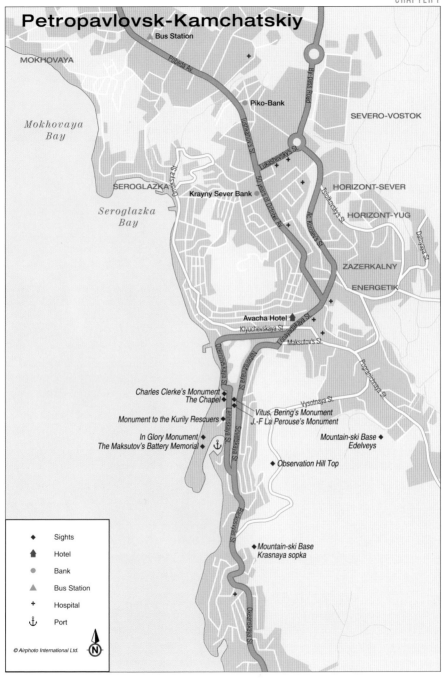

Petropavlovsk-Kamchatskiy

MOKHOVAYA

Bus Station

Mokhovaya Bay

Piko-Bank

SEVERO-VOSTOK

SEROGLAZKA

Krayny Sever Bank

Seroglazka Bay

HORIZONT-SEVER

HORIZONT-YUG

ZAZERKALNY

ENERGETIK

Avacha Hotel

Klyuchevskaya St.

Maksutov's St.

Charles Clerke's Monument
The Chapel

Monument to the Kurily Rescuers

Vitus, Bering's Monument
J.-F La Perouse's Monument

Vysotnaya St.

In Glory Monument
The Maksutov's Battery Memorial

Mountain-ski Base
Edelveys

Observation Hill Top

Mountain-ski Base
Krasnaya sopka

◆	Sights
🏠	Hotel
⬤	Bank
▲	Bus Station
+	Hospital
⚓	Port

© Airphoto International Ltd.

N

VOLCANIC ACTION

VALLEY OF THE GEYSERS. GORELY. MUTNOVSKY. DACHNE HOT SPRINGS. VILJUCHINSKY

VALLEY OF THE GEYSERS. 27 AUGUST

This morning we went to a very pretty place on the Paratunka River to try our hands at a spot of salmon fishing. There are still a few salmon going upstream to spawn, and some pretty well on their last legs – or fins – coming back downstream. Elise, Sergei and I all caught salmon, it's not such a great art here as there are so many fish and by this stage they are not putting up much of a fight. We released two of them as we just didn't need them. Other people were also fishing, to Sergei's disgust, two with just a crude line with spinners and weights – very unsportsmanlike! We passed a very pleasant relaxed morning, waiting to see if we were going to be able to fly to the Valley of the Geysers. We had been told that we should report to the heliport at 1pm, so we stopped fishing, had a quick lunch and duly turned up at the heliport on time.

What a to-do! One chopper did leave OK, but not with us on board. We were then told some more people had to come. Two arrived quite soon and then, after an hour, another four. Still we didn't leave. We started making a fuss and were told that the weather between us and the valley was bad. I think probably this was rubbish, they simply couldn't afford to go without a full chopper, which is fair enough. Finally at 2.30pm we were told we would go in an hour and that we could stay the night there if we wanted, but with no guarantee that we would get back the following day so maybe we would have to stay two nights, and then some. We were told there was a cabin where a couple lived who would look after us. We had to make up our minds then and there, and feeling that it was hardly worthwhile just going for the remains of the afternoon, and because we had heard so much about this extraordinary place, we decided we'd go for it and hope that we wouldn't be left there indefinitely!

A geyser erupts in the middle of the Valley of the Geysers, the most popular tourist site in Kamchatka.

We returned to the hotel to gather up some night things, and sure enough at 4.30 we left, having discovered that the delay was because we had to wait for the new governor of Kamchatka who was flying with us. What a great flight! In perfect weather, with the Pacific sparkling far on our right-hand side, we flew north over and around the volcanoes of Avachinsky and Koryaksky and the brilliant blue crater lakes of hydrochloric and sulphuric acid, looking so pretty – and so poisonous.

The Valley of the Geysers was as picturesque as we had imagined, steep-sided, like a miniature rift valley with a stream running through it, and filled with geysers and boiling mud pools. There were two small, and one larger, new, timbered alpine houses as a headquarters and dormitory.

We were taken on a guided tour of part of the valley, keeping strictly to the wooden walkways due to the danger of falling through the thin crust of earth that lay around us! What an extraordinary place it is, only discovered in 1941 when a group of scientists led by Tatiana Ustinova found their way here, fighting their way through scrub, scree and bogland, to find out why the rivers on this system thawed so much earlier than in the rest of the country. The valley runs north/south and is situated in the Kronotsky Reserve, south of Lake Kronotsky, and although it extends over six kilometres and is the second largest geyser field in the world, none of the native Itelmen knew of its existence.

Much of the rock is quite red in colour. A lot of the area is not open to tourists as the fumes from some of the geysers are highly poisonous. Some of the geysers are over a metre wide while others are pinhead size, all steaming away. Every so often the main ones would blow. They start with an excess of water running out of them, then they boil over and shoot water and steam at huge pressure to a height of up to 30 metres. The water stops and only steam is expelled for several minutes, before the process starts again. The whole valley is like this. It's quite amazing. The reason why this happens so regularly is that there is a deep funnel of steam in a chamber below the surface, and a surface flow of cold water that pours in and fills the chamber. Then steam pressure builds up until it overflows the chamber, consequently ejecting the water at regular intervals.

One horrible mud pool is the site where two girls fell in and were boiled to death – pretty grim – and another very deep boiler makes an eerie, echoing bubbling noise from far underground that's known as the "mouth of hell". You feel as if you're in a landscape from the start of the world. It's very beautiful but rather eerie. If the Health and Safety people got their hands on this place it would be strictly *"verboten"*.

Everyone else on our flight left after supper and we were alone with just the ranger and

the couple who run the place! Not a word of common language between us. Nevertheless we managed to "discuss" the time the generator would be turned off and breakfast, etc. Then I mentioned, *"banyo"*. *"Da, da, da"*, said Misha the caretaker enthusiastically and, before we knew it, he and his wife Svetlana (or Sveta), had produced towels, and she beckoned us to follow her. We went in the opposite direction from the main valley, down a wee, winding muddy path with planks here and there over boiling bits – no wooden walkways here – round strange plants, to a little stream and a clapped out shed. In the shed was an old cast-iron bath sunk into the ground. An iron pipe stretched from it through the side of the shed, over the stream and into a geyser! Sveta filled the bath with a mix of "heart of the world" water from the geyser and bucketfuls of cold water from the stream.

We looked on with growing anticipation until she beckoned us to take off our clothes and share the bath. All bum, belly and bubs we pranced around taking it in turns to get into the bath and have a good soaping. In the middle of Sveta's bath there was a whooshing sound outside as a geyser blew just beside the bathhouse, and covered in soap-suds she leapt out of the bath and, grabbing us both by the hand, pulled us outside where we stood totally in the buff, absolutely entranced, watching as about five metres away water and steam blew high in the air.

Back up in the house, we decided to have a beer to celebrate our somewhat unusual banyo. We were soon joined by Misha and the warden whose name we never grasped, and who is small and slight with high cheekbones and looks rather like the Inuit of North America; he made us understand he was of the Even people. We had a great "chat" with very few words, and when trying to explain Ireland we drew a map on a napkin, showing Kamchatka, then back across Russia, the Baltic, Scandinavia, and the British Isles. They understood totally where we came from, although Misha got quite annoyed when I put Moscow too far south. It's amazing, really, what you can learn from drawings and gesticulations.

PARATUNKA. HOTEL HELIOS. 28 AUGUST

I had woken during the night and looked out the window at a clear sky studded with millions of stars, looking close enough to touch, and reflected on what a strange place we were staying in. Only the five of us in these little cabins, built on such a thin crust of earth, miles and miles from anywhere and surrounded by the evidence of the beginnings of the world. The beds were as hard as iron, but we had made them a bit more comfy, and with my little foam mattress, I had a good night.

The valley was in shadow until quite late in the morning, shaded by its steep sides until finally the sun burst over the rim, and filled it with sunlight. It was clear and very cold. We went off on our own with the permission of the ranger for a walk to look peacefully again at the geysers with nobody to disturb us. We thought it appeared that there was much more steam today, perhaps because of the cold.

We sat and watched the play of light from the rising sun through the steam. With the sun up, the temperature rose dramatically. We made our way upstream, crossing and re-crossing the river, finding more and more extraordinary vents, rock formations and geysers, until we remembered the slide show at Trinity College when we were told that further north along the river is the Valley of Death, where numerous vents in the ground release a heavy, odourless toxic gas. When the wind blows from a certain direction, the valley is filled with hydrogen sulphide which suffocates everything in its path. Dead foxes, bears and birds have all been found. We judiciously decided it was about time to retrace our footsteps and return to the safety of the walkways. It must be fabulous here in the growing season when all the plants are in flower. There were loads of huge seed heads, wild lavender, enormous ragweed and something like a giant Rogersia. Everything seems larger than life.

At around 1pm, having seen the day's visitors arrive by helicopter we returned leisurely to the main cabin, eventually going in for lunch, assuming that we would be here for the

In the absence of trains or a reliable road network, large Russian MI8 helicopters are the most common form of transportation to and from national parks and other isolated locations.

rest of the day, when the guide with the tourists came in and said if we wanted a lift back in her chopper we had 15 minutes to get ready! It's either feast or a famine, and after a wild rush to get our stuff packed, we made it to the chopper with everyone else already on board. Away we flew, on the way delighted to see beneath us several bears at a river, after which, to our surprise, we hovered over a tiny wooden hut, and then landed to bring supplies to some scientists who were staying there and doing research.

We were met in Petropavlovsk by our faithful pair and returned to the hotel. Surprise, surprise, the key didn't fit – wrong one again. This time, in sheer fury I shouted "Oh for fuck's sake!" and stomped off to report to reception. Elise was not going to be the only one to feel the hot wind of my fury. It's absolutely daft how they cannot have a key that is kept labelled for each room – unless, of course someone picks the lock in our absence (there's hardly any incriminating stuff to find in our room – if you could even find it in the perpetual mess of clothes and belongings). Now three handymen were involved in sorting things out. We were unwilling to get involved in the machinations of "The Lock", and repaired to the pool but it was being filled and was much too hot to get into, so, nothing for it but to resort to a small libation before our meal.

HOTEL HELIOS, 29 AUGUST. LUNCHTIME

Our itinerary is absolutely "up the left". According to our original itinerary, we should be up north in Palana, but instead we are now supposed to be going south today to the volcanoes to trek. However it is pouring, so everything is on hold. We had a good lie-in, breakfast and swim. The pool is now at a reasonable temperature and it seemed surreal to be toasting hot in the pool while it poured cold rain. There has been a wee dark man coming to the pool from time to time. He is always the worse for drink (is this the pot calling the kettle black?) but at 10am it seemed a bit over the top! Quite a good way to sober up, all the same. Back in the room it took us most of the morning to sort out our stuff into "needed on trek" and "not needed on trek". You'd think by now we would be better at it than this, but no, we have the room in a complete shambles. Anyway, what's the betting Valya comes and tells us the weather is too bad and we're doing a city tour, and we'll have to unpack again?

TENT, GORELY VOLCANO, STILL 29 AUGUST. EVENING

No, we didn't do a city tour. We played ping-pong till 3pm, Elise beating me soundly, when Valya, Sergei and another lad called Zhenya – plus his guitar – arrived and, though it was still drizzling, off we went, crammed into Sergei's 4WD, reminding me very much of Kenyan safaris.

We had intended going to Viljuchinsky Hot Springs, but the road to it was too wet. We continued on over the Pioneerski Pass in thick mist, and ended up here in the middle of a caldera, partway up Gorely Volcano. Elise and I did a walk in the rain, and then back to the largest tent for a meal, cooked with great difficulty and huge cheerfulness by Valya on a two-ring burner. She is terrific and constantly optimistic. Whenever we say, "we cannot do such and such", she always replies "of course you can, why not?"

It's a lunar landscape here, but there is some growth of low plants, tiny prostrate rhododendrons, pinks and a small conifer, *Pinus pumila*. We are camped in a sandy patch in the caldera and it's still raining with very low cloud, and frankly it's pretty horrible. Unless it fines up tomorrow it will be fairly miserable, but tomorrow is another day. We are finally tucked up in our sleeping bags in bed, at present warm as toast, having kept all our clothes on!

A vast, barren landscape stretches away from the foot of Gorely Volcano.

TENT, GORELY VOLCANO, 30 AUGUST

I spent an amazingly good night – even though there was a heavy frost and the zip on the tent was frozen solid. My bedding is great, thanks to my good friend Jen's goose down sleeping bag and my ancient foam mattress.

We emerged to a cloudless but very cold morning. After breakfast, which we ate sitting somewhat idiotically outside, still in the shadow of the mountain, at 9.30 we set off up Gorely, at this point looking miles away. On the way up we learned from Sergei that this volcano has erupted ten times in the last 175 years and is one of Kamchatka's most active. It contains 11 craters, five of which could still erupt at any time. Many of the volcano's earlier eruptions were accompanied by huge lava flows, which now cover its southeastern slopes. As we ascended, so the landscape opened up. It was fabulous, with layer upon layer of snow-topped mountains: Viljuchinsky looking perfect with a dusting of snow lay behind us; beyond her was Avachinsky, and further Koryaksky, all with snowy crowns. The rain we experienced yesterday fell of course as snow higher up.

Our way up was steep but it was fairly easy going to start with, on stones and volcanic ash like sand. Sergei and Zhenya had bounded off in high spirits, both carrying huge rucksacks. As we got higher it became snowy and the ash was very slick; it gradually got to be really hard going, very steep and slippery. Eventually I thought I could go no further and called to Sergei, just above me, that I had to stop for a minute. Sergei, totally in his element, wearing waders and always ahead of us, turned and called down to me, "come on and see the lake". I struggled on up to where he was sitting, and suddenly I was on the rim of the crater. It was extraordinary. The crater fell straight down, very, very steep-sided to a pale turquoise lake. I didn't want to dare climb on to the rim, as it was only about nine inches (23 centimetres) wide. Elise and Valya joined us, and we stood there, exhilarated, totally thrilled at getting there. We had wonderful views of other mountains into the distance, among them, much closer, Mutnovsky with its smoking crater.

Then we were told that there was a second crater with another lake quite close which

Within Gorely Volcano's crater lies a strikingly coloured acid lake.

we had to go and see. This meant we had to get up on the rim and walk along it. It was terrifying. Quite snowy underfoot, cold and very windy, we looked neither to right nor left. In no time we arrived at the second crater with its milky blue lake, but one with a high toxicity of hydrochloric acid. Fumaroles belched out spurts of gas, firing their poison with ghastly, unearthly noises. Under a bright blue sky, but in the bitter wind, we teetered on the edge posing for photos as though we were in a gentle forest park, and ate a great picnic lunch of smoked salmon and bacon, Sergei and Zhenia rushing off to vantage points to take even more daring photos. Oh, the bravado of the young.

The descent was easier than the ascent; we went down via a small red caldera, very picturesque in the afternoon sunlight, arriving back at camp after nine hours of walking. We sat in the last of the sun drinking beers, feeling euphoric if exhausted. Sergei reckoned we'd walked about 15 kilometres, not too bad for a couple of grannies. Our dinner was watermelon and lots of veggies from Maria's garden. Zhenya played the guitar and sang. A little red fox visited the camp, looking quizzically around, but he seemed quite tame and came right up to us, taking food from Valya's hand as marmots squealed in the distance.

The dangerous 80-metre waterfall at the foot of Mutnovsky Volcano.
(Opposite) Massive glacial ice means the end of the road, even for Sergei.

The sun is nearly away and it's getting chilly at 8pm. It's been an incredible day, we have achieved our objective. You would think we had just conquered Everest. I really didn't think we would do it. Can we also conquer Mutnovsky? And will we be the first Irish grannies to do so? *Guinness Book of Records*, here we come!

Still at First Camp. Gorely. 31 August. 9am

We passed a very stormy night with the wind buffeting at the sides of the tent. There is such a mess of stuff in our tent – so what's new? We had breakfast in the car since, although it's sunny, it is also very windy and chilly. They say the weather here is "softer" than Siberia, only minus 70 in the winter. Everyone digs in to the food, using the same spoon, no niceties here. Valya is coping well with our meals, while Sergei eats mayonnaise by the spoonful. We haven't taken off our clothes or washed since the comparative comfort of the Hotel Helios. For some reason I'm feeling a bit grumpy, I don't really know why, I have absolutely no reason to.

CAMP, MUTNOVSKY VOLCANO, 31 AUGUST, 1PM

We are now camped in what seems to me to be the most exposed situation possible. Mutnovsky is belching away plumes of steam above us. We are on a slope of what is described in our itinerary as "alpine meadow" – I don't think so, it's not grass at all, but a wonderful variety of short, sub-arctic alpine plants, some in flower and others covered with berries. It's quite stony and lumpy and we are exposed on all sides to whatever weather is coming. We were so appalled at our exposed spot that we had to take a little Russian courage in the form of a couple of vodkas, and are now enjoying a beer each.

The route here wasn't fit for a tank, but Sergei managed to get our van – a Mitsubishi 4WD Delica turbo diesel, over impossibly difficult terrain, including a frozen spring, huge icy "moguls" and a frozen lake, where we had to get out and walk as it was so slippery and bumpy, not only for the van but for us also on our feet. I have great admiration for Sergei's driving skills and quiet knowledge. He has a slow smile and understands much more English than he lets on. A volcanologist, he has all the information we need. Valya and he are great friends.

Tomorrow we are supposed to be climbing this smoking monstrosity in front of us. Elise's knee is playing up, so we'll see.

SAME CAMP AND DAY. 9.30PM

After lunch we were all lying back in the sun against a bank out of the wind when superactive Sergei said "come on, we'll go for a short walk to a waterfall".

It's now five hours later, back at camp. I thought this was going to be a day off from Herculean walks, but I was wrong. The "short" walk took us up and down volcanic debris with a scattering of different sorts of herbs and berries. We watched lots of almost tame marmots scuttling about the place diving in and out of holes, Eventually, having moaned a bit at the length of the "short walk", we arrived at a very dramatic waterfall on the Mutnaya River, tumbling 100 metres into a deep, narrow canyon. We stood and watched it for a while, standing beside a long, steep slope of red ash, when, as usual, Valya said "come on, we can go to the edge of the canyon".

So, of course, very daringly, we crept sideways down the almost vertical bank of red ash and cinders, really steep and scary – nothing at the bottom to stop us falling straight down the canyon and into the acidic river rushing along below us. These two have us doing things no ladies, having attained their 60th birthdays, should be even thinking about doing. I know I am really pushing myself some of the time, it's all very well doing these big hikes if there is a hot bath and a warm bed at the end of it, but the joy of coping with camping with just a cold stream for washing in is, just possibly, wearing a bit thin! Like "marriage" and "having my hair permed", both of which I have experienced to my cost, and have sworn never to do again, camping and climbing volcanoes are beginning to come under the same category!

Nevertheless, I had to admit, the waterfall was wonderful. We all took loads of photos with Sergei as usual finding dramatic vantage points from which to photograph. The walk back from the waterfall seemed easier, although you have to watch every footfall as the

black lumps of lava are rough and unstable, and it would be just so easy to twist an ankle. This gentle little stroll today is supposed to be a limbering up exercise for tomorrow. I shudder to think what awaits us for the morning's jaunt.

After dinner we found a tiny stream

in which to have a cursory wash. The water is freezing cold so we only wash the really necessary "parts" – and that feels good. Amazing how you just get on with it.

CAMP MUTNOVSKY, 1 SEPTEMBER

We've bloody well done it! Been there, seen pretty well all and now absolutely exhausted but thrilled at our achievement. It's after 7pm and the sun is setting in front of us and you can see for miles and miles – the visibility is amazing.

We set off this morning at 10.30am on our conquest of Mutnovsky, over awful terrain, not too steep but very rocky. Over little rivers, and bigger rivers. The greenery soon faded, just little patches of a sort of stonecrop, then finally nothing but stone. Up and up to where this year's eruption has split the big glacier and it is all ice, glacial moraine and ash. A large part of the glacier vanished and a green acidic lake appeared amongst the broken ice.

Mutnovsky, at 2,323 metres high, surpasses even Gorely, in that it has erupted more than 15 times in the past 150 years. On a clear day steam from the fumaroles can be seen from Petropavlovsk, 70 kilometres away. We had already crossed several ice fields which didn't pose too much of a problem, but then we came to a very steep glacier. Valya crossed safely holding on to Sergei, then he came back for Elise. It was awful. She slipped a lot and I thought they would both go together, non-stop for hundreds of feet, down to certain death. They couldn't turn and come back, and I kept thinking what I would have to tell Jimmy, her husband, if she were killed. I could feel her fear, and hear her whimpering with fright. She kept slipping and sitting down and was then unable to get up – just frozen to the spot. But Sergei was amazing. Wearing, of all things, waders, he kept his feet, using them to anchor Elise's feet and gradually they made their way round a bluff and to safety.

This left Zhenya and me to go. With Elise and me, if one of us does something a bit "off the wall", the other would be damned if they don't do it too, but this time I had to admit defeat and said no way. I have done some daft things in my life but this was beyond a doubt the daftest and most dangerous. So I told Zhenya to go on without me and that I would wait for them all to return. He, of course, wouldn't hear of it and so we decided to try and go upwards over the top of the glacier. But this was a massive, steep bank of wet mud and stones, and every time we tried to climb a step it all just collapsed. Having Zhenya in front of me was hopeless as all the wet mud kept falling on top of me.

Then suddenly Sergei appeared well above us and from the top was able to pass down the end of Elise's walking pole. "Come up really fast," he urged, so with Sergei pulling us up from above, both Zhenya and I were able to scramble up the slope really quickly before

Trekkers are wise not to get too close to sulphurous mud pools in Mutnovsky Volcano crater.

it had time to collapse, and arrived at last with Elise and Valya, who had amazingly met up with a Finn and a Russian who had been into the crater and were exchanging notes on their route. They were full of encouragement for us before returning to their camp.

We continued on into the crater on top of the broken glacier, which had been reduced to enormous pieces of ice all coated with ash. We went along a narrow path in single file through a high-sided canyon, a river rushing along below us, massive holes and cracks in the glacier which groaned around us as it melted and moved, the ice looking like colossal chunks of marble. Every so often we had to use our sticks to try and knock off the wet ash clinging to our boots in great big gobs, surrounded by more unearthly noises all the time from fumaroles, the smell of sulphur almost overpowering.

3.15PM. My diary reads: We are in the first fumarolic field of Mutnovsky. It is almost indescribable. We are surrounded by towering crater walls with a huge broken glacier in front of us. The sun is shining but almost hidden behind clouds of steam. There are fumaroles everywhere spurting steam and gas. We have just walked (slithered) along a six-inch path between on one side a bright yellow sulphur fumarole gushing steam, and on the other a pool of vile, green and putrid-looking boiling "matter". The noise of it all is appalling. I feel miniscule, unimportant and totally vulnerable, I imagine it is like being at the beginning of the creation of the world and ask myself the unanswerable question posed by Arthur Rimbaud and many travellers since: "What am I doing here?"

This is where we chose to sit down and have a picnic!

Sergei and Valya went on further into the crater and out of our sight. They photographed an enormous bear's footprint. Now why on earth would a bear venture into here? I know we are really keen to see a bear, but I do think one scary thing at a time.

Our journey back to camp seemed endless although we are both thrilled with ourselves. Gradually the huge boulders gave way to stones and then to smaller ones and then the stonecrop and moss round a little stream began to appear until we eventually arrived safely back at camp. We are tired and aching but, once again, euphoric over what we have achieved. Valiant Valya once more produced an excellent supper and we toasted one another liberally with vodkas.

DACHNE HOT SPRINGS, 2 SEPTEMBER

Another heavenly morning, with not a cloud in the sky. I am feeling great today, well rested and still amazed at all that we did and saw yesterday. We had a river wash again. It is just possible to get to the river wearing flip-flops, but the going is so rough that it is really more comfortable to wear boots; they are beginning to feel like part of my body. We are drinking the icy river water also, occasionally boiled. There is not another soul around, so I imagine the water must be pristine clean. After breakfast we struck camp and set off.

We travelled all day over streams and round boulders, occasionally having to walk when the going got really rough, until about 3pm, when we reached Dachne Hot Springs. We left the car and carried what we needed for lunch up a track beside the hot stream, which fell in a series of waterfalls down the hill. Here, in bathing suits and bikinis, we sat about eating a picnic lunch in this most bizarre place. There is a new geothermal power station being built here, surrounded by the broken remains of the old one, and broken and abandoned machinery. The building site was terrible; mud, tractors, *veshdehods* (tank-like all-terrain vehicles), men, rubbish. Pipes here and there gushed uncontrolled boiling-hot steam. It all seemed terribly casual and dangerous. There were no barriers or gates or safety precautions of any sort that we could see, but, as usual, we just went along with it as do, apparently, dozens of other people. It is not too far from Petropavlovsk and as it is the weekend, lots of folk are picnicking and enjoying the hot springs and lovely weather. It is incredibly ugly, but a new and very modern restaurant is also being built, and I suppose some day it will all be tidied up – well, maybe.

We made camp with a little fire over which I hung my nasty wet socks. It is the one, small, flatish area to pitch the tents, but it is beside a creepy looking hot lake surrounded

Curious rock formations at Avachinsky Volcano.

by a steaming marsh. When we had sorted our things, we walked through the building site to a man-made pool of about seven square feet, probably made for the workers, Sergei told us. Again natural hot and cold running water, but this time a bit murky looking. Regardless, we all got in with of course lots of giggling and laughter, until three men arrived, probably workers, and we had to get out. The evening was simply beautiful with the sun slipping down behind the nearby volcanoes. It was so still and silent with everybody having gone home but us, and then Zhenya entertained us on the guitar, learning the songs from my Celtic Classics tape. He is really quite good, and we all had a couple of drinks to soften the blow of this horrible industrial site after the beauty of the mountains.

Viljuchinsky Hot Springs, 3 September

During the night my mind was tying itself in knots, my imagination running riot in a strange dream world of escaping gases where we were being poisoned to death and nobody knew where we were. I'm sure these hallucinations were brought on because I had a slight headache and sore throat. The morning, of course, was fine and everything was normal in the bright light of day. The old legs were a bit tired this morning but after a little walk all felt great again. It is yet another cloudless day – we are so lucky. There was no frost last night but a very heavy dew.

After breakfast we climbed back up to the pool partway up the hot stream, which was too occupied yesterday, and had the most wonderful bathe and hair wash in the sun. Really, really wonderful but still in sight of the construction works. However, although it was Sunday, there was nobody else around, and we spent ages in the water and then lay around on the bank drying off before setting off once again for Viljuchinsky.

Here we are now, and this is the first time we have had any mosquitoes. Certainly not a lot but enough to warrant spraying ourselves with insect repellent, and Elise has her hat with the mosquito net on. We are beside a river in woodland with the perfect cone of Viljuchinsky Volcano above us. This valley, which runs on down to the sea, was filled with cloud and sea mist when we saw it from above on the way here, but that has all gone now and there is just the sound of the Viljucha River and it's very, very peaceful.

The track down here from Pioneerski Pass was dreadful, very steep with a huge drop on the left-hand side into a ravine and the river, and littered with huge chunks of rock which we had to dodge. We got the car almost to the bottom, and then the track became totally impassable and we had to unload and carry stuff down to a collection of huts that have been built here to accommodate schoolchildren and students for trekking and nature outings. The warden said there could be no camping which upset us somewhat, however, wonderful Valya sweet-talked him into letting us stay, after which he couldn't have been more accommodating – I don't know what she promised him but she really is amazing.

After we had unpacked everything, we discovered one of Elise's boots was missing and we deduced that it had fallen out of the car at the pass when she and Valya exchanged places. Poor, valiant Sergei was the only one who volunteered to go all the way back up the dreadful track and hope to find it, which, luckily, he did, otherwise Elise would have been, almost literally, up the creek without a paddle!

VILJUCHINSKY HOT SPRINGS, 4 SEPTEMBER

This was a brilliant day. In the morning we fought our way downstream through huge plants, often with seed heads, willow and hazel to a place on the river where, late in the season, salmon still lurk. We had to cross the river three times – a bit of a pain repeatedly getting out of our boots and into our gutties. We climbed over trees and under branches, making our way, most of the time along a very narrow bear path. Twice we passed recent

A thick ice bridge provides a close-up view of an impressive waterfall on Spokoyny River.

bear droppings consisting mostly of red berries.

After about an hour we came to a deep hole in the river and there we must have surprised a large bear, for we could just discern him ambling off into the vegetation where he was totally lost from view. So disappointing – we were hoping to see bears here where there are still salmon in the river.

We ventured out of where we were hiding and took over the bear's patch on the river. The water was beautifully clear. Elise and I sat on top of a steep bank salmon-spotting, and watching Sergei fishing. We managed to catch three enormous salmon, me using a horrible three-hook affair, not sportsmanlike at all. We had a picnic and spent hours hoping to see another bear, of which there were obviously plenty. However, Valya was not at all sure that she wanted to; she said they are very aggressive and she is scared of them. Wow!

Back at the camp Elise, Valya and I clambered up the little track to the topmost thermal pool. It was gorgeous but took us ages to get in the very hot, just about bearable (excuse the pun) water, somewhere between heaven and hell! We stayed in a long time getting redder and redder, somewhat resembling three boiled lobsters, then went down the hill to a much bigger and cooler pool, just large and deep enough to swim about in. It's all quite unreal, these hot natural pools in the most beautiful surroundings, always with the silhouette of the perfect cone of Viljuchinsky above us and not another soul around.

Meanwhile back at our camp, Zhenya had cleaned and gutted the fish, and Valya set to work on the female fish, taking out the roe and parboiling it, then putting it into a little bag and hanging it from a tree. The head was cut up and put with the filleted bones and some vegetables to make soup. Eventually at about 9pm we had the most delicious dinner – fish soup, fried salmon fillets with spuds mixed with bacon and onion and big chunks of cucumber, all washed down with vodka and/or beer. You cannot get food like this in the poshest restaurant in Petropavlovsk. At this point, Sergei got up and went off in a bit of a huff because Valya had teased him about something; we thought it was quite funny, but she went to find him and they disappeared for a while to have a walk and sort out their differences.

PETROPAVLOVSK. 5 SEPTEMBER

This morning's breakfast was fish soup and caviar – if you like that sort of thing for breakfast! The swamp beside us steamed gently in the cold morning air while the sun rose yet again into a clear blue sky. A mist was rolling in again from the direction of the sea and we hoped it wouldn't block out the sun. There were indeed mosquitoes during breakfast as the air was so still. It's a bit of a laugh trying to eat and drink wearing a midge mask!

Every now and then the discomfort of camping impinges on us oldies; this time we were both feeling tense sitting on a log to eat as the chairs were still in the car. It is very uncomfortable not being able to stretch out one's legs or have something to lean against. Our clothes were by now pretty filthy, but there was no way we were going to try and wash them even though there was no lack of hot water.

At Zhenya's suggestion we spent three hours trying to reach another waterfall. We started off up bear tracks, climbing over chunks of granite and fallen trees, then teetering along the river's edge, fighting our way through high grass, huge, very prickly thistles, Rosebay willow herb and an enormous kind of cow parsley. Some plants sported bluish berries and many more were covered with red berries. It's quite extraordinary how huge everything grows here, given that the winters are so long and severe and there are only about four growing months. I suppose that's what underground heating does.

Our scramble up the river was, in fact, the hardest going so far. We constantly tripped and fell as we climbed over and crawled under the branches of bushes and trees. My knees

started complaining, then screaming "enough, enough!" Eventually Elise and I came to a grinding halt, with a sheer cliff on our side of the river dropping down to the water. We had to try and cross over, but the river was a raging torrent, and even the others decided it was too dangerous. Sergei managed it in waders, by now carrying my backpack, and Zhenya, of course, did it by leaping from rock to rock, but it was very slippery, so Valya, Elise and I regretfully turned back.

In fact the boys never made the waterfall either. Everywhere had changed since the last time Zhenya and Sergei had done it, a year ago. Each year's winter brings changes to the landscape; a landslide had blocked the way with two huge rocks on either side of the now torrential river, and they couldn't make it up and over or round them. We were glad we had turned back when we did, and instead made our way to the top thermal pool and steeped our aching limbs in the comforting warmth.

During the late afternoon we packed up camp. Our tent, as usual, was a wreck – I don't know what I learned as a Girl Guide, but I've obviously forgotten most of it. We had to make several trips up and down to the car carrying all our equipment, to return to Petropavlovsk. Then we had to walk

the whole way up to the pass as it was far too steep for the car, heavily laden even without us in it. And anyway, Elise and I thought it would have been much, much too scary in the car, skidding and sliding around so close to the ravine. We passed the top of the waterfall and were able to peer over trees and shrubs to see the landslide at the bottom; no wonder we were unable to reach it. We called at the dacha again to be fed and fussed over by Maria who, I am sure, thinks we are totally mad. Once again we were given the run of the garden so couldn't resist a few more raspberries and blackcurrants.

We dropped Zhenya off near his apartment and turned into what looked, to our spoilt Western eyes, like a scrapland. Unmade roads, horrendous blocks of flats, unkempt, unpainted, indescribable... when to our horror, we stopped at a building that was our new hotel. We were aghast – we simply cannot get used to the state of the hotels. The room we were brought to stank of cigarette smoke. We asked if there wasn't somewhere better, in a nicer location, and Valya said it was a good area and where she lived – oh God, we stepped right into that one! We were overcome with embarrassment. She assured us it really was a good hotel, so we settled for a different room and the bliss of a shower, clean clothes and *beds*!

PETROPAVLOVSK

HOTEL RUSKI. PETROPAVLOVSK. 6 SEPTEMBER

Well here we are in relative normality. We have come to a hotel here in Petropavlovsk from Paratunka as it is nearer all that we now want to do.

Today we had a city tour with a different guide whilst wonderful Valya came to the hotel and took away all our dirty clothes, saying she would do our washing, bless her. We are being incredibly lucky with the weather and it was yet again a gorgeous day, with Avacha Bay looking dreamy and far across the water a little shimmer of mist hanging over the entrance to the harbour. We thought it would be a rather boring round of monuments and parks as per the itinerary, but it was a good experience to see around the town and learn a little bit about it.

The town of Petropavlovsk was founded in 1741 by Vitus Bering and is one of the Far East's oldest capital cities. Bering was a Danish Russian who named the town after his two ships, the *Svyatov Pyotr* (Saint Peter) and the *Svyotov Pavel* (Saint Paul). Tragically, Bering and many of his crew died of scurvy and he was buried on the Komandorsky Islands. Although Petropavlovsk became the Tsar's major Pacific sea port, it developed very slowly and even by 1866 it was still only a small village of log cabins. Near the harbour in Petropavlovsk, where there is a memorial to shipwrecked sailors, there is also a monument to Vitus Bering.

Petropavlovsk is situated on the northeast shore of Avacha Bay, a long, thin city snaking around the bay between the mountains. It has two main areas: one centres round the bay and Lenin Square, while the other is a bus ride away near Komsomolskaya Square. Built in 1978, Lenin Square used to play host to the May Day and other military parades. It is the administrative and cultural centre of the city, with the theatre and museums nearby. Beyond the theatre, and continuing on up Leninskaya, a path on the right leads

The drab concrete blocks of Petropavlovsk's Soviet-era expansion are dominated by volcanoes.

up to a small chapel. This was the first monument erected in Petropavlovsk in 1854 to commemorate the defenders of the town during the Crimean War. The Russian defenders are buried under the right cross (their cause being righteous), the English and French under the left one.

Farther up the street on the left is a department store, and past that a grey obelisk. One of the very few foreign monuments in the Russian Far East, this was brought to Petropavlovsk from England in 1913 and marks the grave of Captain Charles Clerke.

In 1766 Clerke had joined Captain Cook's ship, the E*ndeavour*, for Cook's first voyages in search of Australia, and he stayed with Cook on both of his successive voyages, the third being in search of the rumoured North West Passage. Cook's death at the hands of angry natives in Hawaii put Clerke, as captain of the companion ship, *Discovery*, in charge of the expedition. After Cook's death he took command of his ship, the *Resolution*. The two ships had already been as far north as Kamchatka but fatefully returned to Hawaii before making a second attempt. The loyal Captain Clerke, although seriously ill decided to have another go and successfully landed in Kamchatka. It was only then, from Petropavlovsk, that the news of Captain Cook's death was sent home – news travelled slowly in those days, a far cry from the speed of communications today. Captain Clerke died at sea soon after, and was buried here in 1779.

Across the road is the monument to the liberators of the Kuril Islands from the attack launched from Kamchatka during the Second World War. Four thousand Japanese died in the assault to recapture these strategic islands in August during the last days of the war.

Back on the right-hand side of Leninskaya we took a right into Krasintev Street and walked up to a large gate. This path led us up to Nikolskaya Hill. This is the spot where the English/French landing during the Crimean War was repulsed. From here one has a wonderful view of the city and bay, and it is easy to see why this hill was the focal point of the city's defences. Nearby stands another memorial to those of the Third Battery, who fell in defence of the city in 1854. Replicas of the cannons used at the time are placed along the embankment.

This is a lovely place on a good day to enjoy a picnic and watch the ships go by, slightly spoiled by the wreaths of telephone wires draped across the view. It is also known as "lover's rock" due to the numbers of couples found here, hoping to find a secluded spot. Sadly, only around six nice old wooden houses are left from the old days, but nothing earlier than 1906; otherwise most of the town consists of fairly dreadful concrete apartment blocks.

After our long tour, we had quite a good lunch of crab salad and fish cakes with a very good ale, a bit like malty Guinness. In the afternoon we visited a lovely little museum where we spent a long time looking at an interesting exhibition on the indigenous peoples of Kamchatka.

Our itinerary changes by the day. We thought we were going mountaineering again on the morrow, but instead we will be going to the Institute of Volcanology – however, we'll see. Our rather dull room has the benefit of a tiny balcony facing west and oh joy, drinks in the late afternoon sun. This has been a really touristy sort of day, just doing what we were told, in the hands of our guide, very calm and restful and with no physical exertion!

A snowboarder grabs some air on a man-made snow ramp against the backdrop of Petropavlovsk port.

HOTEL RUSKI, PETROPAVLOVSK, 7 SEPTEMBER

This morning we went with Valya to see about an e-mail I had sent rather hopefully some days ago from the post office, only to find that it never left the post office – surprised? So off we went to the public library which was apparently "online". We made our way through the large library, full of dusty tomes and ancient shelving as one might expect, through two or three old offices and there, lo and behold, was an up-to-date room with a choice of computers. By dint of my half-reasonable knowledge, with Valya translating and another girl's help, we found I had a hotmail message from my sister Jill. I got great satisfaction from this, and was able to reply – but heaven knows if she will get it. She should, but I've given up trying to do any further communication; Jill will be able to let everyone know that we are still in the land of the living.

Our next appointment was with Vitaly Ivanovitch, a tiny, dark, dedicated man, who is the director of National Parks. He seemed pleased to see us and showed us two videos of one national park and another of the setting-up of a film about Kamchatka's wildlife. The five national parks have only been in existence since 1998, and there is of course a constant problem of funding. Much of the government from Moscow is against the idea but Vitaly has had some funding from a wealthy American and also some from the WWF for Nalychevo Park as a World Heritage site.

He is upset that the Valley of the Geysers is pretty well unavailable to ordinary Russians because of the need to have a permit and the prohibitive cost of the helicopter. It is possible to walk from Milkovo and camp on the way but it takes about four days to get there and the same back and there's still the permit, so in reality it is only available to VIPs and tourists. Unfair, without a doubt. It was a very interesting meeting and quite a privilege to get such first-hand information. There was wine, tea, raisins, nuts, redcurrants and chocolates at our disposal. Again, everyone is so very hospitable.

After lunch in a local cafeteria we went to the Institute of Volcanology to meet Viktor Mikhailovitch, the director, and Sergei's boss. This was tremendously interesting. We saw a map of the Pacific volcanic activity, showing constant movement, and the computer room of seismic readouts from the six volcanoes in southern Kamchatka, the needle vibrating on Koryakskaya where small eruptions were taking place. There were constant tremors, some quite long and big. Again we were made aware of the earth's instability. We were shown lots of maps, photos, volcanic rocks and a great cross-section of a volcano, explaining the various layers. Viktor remembered Adrian Phillips quite well from the recent visit by Trinity College, Dublin. When we had finished our tour, we found that we had no car to take us back into the city centre, so, nothing daunted, Valya flagged down a car and we had an impromptu taxi with a very nice, friendly man.

An amusing end to a most informative day. Meeting these two men, top in their professions, was a real bonus and a privilege. We were, by now, psyching ourselves up for our next ten-day up-country spree. What excitement and adventure, we wondered, would it hold for us?

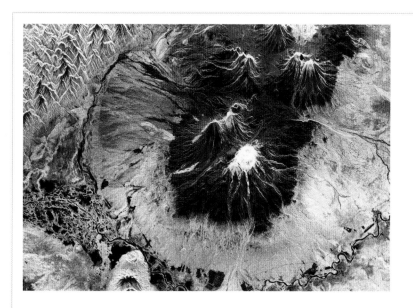

Space Radar Image of Kluchevskoy Volcano.

Kluchevskoy Volcano began to erupt on 30 September 1994. Kluchevskoy is the blue triangular peak in the centre of the image, towards the left edge of the bright-red area that delineates bare snow cover. The image was acquired by the Spaceborne Imaging Radar-C/X-band Synthetic Aperture Radar (SIR-C/X-SAR) aboard the space shuttle *Endeavour* on its 88th orbit on 5 October 1994. North is toward the bottom of the image. The radar illumination is from the top of the image. Kamchatka's volcanoes are among the most active in the world. The *Endeavour* crew obtained dramatic video and photographic images of this region during the eruption, which will assist scientists in analyzing the dynamics of volcanic activity.

No authenticated original portrait exists of Vitus Bering. The only reliable likeness is this bronze bust by the sculptor Y. Chernov, who created it from a reconstruction of Bering's skull bones after his grave was discovered. The bust now belongs to the collection of the Central Navy Museum in St Petersburg, Russia.

VITUS BERING

The Danish explorer Vitus Bering served for most of his life in the Russian Navy and is renowned for exploring Kamchatka and the strait between Asia and America that now bears his name.

Bering's first expedition was ordered by Peter the Great in 1725, just before the death of the Tsar. Peter had told Bering to go to Kamchatka, and find out how the Siberian mainland was (or was not) connected to the American continent. Bering and his group travelled overland and by river from St Petersburg to Okhotsk, a small, miserable settlement across the Sea of Okhotsk from Kamchatka. This incredibly difficult journey took Bering through the forests, swamps and ice fields of Russia and Siberia, and by the time they reached Okhotsk the group's situation was desperate. Their food had been rationed to the very minimum and they were only able to build a boat with what materials were available locally. Large, strong trees were unable to grow in this windy northern area and they were without nails, so they made a

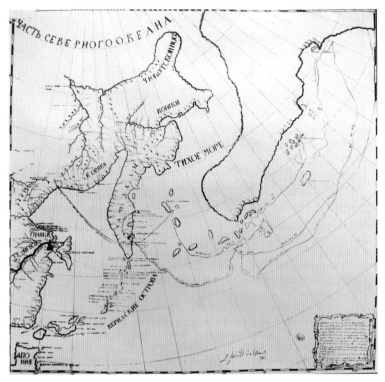

The 1741 map that resulted from Bering's nautical campaigns.

makeshift boat bound together with leather strips. Amazingly, this got them across the Sea of Okhotsk to the west coast of Kamchatka, and from there the expedition travelled by dog sled over the miles of swamp, tundra and mountains to Nizhnekamchatsk on the Pacific coast. Here they were able to set about boat-building in earnest, while trying to stay alive in the terrible weather conditions, living on fish, roots and berries.

In the summer of 1728 they were finally more or less ready to begin exploration. Bering sailed north along the coast of Kamchatka and rounded the Chukchi Peninsula, without knowing, passing through what is now the Bering Strait. As the ship continued north and the coast they were following turned northwest, Bering believed that they had established that Russia and America were unconnected, and since the winter weather was almost upon them, he turned the ship around and returned to Kamchatka.

In the summer of 1729 Bering set out towards the east. Again he did not sight the coast of America, and, again presuming that his task seemed to be accomplished, he headed south round Cape Lopatka, onwards to Okhotsk and subsequently overland again to St Petersburg, submitting his report in 1730.

In St Petersburg the Tsarina Anna was still interested in Siberia and its relationship with America. Under her authority, a second expedition was organized, called the Great Northern Expedition. This was a massive operation which included a large party from the Academy of Sciences, among them Johann Georg Gmelin, Gerhard Friedrich Muller, Johann Eberhard Fischer, Georg Wilhelm Steller and Stepan Krasheninnikov. The intention was to determine not only once and for all the Asia/American connection but also to map the Arctic coast and conduct geological and other scientific research throughout the north of Siberia. Bering, as head of this expedition, also had orders to map the American coastline. This huge expedition took nearly two years to organize and included over 3,000 people. Bering and his party left St Petersburg in 1733.

As one might imagine, once the project got under way, it became a logistical nightmare, full of political infighting and personal conflicts. It took two years for the main body to travel overland to Okhotsk, yet again over the wilds of Russia and Siberia, and build the necessary ships. In 1740 Bering sailed around the coast of Kamchatka and into the natural harbour of Avachinskaya (Avacha) Bay, founding the town of Petropavlovsk, named in honour of his two ships, the *Saint Peter* and the *Saint Paul*. In late spring Bering again set sail to seek America. Despite the hardships of poor food, bad weather and being separated from the *Saint Paul*, he finally sighted land in July of 1741. This proved to be Kayak Island off the Alaska coast.

Sick, exhausted and wary of bad weather, Bering turned the *Saint Peter* back towards Kamchatka. Strong headwinds, storms, miscalculations and mass cases of scurvy among the crew slowed their return. With most of the crew dying and Bering himself sick from scurvy, on 4 November the ship sighted land, one of the Komandorsky Islands. Bering decided to spend the winter on the uninhabited island to recuperate and prepare for the spring, but died a month later on 8 December 1741 on the island which was later to bear his name. By the following summer the remains of the crew were able to build a boat and return to the mainland.

Despite its tragic end, the Great Northern Expedition did achieve some marvellous results. Although the scientists had gathered a massive amount of new information, unfortunately there was no plan to systematically evaluate and publish it for some years to come. However, the city of Petropavlovsk was founded, the Siberian and Arctic coasts were charted and the Komandorsky Islands discovered, not to mention the fact that Bering's expedition was the first to explore that now famous body of water – the Bering Strait.

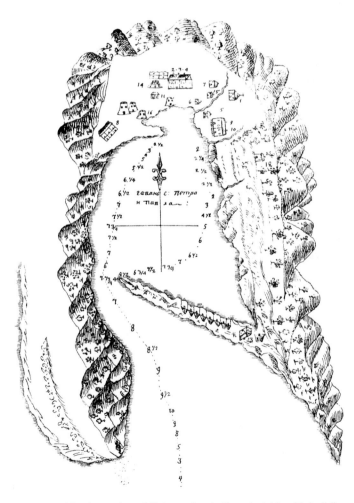

A harbour plan of Petropavlovsk-Kamchatskiy with buildings marked, created by I. Elagin in 1740.

THE "VOLCANOES OF KAMCHATKA" WORLD HERITAGE SITE

The tiny figure of a trekker gives perspective to Gorely's crater and the inspirational surrounding landscape.

The first protected areas in Kamchatka appeared at the end of the 19th century in order to protect the habitat of the valuable sable. In 1882, the Kronotsky area received the benefit of an imperial decree ordering the protection of sable, snow sheep and reindeer, and in 1926 an executive committee officially designated the area a "*zapovednik*", a strictly protected federal nature reserve, where theoretically all forms of commercial activity are prohibited and human movement is restricted to scientific research. Today, protected areas occupy approximately 27 percent of Kamchatka's total land area.

In 1996, UNESCO designated five protected areas on Kamchatka a World Heritage Site, "Volcanoes of Kamchatka", and in 2001 Kluchevskoy was added to the site. The concept of World Heritage originated in 1972, whereby nations agree to identify sites in their countries that are of "outstanding universal value" from either a cultural/historical, natural, (such as Kamchatka) or mixed cultural/natural criteria. There are four major criteria for selecting World Heritage natural sites; they should:

1. Be outstanding examples representing major phases of the Earth's history.
2. Be exceptional examples representing ongoing ecological and biological processes.
3. Contain the most important natural habitats of endangered species of universal value.
4. Contain superlative phenomena or areas of exceptional natural beauty.

The "Volcanoes of Kamchatka" is one of the few sites that fulfil all of these criteria. It is one of the most outstanding volcanic regions in the world, with a high density of varying types of active volcanoes, with a wide range of related features. The variation of landscape between active volcanoes and glaciers makes for the most dynamic and beautiful scenery. The six sites contain a great diversity of species, including the largest known variety of salmonoid fish and exceptional numbers of brown bear, sea otter and Steller's sea eagle.

The Volcanoes of Kamchatka site comprises the following protected areas:

- KRONOTSKY STATE BIOSPHERE NATURE PRESERVE with an area of 1,0007,134 hectares, plus a three-mile ocean buffer zone

- BYSTRINSKY NATURE PARK*, 1,500,000 hectares

A sturdy lodge between Avachinsky and Koryaksky volcanoes.

- NALYCHEVO NATURE PARK*, 265,000 hectares

- SOUTHWESTERN TUNDRA NATURE RESERVE*, 123,000 hectares

- SOUTHERN KAMCHATKA NATURE PARK and the SOUTHERN KAMCHATKA STATE NATURE RESERVE*, 1,025,000 hectares, created under an agreement between Russia and Japan to protect migratory birds

- KLUCHEVSKOY NATURE PARK*, 375,981 hectares

- KOMANDORSKY ISLANDS STATE BIOSPHERE RESERVE, 3,648,679 hectares

These reserves are "zakazniks", ie an area set aside for the preservation of smaller ecosystems or individual species. Zakazniks may be protected federally or regionally. Restrictions on commercial activities are sometimes limited to certain seasons. As with zapovedniks, they have been established in order to regulate hunting so that viable wildlife populations may be maintained.

KRONOTSKY ZAPOVEDNIK is located within eastern Kamchatka's volcanic belt, whose influence on the territory's topography, flora and fauna is readily apparent. Here the full diversity of volcanic activity is found – from 12 active volcanoes, to post-caldera formations and a multitude of thermal springs. The Russian Far East's greatest prevalence of glacial alpine landscapes is here as well; glaciers, including some of the peninsula's largest, cover 14,000ha of the zapovednik's territory. The zapovednik also includes large areas of forest, wetlands, open dry range and a large system of rivers and lakes all of which drain into the Pacific Ocean. One of the largest lakes in Kamchatka, Lake Kronotsky, covers 242 square kilometres.

A number of unique natural objects can be found in the zapovodnik that have great scientific, recreational and aesthetic value. The famous Valley of the Geysers is a collection of volcanic phenomena whose scale and localization are rare; 20 large geysers, over 200 thermal springs, and a multitude of mud pots, thermal vents and other volcanic formations. The largest geyser, Velikan, shoots boiling water to 30 metres and steam to 300 metres. The valley is a beautiful landscape of multicoloured rocks against the bright green of lush plant life and wildflowers. The Uzon Caldera, formed some 40,000 years ago, is a giant volcanic bed with steaming warm lakes full of geothermal activity. Uzon has hot springs and a landscape painted with an amazing array of colours from the minerals deposited here.

The huge boiling mud pools found in the Uzon Caldera were once feared by the indigenous people of the region, who considered them the homes of evil spirits.

A facility for observing bears gives visitors an opportunity to view these animals with a preserve researcher providing information about the bears and their territory. As well as bears there are around 2,500 wild reindeer in the area along with Steller's sea eagles and Aleutian terns.

This zapovodnik is not a national park and has a much more limited mandate for public use than the other zakazniks. The special status of the preserve places the wilderness value, its preservation and research at the highest priority, but has designated specific areas for limited human utilization.

BYSTRINSKY NATURE PARK (a zakaznik) is located in the heart of the Kamchatka Peninsula with several peaks or more than 2,000m; the active volcano Ichinsky, at 3,607m is the highest summit in the area. The park's largest river, the Bystraya, serves as the headwater for the Kamchatka River, the country's longest. Many smaller rivers and streams also flow into the Kamchatka River, creating large wetlands in the river valleys. All the ecosystems found in central Kamchatka are to be found in the park in their virgin state. The high biodiversity of these ecosystems resulting from the area's volcanic activity and numerous hot springs, add to the park's value for conservation and tourism.

This zakaznik is home to a sizeable population of brown bear, snow sheep and sable, and the density of introduced muskrat, American mink and Canadian beaver is high. Siberian lemming, wild reindeer and Kamchatkan marmot are among the rare species that inhabit the park. All species of Pacific salmon, Arctic grayling and Dolly Varden trout are to be found in the rivers throughout the park.

A wide variety of arctic plants inhabit the high plateaux and relict cryophilic and steppe species are found among the cliffs. The park forms the southern extent of many species' geographical distribution. Much of the land is forested with Japanese stone birch, shrub alder, stone birch, Ayan spruce and Dahurian larch.

Indigenous Even, Itelmen and Koryak live in the park practising traditional subsistence activities such as fishing, hunting, gathering berries and mushrooms and reindeer herding. Two settlements, Esso and Anavgai, are located within the park.

Two healthy reindeer prance across the open spaces of the tundra. Their huge antlers are used for display, defence and attack – but the reindeer herders find many more uses for them.

NALYCHEVO NATURE PARK is situated north of Avacha Bay; its proximity to Petropavlovsk and Yelizovo making it a favourite place for recreation and tourism. Whether hiking in the park – there is no road access – or arriving by helicopter, visitors have the opportunity of seeing brown bear and Steller's sea eagle; of fishing (the Nalycheva River provides spawning habitat for five species of Pacific salmon); or climbing an active volcano.

This zakaznik incorporates the volcanoes Zhupanovsky, Koryaksky, Avachinsky and Dzenzur, which surround the Nalycheva River valley. A few hundred hydrothermal and cold mineralised springs are concentrated in the upper reaches of the Nalycheva River. The thermal springs range in temperature from 14–75°C. The waters of the largest hot spring, Nalychevskie, are the only known example in the world with such carbonaceous, arsenic and boric concentrations.

The park combines stunning mountain scenery with vast expanses of tundra and coastal seascapes. The presence of volcanic and ancient glacial landscapes, together with the specific microclimate conditions of the river valley have produced unique richness and diversity of flora and fauna, many of which are presented in Russia's Red Book. Thirty-three mammal species are found in the area. As well as brown bear and Steller's sea eagle, the volcanic cones and cliffs of Nalycheva Point provide habitat for snow sheep. The valley is frequented by 145 species of bird; rare species include the black brant, white-tailed sea eagle, gyrfalcon, peregrine falcon and golden eagle. The forests of Ermins birch (stone birch) around the hot springs have a variety of wildflowers including the rare Lady's Slipper orchid.

Nalychevo Park can be visited at any time of year with many hiking, skiing and dog sledding opportunities. In the centre of the park there is an eco-educational centre where visitors can obtain information about the environment and activities available. There is also a little shop and a few tourist cabins are located here.

THE SOUTHWESTERN TUNDRA ZAKAZNIK is a Habitat/Species Management Area comprising uninhabited, coastal/flatland covered with lakes, pools and peat, very attractive to migrant waterfowl.

THE SOUTHERN KAMCHATKA NATURE PARK and the SOUTHERN KAMCHATKA STATE NATURE RESERVE (Yuzhno-Kamchatka) is a huge area covering territory from Avacha Bay on the east coast, south to Cape Lopatka on the southern tip of the peninsula. The northern part

Marmots, or ground squirrels, are amusing animals to watch, and ideally suited to the Russian tundra.

of the park's territory encompasses several volcanoes, including one of Kamchatka's most active, Mutnovsky. Fifty-nine mammal species inhabit this area. Snow sheep, brown bear and sea otter are the most valuable but there are also large communities of fox, sable, river otter, wolverine, American mink and Arctic ground squirrel.

The park boasts one of the largest populations of peregrine falcons in Kamchatka and also has a number of nesting pairs of Steller's sea eagles, some ospreys and golden eagles. Nesting colonies of seabirds, including long-billed murrelets, slatey-backed gulls, tufted puffins and pelagic cormorants inhabit the shores of the Pacific coast and islands. Sharing this coastal habitat are colonies of ringed seals, sea otters and the endangered Steller sea lion.

In the southern part of the territory lies Lake Kurilskoye, Kamchatka's second largest freshwater body with a depth of 306 metres. It is dramatic, surrounded by a theatre of active volcanoes, Kambalny, Ilinsky, Diky Greben and Kosheleva. In autumn the lake shores and the rivers in the area teem with hundreds of bears that feed on the massive salmon run. In the summer, millions of these fish pour into Lake Kurilskoye, entering the Ozernaya River from the Sea of Okhotsk. This is the largest sock-eye spawning run in Asia and accounts for between 1.5 and 3.5 million fish.

Besides bears, there is always a chance of seeing red fox, river otter or mink trotting along the lakeshore, and varieties of duck and whooper swans gliding along on the lake surface. Rare birds such as the yellow-billed loon, black brant, lesser white-fronted goose and the Aleutian tern are to be found here. The area also boasts the highest population density of Steller's sea eagle in the world. Every winter as heavy snowfall covers the land, anything from 300 to 700 of these enormous raptors winter along the shore, as well as 100 to 150 white-tailed sea eagles and 50 golden eagles, making this park one of the most important raptor refuges.

KLUCHEVSKOY NATURE PARK is a relatively small zakaznik about 350 kilometres northeast of Petropavlovsk. However, it contains 12 volcanoes, 47 glaciers, 400 cones and hundreds of lava flows. Because there have been so many eruptions in this area, it has caused a wide lava plateau which is the biggest and most powerful volcanic mass in Russia. No fewer than two eruptions occur annually, lasting from probably one or two days to a few months. Kluchevskoy, Eurasia's highest volcano (4,750m) each year emits around 55,000,000 tons of basalt from a depth of 30 kilometres. 1975 saw the massive 18-month eruption of Tolbachik Volcano. In total size the eruptive material and activity was the sixth largest volcanic event ever recorded.

Bezymyany Volcano is situated in the centre of the park, surrounded by beautiful river valleys and lakes where wild geese, ducks, swans and Steller's sea eagles nest. Fir, larch and birch forest, alpine meadows and mountain tundra provide habitat for diverse flora and fauna where there are about 400 species of plant. Snow sheep, black marmot, capercaille, wolverine, lynx, bear and moose thrive here. A massive salmon spawning area is located here also in the peninsula's largest river – the Kamchatka River – which runs southwest to northeast.

On the banks of the river are forestry harvesting, fishing and hunting settlements. Itelmen and Kamchadals, original inhabitants of Kamchatka, live in this valley. Klyuchi is a small local town where everyone depends on the wilderness for survival. Almost everybody goes fishing and in the spring and autumn many people hunt the brown bear. A single bear can provide several hundreds of pounds of meat, which is salted and then boiled for hours to make it safe and soft enough for consumption.

In 1935, Klyuchi village opened its first volcanology station. In 1958 in Kozyrevsk, a seismic station was established and now the park operates seven field stations and five field points of the Geophysical Service of the Russian Federation where international research on volcanoes and glaciers takes place.

THE KOMANDORSKY ISLANDS NATURE RESERVE is a biosphere reserve situated in the Bering Sea east of the Kamchatka Peninsula that boasts mountain tundra, motley grass meadows, wetlands, coastal and marine zones. The flora and fauna of the Komandorsky Islands are remarkable because of the unusual combination of species of Asian and American origin. Its coastal ecosystems are unique because of their diversity of marine mammals and birds. The islands were discovered by Vitus Bering, and it is here that he died and is buried.

The "Volcanoes of Kamchatka" World Heritage site is under-funded and consequently undermanned. With the local population finding it hard to make a living, quite naturally logging, illegal hunting and poaching occur throughout the

site, and in Kronotsky Zapovednik, which, by its very name should be used only for scientific and environmental research, tourism, particularly to the "Valley of the Geysers" continues unchecked.

The fact that Kamchatka possesses this site, offers greatly enhanced prospects for balanced, environmentally and socially friendly economic development. However, it's potential will only be realized if communities and government officials in Kamchatka work together to maximize the opportunities it presents.

There is, of course, great competition among countries to have sites chosen for World Heritage designation, not least because inclusion makes an area an international focus of attention for tourism and sometimes attracts financial support from international organizations. If inappropriate development or poor management endangers a site, the UNESCO committee can declare that the site is "in danger", creating substantial embarrassment for the government concerned.

For international support and tourism to materialize, there is a need for local communities and authorities to cooperate to effectively manage the sites; unfortunately, it would appear that at present the parks constituting the Kamchatka World Heritage site are not, in fact, being developed coherently.

Based on information in The Russian Far East *by Josh Newell,*
published by Daniel and Daniel .

It took the photographer hours to get near a den of red foxes, but once they had accepted her as harmless, they relaxed completely.

THE ROAD NORTH

MILKOVO. HOMESTAY. 8 SEPTEMBER

A horrible wet morning greeted us. We were actually ready and waiting for Valya and Sergei, for once, at 10.30am. By 1.30pm we had done the shopping for provisions, except for the booze which we couldn't find until I went off on a sortie, meeting with some success. We left our spare bags with Maria at the dacha and left Petropavlovsk for Milkovo. Maria had, as usual, fallen upon us making a great fuss and plying us with flowers, fruit and veggies, fussing that we were going so far away.

The road to Milkovo is metalled part of the way north as far as the hot springs at Malki. Valya was very excited about it and was looking forward to having a bathe, but we thought it was a really vile place with a dirty car park, rubbish everywhere and four men in one of the hot pools. It was still drizzling and even Elise, who is almost always game for a dip, said "no way". We had an Irish-type picnic in the car in the rain and Valya kept on trying to coax us into the water. However, we were not to be tempted and went for a walk along the river instead but were soon totally put off by the litter of plastic bags, loo paper, sanitary towels and other unmentionables! We repaired to the car and had a quick "reviver" while Valya and Sergei had a bathe.

We continued on to Milkovo, now in brilliant sunshine, on what was basically a dirt road, through the taiga, crossing many rivers, with me dozing off from time to time, arriving at the home of Alexei and Nina in the late afternoon. They are an elderly couple, retired from the Russian Army, who run a sort of B&B. She was a vet and he a driver and they are now both 72. They had lived from time to time in Kazakhstan, Tajikistan and the Ukraine. They didn't have a word of English and so conversation was pretty limited. He had built the house with the help of friends and there is a flush loo inside and a banya outside, these two amenities qualifying the house for paying guests. The couple were very

Vladimir, one of a growing number of tourist guides, prepares a meal by the fire outside a hut in Kronotsky National Park.

friendly, kind and curious and our bedroom was basic and OK but the kitchen area was so dirty and somehow squalid, not one single decent cooking implement, or pan. The water comes up from a spring so probably it was fine. The cooking and heating is by way of a big wood burning stove. The one amazing luxury was the stunningly beautiful Kazak carpets – on the walls unfortunately, not the floor.

We were plied with loads of smoked fish, bread, rock-hard biscuits cooked by their daughter-in-law, cakes and rather watery wild mushroom soup, plus copious quantities of tea. They also ate boiled and unboiled condensed milk from the tin.

Alexei and Nina have been unhappy since perestroika because their pensions have not risen with the cost of living and there are serious worries among older folk as to just how they are going to manage in the future. There were many other reasons for their discontent, but they are the people who lived with, and gained from, communism, always in work, kids educated, bright enough to have good jobs and unquestioning. All that we were told was interesting and a real "in your face" example of how different the Eastern and Western worlds' view is of "freedom". How very difficult it must be to be brought up to believe absolutely in communism, and then, overnight, be told that it was all wrong. We felt terribly ungrateful by not eating all in front of us.

We did, however enjoy a wonderful sauna in a dilapidated back shed, Elise, Valya and I, yet again, leaping about, beating each other sadistically with birch twigs and dashing between roasting sauna and standing naked in the rain until we all felt clean, refreshed and tingling all over!

The whole house was very open-plan. We didn't know where anyone else was sleeping, and I just prayed I wouldn't have to go to the loo during the night. The loo paper was old torn-up magazines; the seat was covered in a sort of black satin quilting – very unusual; and the cistern was very noisy!

ESSO. REST HOUSE. 9 SEPTEMBER

Breakfast, with our kind Russian hosts was a complete disaster! After saying grace – they are strictly religious and grace is said before every meal – (can you be both Russian Orthodox and Communist?) we were served fish soup which we politely refused saying we didn't eat soup for breakfast at home, followed by the inevitable fishcakes and mashed potato. I managed one fish cake and excused myself for a handkerchief and got a plastic bag into which I surreptitiously slipped my other fish cake, and into which Elise managed to put both of hers. I toyed with the spud but couldn't manage to bag it! It was awful, the

trick was not to get caught as the old pair would have been so hurt; it was all rather schoolgirlish.

After this debacle we went and met Misha, an incredible ex weightlifter from the Ukraine. A strapping man with blue, blue eyes and a bush of greying red hair and beard. He had built, with the help of his family, an extraordinary church in the shape of a cross. It housed different ethnic and religious artefacts in the four sectors, along with paintings done by his wife and daughter and paintings and carvings by himself, including a beautiful ceiling made from different coloured pieces of cut wood, fitted together, almost like a jigsaw, to make a sort of collage. His religion is a sect of the Russian Orthodox, but they don't worship the cross or Mary – a little more like Protestants perhaps. As Valya knows absolutely nothing about religion, it is difficult to get her to translate.

From this church cum museum Misha took us to a place where he had built a huge, life-size wooden replica of the fort the first Cossacks built on their way north to Esso. Sadly someone had set fire to it and he now finds it hard to start to resurrect it. Misha also runs an art gallery housed in a wonderful old wooden house, full of quite unexpected treasures, by his daughter, himself and other artists. We thought they were all for sale, and will call again on our return. Misha was originally trained as a scientist in Novosibarisk, and is a dynamo of artistic, creative and scientific energy. He is a bit of a mystic and a healer. What a fascinating person.

We stopped around lunchtime for a picnic well off the road in a little clearing up a grassy lane in the endless taiga, where we all enjoyed a good walk through tracts of birch, larch, hazel, ash and aspen, all of which I recognized. There were occasional sightings, when we hit higher ground, of Kluchevskoy Volcano, already wonderfully dressed in snow. We had odd stops throughout the afternoon to view rivers and gather berries and at 1pm, met and had tea with some hunters on a riverbank, having a few days off to gather berries for the winter. We chatted about animals, hunting, bears and the price of bear bile to China and Korea – all in the same way you would discuss the price of eggs at home.

We finally arrived at the house of Gnadig and Frida in the enigmatically named town of Esso. Gnadig is a hunter and taxidermist, and we had tea in his *"yaranga"*, a Koryak type of tepee very similar to those of the American Indians. It had a paved floor with a fire in the centre, and skins, utensils and totems hung round the walls. Gnadig was a short, muscular man in a black vest and trousers with a fierce, strong handshake – almost bone crushing. Another vital, energetic, very humourous man. He showed us his work shed full of bearskins, stuffed eagles, swans and all manner of other birds. He had two new-looking skidoos and a terrific work bench with modern lathes and machinery. Outside he showed us over and into his veshdehod – a cross-country tank on tracks for negotiating the wild rough terrain. A couple of trailers, sleds and an estate car completed his vehicles.

We should have been staying here but they already had guests, so disappointingly we set off to another house. It was great, brand new, and only us in it. After tea – again – we went off to another hot spring. This time it was a wonderful surprise, an enormous warm pool deep enough to swim in. By this time it was late, dark and freezing cold under the stars; there were not many people about, and although it was horrible undressing in the freezing darkness, we quickly stripped off and luxuriated for ages in the warm water.

Kamchatka's combination of geothermal activity, fertile volcanic soil and sheltered valleys make plant and fungal life grow to prodigious proportions.

ESSO. REST HOUSE, 10 SEPTEMBER

Valya had numerous visitors during the morning, including the hunter from the riverbank the day before. We fiddled about getting ready for our day with Gnadig, to walk to see wildlife and, hopefully, more bears. We finally left at about midday, not with Gnadig but with Sasha, the hunter from the riverbank.

We started off going to yet another hot spring, just a little one, so it was feet only, and then into a car and Valya, Elise and I set off with Sasha, up the hillside complete with shotgun, to go on a bear "hunt". We kept seeing bear's footprints but no bears; we really thought this place was going to be virtually "alive" with bears, but obviously they are not always exactly where you expect to see them.

Sasha kept us amused with a fund of "shaggy bear" stories, which were not quite the same as seeing the real thing. We amused ourselves as we walked the final seven kilometres or so, picking berries as we hiked on to a pretty lake. It was very windy so it was not so easy making a fire for lunch, during which we had yet more tea but this time made with some berries and pine needles. Everyone uses all the natural products around them; there is so little to buy up here in the north, it seems only sensible to use nature's bounty. Although we were getting a bit tired of smoked fish at meals, the good stuff was excellent; however, what we were eating today was terribly salty and my hands now smell constantly of fish.

Back in Esso, we brought Sasha home to his workshop; full of skins, saddles being repaired, carvings made from bone, reindeer antler and mountain sheep horn. It was beautiful work, all of which we greatly admired before making a couple of small purchases.

Esso is a village of small, wooden chalet-type houses, each with quite a good garden, growing potatoes, carrots, spinach, hops and flowers. It has a sort of microclimate due to the thermal effect from underground. Everyone has roasting hot, geothermal central heating, costing almost nothing. The town is situated on the Oxygiana, a small tributary of the Bistraya River which, in turn, is a tributary of the Kamchatka River. The beauty of the rivers is spoiled rather by the very obvious water pipes everywhere, but they do bring hot and cold water into everybody's houses, so there are no complaints. The village has a gorgeous setting surrounded by mountains and, at this time of year, the wonderfully coloured autumn hues of the woods in the middle of the huge Bystrinsky Nature Park. Here is the end of Kamchatka's "M1", its main highway; after Esso it is Shanks' Mare! Or indeed, anybody's mare, or, with luck, a helicopter which we hope we will get to take us further north to the reindeer herders.

However, during dinner (our favourite old dish, *plov*, from Uzbekistan) Valya told us that our flight to the reindeers the following day had to be postponed. Apparently the other people sharing the chopper would not be with us till the following evening and we couldn't take the chopper on our own. We were pissed off, to say the least. We are almost always ready on time, and seem to get messed up by others. However, luckily we had built in two or three extra days to our itinerary for just this kind of eventuality. Valya and Sergei kept disappearing into their rooms – she was constantly cheerful, while we began to go into deep decline. We knew we were bloody stupid getting grumpy like that when we knew there were likely to be postponements, so we decided we would go for a walk in the beautiful evening light. Looking up, we saw dark clouds on the horizon – oh please don't snow just yet!

Esso. Rest House. 11 September

11am. It was really cold last night and this morning the near mountains are covered in snow; thank goodness we are tucked up warm in this nice little house and not having to put a brave face on it in a tent! Valya has discovered that after all we may go in the chopper at 5pm today. This time we are neither surprised nor optimistic – all will be revealed later. Valya is ecstatic; she has bought fresh milk and a delicious sort of mix between cream and cottage cheese. We are not long after breakfast and cannot eat more, but maybe we'll sample it for lunch, whenever that will be.

Rest House, 5.15pm. We have been to a small but very attractive museum, quite one of the nicest ethnic museums I've ever seen. The girl there is half Koryak, half Ukrainian. Lots of artefacts from the Even, Koryak and Chukchi tribes, all well displayed in a pretty wooden building. We also saw slides of the reindeer herder's camp where we hope to go. We have had a nice walk and wait for news of the flight.

Rest House, 11.45pm. Well, we didn't get our flight. By 7pm the couple who are to go with us up-country arrived, a Swiss couple who have been photographing bears in the Kronotsky Reserve – hundreds of them! Their interpreter arrived to say that the weather at some pass we have to negotiate, was too bad – snowing apparently – although it's OK here. Elise and I were in very bad form and behaving like spoiled children so we decided to go for a really good long, four-hour hike along the Oxygiana River. We returned refreshed and in much better humour. It is all so pretty and unspoiled with the lovely

autumn colouring and the sun shining on the distant snowy mountains. There was nobody else around and we saw loads of small squirrels, presumably stocking up for the winter. Back at the house and the four of us traipsed off to the pool again. It's bizarre; it's freezing and the last thing one wants to do is get undressed, so it's horrible getting into your costume, but then its simply wonderful getting into a hot thermal pool under a canopy of brilliant stars.

Esso. Rest House. 12 September

We had thought the earliest we might leave for the herders would be around 1pm, so we were about to go for a walk and see the church when the herders' liaison man arrived about 11am and we had to pack up everything again while Sergei left with the car and provisions. We pay the reindeer herders with food, so that was why we bought so much at the market, sacks of flour and sugar and crates of fruit. I did wonder at the time how we could possibly get through all the provisions that we had bought in Petropavlovsk.

The morning was beautiful, not too cold but bright and sunny. We arrived at the heliport to find a chopper OK, but being boarded by an American hunter and his entourage of six, plus massive provisions, about to set off into the mountains to shoot big horn, or snow sheep. We watched him for some time standing directing operations, feeling a bit like the poor relations – it looked as though they were off for a month or two.

Eventually I got really shirty and my anti-American feeling came bubbling up. This was just the type of American that gets me going – obviously wealthy, loud laugh, thinks he owns the world, etc. I was sure he must be a horrible man. Elise had seen him the previous day, very much the worse for drink and giving off rings round him to his team. I went marching over to him and started haranguing him. I was probably very rude and uninformed I know, but I just couldn't help it.

A friend once told me I was a "woolly-headed idealist" – well so be it. I said did he know he had taken our plane, and then, nothing daunted and getting well into my stride asked him if he got pleasure out of killing endangered species and what on Earth did he do with them? He said he had a big house in New York where he hung the heads as trophies. I asked what his wife thought of his hobby, and when he said he didn't have one, I said no wonder; he would probably hang her up as a trophy also. I finished off my tirade belligerently saying I hoped he didn't get his snow sheep. He laughed at me of course, and said that he almost certainly would.

The Kamchatka bighorn sheep, (*Ovis nivicola nivicola*), also known as the snow sheep, is the biggest among the various species of snow sheep. Among the males, dominance is based primarily on the size of a male's horns, which can be anything from 85–105 centimetres long. If males have similar-sized horns they will duel, ramming their horns together until one emerges as the winner. These magnificent animals live high in the mountains from 1,500–2,000 metres, where they have adapted to walking on uneven surfaces. Their population is sadly in decline.

What is it about Mankind that we have to have trophies, have to possess the biggest, best, most beautiful, most rare, most endangered animal, and in order to have it we must, perforce, kill it? Why, I wonder, are we not content to know that these wonderful creatures simply exist, and that they should be able to exist in their own environment? I retired from the fray as graciously as possible, feeling that at least I had made my point and vented a bit of steam. He, of course had made his point that he was paying a lot of money to the people of Kamchatka for the privilege of hunting – somewhere in the region of US$10,000 for shooting one snow sheep – whereas we were on a fairly lean budget.

Anyway, we didn't get the chopper. Next a group of children flew off at around 3pm and we were told to come back at 6pm. We went for another walk, returned at 6pm... no chopper... desperate, we went for a drink and tried our luck at 7pm, feeling it was all such a waste of time. Why is our Western world so impatient, making us expect everything to happen exactly when we want it to? With all our Third World travels we still have not learned to be patient. How pathetic we are.

THE VEGETATION OF KAMCHATKA

by David Jeffrey, Professor Emeritus, Trinity College Dublin

The glorious burst of Kamchatka's spring bloom is due to the peninsula's volcanic origins.

In 1996 I visited Kamchatka as a member of Dr Mike William's (Institute for Hydrology and Ecology, Wallingford, UK) expedition supported by the E.U. INTAS scheme. My specific role was to interpret the vegetation of southern Kamchatka to enable "ground-truthing" of a satellite image of the region. Also from Trinity College, Dublin, were geologist Professor Adrian Phillips, and my daughter Dr Rebecca Jeffrey, zoologist and cameraperson for the expedition. We were accompanied by three Russian geologists from the Russian Academy of Science, Institute of Geology, Vladivostok.

Kamchatka may be regarded as an island of largely temperate vegetation. The eastern shore fronts the North Pacific and is dominated by the icy Kamchatka current. The western coast fronts the Sea of Okhotsk. Its coast eventually curves to the south and the island of Sakhalin. In the north, isolation is maintained by boreal and tundra vegetation. This sweeps west across Russia and east across Canada to constitute a circumpolar belt.

Throughout the world temperate vegetation is interpreted in terms of the recovery of plant cover since the close of the glacial period some 13,000 years ago. The first post-glacial vegetation was undoubtedly tundra, but this has gradually been replaced by the present temperate flora.

Islands pose interesting problems when viewed in this light. By what paths can plants advance? Here the answer lies in the island arcs that link Kamchatka to the nearest mainland masses. These arcs are related to the volcanism of Kamchatka.

Fertile soil produces a rich diversity of vegetation: a mushroom itself serves as a bed on which other plants grow (above), while thick-trunked birch trees (opposite) carpet the mountains' slopes.

The Aleutian chain is a link to Alaska and North America. The Kuril Islands extend to northern Japan and thence to the great forests of Manchuria. Any species may be analysed for its biogeographic origins. A further possibility is that it has evolved uniquely in the Kamchatka environment to be significantly distinct from its progenitors and be deemed an "endemic" species.

The term "plant community" will be used to describe readily recognisable groups of plants occupying similar environmental conditions. Use of this term is a way of avoiding the controversies which exist in ecology regarding the best method to classify vegetation. Plant communities frequently include variations in species according to minor environmental changes, eg in soil, moisture or aspect. Intermediate communities often occur at boundaries.

Hill Woodland

All the middle slopes of the hills are clothed continuously with a woodland of "Erman's Birch" (*Betula ermani*), a robust and sturdy tree with a broad crown and heavy trunk. The bark is predominantly white with much brown/black marking. This vegetation exists on a range of soils derived from old and modern volcanic materials. The species is common in Manchuria and may be assigned to this source. The woodlands remain largely unutilised, and may represent a sample of the last primeval temperate woodlands of the world. There is no evidence either of widespread incidence of forest fire or of wind-felled trees.

The woodlands are relatively open and easily penetrated on foot with a low ground flora and a sparse under-storey of smaller trees. This includes a beautiful mountain ash (*Sorbus sambucifolia*) with attractive autumn colours, red against the yellow of the birch. The ground flora comprises grasses, ferns, herbs and dwarf shrubs.

There are two variants of the *Betula ermani* woodlands. For the greater part of Kamchatka the hills are steep and the soils shallow. On this ground so-called "dry" woodland predominates. This has a characteristic under-storey of *Geranium erianthum, Epilobium angustifolium, Thalictrum kemense, Allium victorialis subsp platyphyllum, Carex sp., Saussurea sp. Majanthemum dilitatum* and *Trientalis eoropaea var arctica*. Also characteristic but not constant are *Sorbus sambucifolia, Calamogrostis langsdorfii, Artemisia vulgaris, Cimicifuga simplex, Lonicera chamissoi, L. edulis* and *Coelopleurum gmelini*.

Where sites are more level or abutting the alluvial ground on the fringes of rivers, the ground flora merges with that of the river bank communities, namely *Betula ermani, Geranium erianthum, Cirsium kamtschaticum, Filipendula kamtschatica, Dryopteris linnæana, Majanthemum dilitatum, Trientalis europaea var arctica, Salix hultenii, Sorbus sambucifolia, Cimicifuga simplex* and *Lonicera chamissoi*.

RIVERINE FOREST

The Kamchatka River drains the interior of the peninsular. It is a very seasonal river, swollen with snowmelt in spring, at a low level in summer and autumn and almost static under winter snow. One of the most remarkable phenomena that affect the river is the annual spawning migration of the cohoe salmon. These fish migrate from the sea to their freshwater spawning grounds and after spawning die in their thousands. This has been described in the literature as a rare example of nutrients being returned from the sea to a freshwater environment.

The gravel beds of the main river channel are flanked by a woodland manured by salmon corpses and always well watered. Large willows (*Salix sachalinensis*) abound with *Alnus hirsutus*. On the upper slopes above the river channel the occasional broad-leaved birch *Betula platyphylla* also occurs. Here are to be found the giant herbs for which Kamchatka is famous. One of the most spectacular is a giant hogweed, *Angelica ursina*, up to three metres tall. This is most prevalent in western Kamchatka.

Where the river valley broadens into an alluvial floodplain, a meadow-like vegetation is present. This has many affinities with the riverbank community above. In all areas affected by the river, on alluvial ground and continuously moist, meadowsweet (*Filipendula kamtschaticca*) is abundant. It is frequently accompanied by shoulder-high stinging nettles (*Urtica platyphylla*).

Where tributary streams flow into the alluvial ground of the meadows, drainage is impeded and patches of boggy ground develop. Sphagnum mosses are present accompanied by sundew (*Drosera rotundifolia*) and cranberry (*Vaccinium oxycoccus*).

The stony beds of Kamchatka's rivers cut through woodland and meadow before reaching the sea.

SUBALPINE HEATH

The alder woodland abruptly ends at the tops of the hills to give rise to subalpine heath. Heaths are common to temperate mountaintops and lowlands devoid of soil nutrients. The Kamchatka version is bio diverse compared with the woodlands. Heath is predominately woody with thick, long-lived leaves. Many are members of the plant family *Ericaceae*. This includes *Rhododendron spp.* and berry bearing types such as *Vaccinium sp.* The black-berried crowberry (*Empetrum nigrum*) is also present. These provide an abundant source of autumn food for mammals, e.g. bears and birds such as the ptarmigan. Whilst many species are evergreen, some deciduous arctic and alpine shrubs occur like willow (*Salix*) species and the dwarf arctic birch (*Betula nana*), a circumpolar plant. Generally speaking these plants are derived from tundra floras and may have preceded the Ice Age clearance. There is also a sign of North American influence in the form of a *Castilleja* species (Indian paint brush) which may be related to the alpine flora of Washington.

This attractive vegetation survives on suitably moist and relatively level sites at high altitude. This includes the Uzon Caldera. Some species are common to the tundra of the north. The ground of the subalpine heath is not uniform and may yield rock outcrops with shallow soils. These are often occupied by a dwarf pine (*Pinus pumila*) observed as dark patches on the hillsides.

A three-dimensional perspective view, looking up the Tigil River, showing how volcanically active the western side of Kamchatka is. The image shows that the Tigil River has eroded down from a higher and differing landscape and now flows through, rather than around, the large green-coloured bedrock ridge in the foreground. The older surface was likely composed of volcanic ash and debris from eruptions of nearby volcanoes. The green tones indicate that denser vegetation grows on south-facing sunlit slopes at the northern latitudes. High resolution SRTM (Shuttle Radar Topography Mission) elevation data is used by geologists to study how rivers shape the landscape, and by ecologists to study the influence of topography on ecosystems.

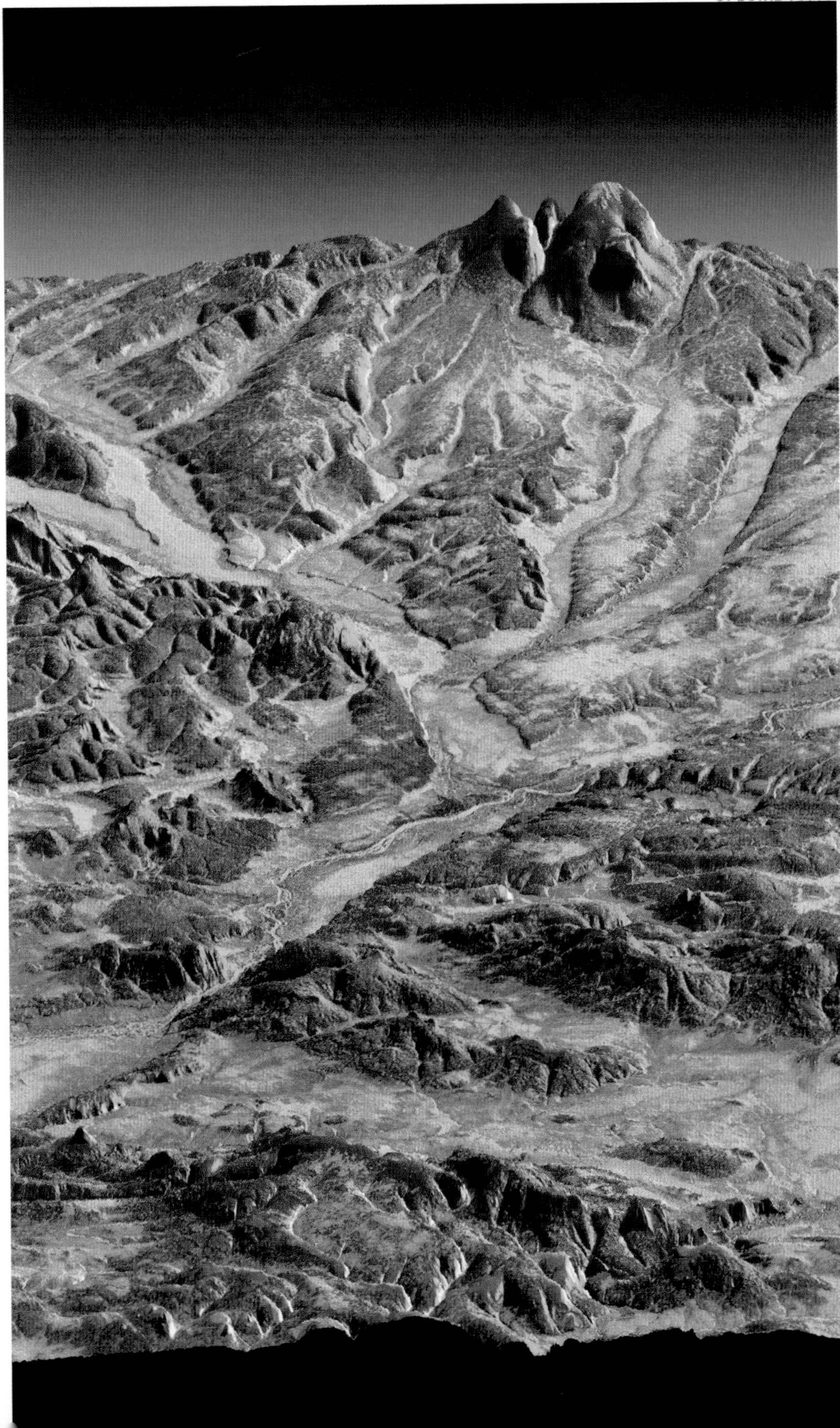

The Fur Trade (Circa 1910)

The people of Kamchatka depended mainly on hunting and fishing for their livelihood. Hunting species included sable, fox, bear, otter, ermine, reindeer and mountain sheep, but of all these the sable was the most important. According to Sten Bergman in his book *Through Kamchatka by Dogsled and Skis*, published in 1926, sable and salmon were Kamchatka's alpha and omega. These are what attracted so many other nationalities to the country and reconciled them to its inhospitable climate.

The sable belongs to the marten family (*Martes Zibellina*) and is found in both pine and birch forests. It is a carnivore, feeding on chipmunks, squirrels, mice, small birds and fish. During long periods of bad weather they have been known to remain in their dens for days at a time. The males are longer and heavier than the females. The gestation period is 250 to 300 days, leading to a birth of from one to seven young. The Russian sable is similar to its European and American cousin, but its coat is denser in colour and much silkier.

Nomad portrait in traditional costume. In this incredibly harsh climate there is simply no substitute for fur.

This valuable little animal is held in the highest esteem by connoisseurs for possessing a combination of rare qualities: The underwool is close, fine and very soft. The top hair is regular, fine, silky and flowing, varying in depth. Colour ranges from pale stone or yellowish to rich brown and almost black. Although light, the skins are very durable, and articles made from them produce a sensation of warmth almost immediately.

Sable hair is also used for paintbrushes, making the finest water colour or oil paint brushes and is particularly sought after by artists. Kolinsky sable paintbrushes, made from the winter pelage of the male sable, are considered the finest artist's brushes available. The Kamchatka pelts are the largest and fullest furred but less dense in colour than those of Yakutsk and Okhotsk.

The sable was hunted from late autumn until about March, the winter pelage being longer and more luxurious. A hunting party would have consisted of at least two men plus one or two sable hounds. They would have stayed in a hut or tent for most of the winter, existing only on tea and *jukkola* (sun-dried salmon). The traps were mostly baited with hare. It is amazing to think that such a little animal should be responsible for a country's economy. It might be said to have been the financial unit of Kamchatka. All business was transacted in furs – the only form of currency known to the people.

At this time the town of Klutchi was the centre of the fur trade. Two major fur trading businesses – the Hudson Bay Company and The Olaf Swenson Company – operated from here. Every spring Olaf Swenson would come over from Seattle with his steamer loaded up with goods for the people of Kamchatka, from guns, cartridges and traps to sewing needles and chewing gum. The furs would be valued by Swenson and the hunters would start purchasing. He would return to the States in the late autumn loaded with millions of dollars worth or pelts. In the meantime he would have kept himself posted as to the market value of skins by means of his radio.

Today a complete, good quality, Russian sable coat could cost around $50,000.

The Koryak are renowned among Kamchatka's indigenous people for their generosity. This postcard illustration shows a family wrapped up in attractive winter clothing. (Following pages) Winter is a time to keep the herd together.

CHAPTER 5

WITH THE REINDEER HERDERS

THE KILLING FIELDS. NULGUR DANCERS

REINDEER HERDERS CAMP OF LUBA AND KYRIA PETROVITCH. 13 SEPTEMBER

Yes, we've made it! At 8pm last night we got our whirlybird. As usual, it all happened at the last minute and was a wild rush to get everyone and everything on board a very old, maybe ex-army, rather battered looking chopper now used for transporting goods – and full of barrels of caviar from Palana! We got ourselves, the two Swiss photographers and all the food on board and away. The interior of the helicopter was very basic, like a huge tin box. There were two long metal seats along either side, and the rest of the area was taken up with containers and boxes.

I sat, to my amazement, at an open window. It hadn't occurred to me that you could of course open the window in a chopper. What a totally exhilarating flight. This has to be one of the best experiences I have ever had, flying into, then around mountains and volcanoes, over passes and rivers; taking lots of photos actually leaning out of the window, the setting sun lending colours and long shadows to the already dramatic scene unfolding below and around me. I couldn't believe just how close we could be to the snowy mountainside, I felt as if I could just lean out a little further and catch up some snow in my hands. It was surprising how little draught there was, perhaps something to do with the vacuum caused by the rotors, I don't know… but whatever it was, it was brilliant, quite brilliant.

We landed safely and very noisily, and with the rotors still turning over our heads, bent double, we scurried off to safety. After the departure of the chopper, the silence was absolute and we made our way to the headman's *yurta*, where we were told where to make our own small camp, a little way from the main one. When we had everything in place we all went into the headman's yurta with all the other herders for the evening's tea and chat;

Nomads gather around the fire in a *yurta*; reindeer herdsmen eat virtually the entire animal to compensate for the vitamins missing due to an absence of fruit and vegetables in their daily diet.

that is, Valya chatted and now and then translated for us.

The first thing they wanted to know was how old we were, then what we did and how much we paid to get there. Not easy questions. We told the truth about our ages, which absolutely threw them. We told them the truth again, that my husband had been a neurosurgeon and had been able to leave me some money for travelling, and that Elise kept a B&B and saved up for the travel. But of course, the very fact that we were there signified that we had, to them, riches beyond the dreams of avarice. It's always an embarrassment trying to explain that we are not actually wealthy by Western standards. There was a fire going in the yurta and it was roasting hot, but my goodness it was cold going to bed, and freezing during the night.

Valya thinks Kyria, the headman, is a shaman; he apparently has all the attributes, perception, intuition and knowledge. He is 48 but looks 70. Small and lean with Red Indian type features and almond-shaped, pale-green eyes, he is pure Even. His wife Luba is mixed blood. She has a lovely smile and is permanently surprised looking, with raised eyebrows over round, thick, milk-bottle-bottom spectacles. We wonder does she look like this in bed! These are mostly Even people although some are Chukchi mixed. None of them are Koryak. Although they are all dark, some have quite light eyes and others almost black. Among the chat that was translated for us, we understood that it seems that the reindeer market since perestroika is very bad. The government doesn't give regular standing orders for reindeer meat any more. It's an anachronism that pre-1990 everyone

(Above) Kyria, an Even headman, his weathered face speaking of the hardships of a herder's life. (Opposite) Reindeer graze on lush pastures in the brief autumn. For the nomadic reindeer herders, wealth is directly proportional to the size of your herd.

was "Sovietized" and they were better off, and now the ethnic groups are recognized yet they are much worse off.

Tomorrow at 4am the men will go and bring the reindeer down from the high tundra where they find grazing. The camp is in a perfect setting of a long narrow river valley surrounded by high, steep hills.

This morning when we got up, we were a bit annoyed that there was no fire going as it was bitterly cold – Sergei was getting a bit too "laid back", we thought! Elise was the first to get up, being that she was very cold; I was loath to as I was very snug in my sleeping bag. She ventured out and rushed back immediately saying it was all so beautiful in the frost that she wanted to take photographs before it all melted. But she couldn't find her camera among the normal chaos of our tent and threw a real wobbly; of course, I couldn't resist giggling as she stomped around the place swearing, desperate to take photos in the wonderful clear early sunshine. Eventually she found the camera, the fire got going and all was peace again.

We went off to explore and to take a look at the family's white horses grazing near-by. At this time of year the horses are hobbled as they start wandering off down towards Esso where the grass is sweeter – the grazing is getting poor up in the mountains by the autumn and is much better down in the valley.

The two young sons of the family took us up the mountain to await the arrival of the reindeer. We had to cross a little river which the boys skipped over without a backward glance – we were more cautious and took off our boots, just in case we slipped and filled them with water, but kept our socks on, and managed the crossing with the boy's help without actually falling over. Up we climbed to a patch of the delicious cloudberries, where we sat and waited for the reindeer.

Gradually they started to appear up the valley, streaming slowly down like a soft beige river of dun, brown and white animals. The reindeer are quite big with enormous antlers. It's the rutting season so the big males are quite aggressive, pushing away the smaller ones. Some were losing the velvet off their antlers, and one already sported totally naked, pink antlers. There were about 1,500 animals in all.

The killing of a reindeer follows a familiar routine: the body is skinned, the entrails and head removed, before finally the fat- and meat-rich carcass is carved up to be shared among the community.

REINDEER HERDERS CAMP,
14 SEPTEMBER

I have been lying on my back in the tent, watching the raindrops on the window and listening to the wind and river while contemplating yesterday. I couldn't write about it last night, I was too involved with the reindeer, and feeling much too emotional to put pen to paper.

When the reindeer arrived in the camp, they were given a couple of hours to settle down. We watched them for a while as they rested, remarking on their size, heads of antlers and so on, the soft grunting interspersed with the occasional spat between old and young males. They settled down quite soon and started grazing quietly. We sauntered off, and then, just as we were having a cup of tea, the herders came for us from the yurta and said "come".

They had the reindeer going round and round in a large circle. As I watched them striding out, they seemed almost to float on the air, while the men looked for specific animals to cull (although we didn't know this at the time). They look for old, injured or white beasts. We arrived in time to see the first reindeer lassoed, then wrestled to the ground; a direct stab to the heart with a knife meant instant death. I was really shocked at first and couldn't help crying. It seemed so primitive and sudden – we hadn't realized this was going to happen. But this is their way of life. We had thought we were just going to look at the animals – we didn't really know, but of course they are hardly going to put

The killing of a reindeer, which can appear horrifying to our eyes, is for the reindeer herders simply a matter of survival, repeated week by week.

on a show for a few tourists. It just so happened that we had arrived at the time they were going to do a cull, to replenish their stocks of meat and pelts. Lucky for us, really.

Everyone was at the butchering. Luba did most of the skinning with a deftness borne of years of experience. The stomach was emptied of grass and then filled with entrails and blood and lots of blood was drunk out of a cup by all the workers! We were offered some but politely refused. Most of the time everyone was too busy even to notice our existence. There was blood everywhere, with anyone doing the butchering literally up to their armpits in blood.

After the initial shock of what was happening I got totally engrossed with watching the skill of everyone involved – the butchering was done so swiftly. The tendons were pulled for sewing thread. Heart, lungs, brain and liver were eaten raw as they are full of vitamins. Daisy, the Swiss photographer, said she had seen many squeamish things but had never photographed anything like this before. The pieces of meat were put on clean willow branches, the skins laid upside-down to dry in the sun. Later, tripods of branches were built, and the meat hung on them to dry. In all, three beasts were killed which was unusual, but one was for a visiting family to take with them, one for Luba to take to Esso for the winter, and one for the herders.

Mid-afternoon the herd was driven back up to the hills and we went on horseback up the valley after them. Five of us went riding on the small, sure-footed animals, up over fallen trees and across streams until we spotted the reindeer, already high above us on the mountainside. These little ponies could be pretty intransigent at times; my pony kept kicking Valya's as she came too close behind, then, when we turned for home it decided to do a bucking act. However, I gave it a couple of good skelps up the backside to the amusement and approbation of our leader, a herder named Alexei.

Another evening spent back in the yurta with a big fire roaring away, and the men in festive mood after some vodka we had brought for them was passed round. We gathered that vodka goes to their heads terribly quickly – and so it appeared! I can just imagine the euphoria that sets in after the day's activities and the consumption of so much reindeer meat. There was lots of singing by all the herders except the headman, Kyria, and we were eventually persuaded to perform our party piece, the rendition of Patsy Fagin to great applause, it didn't matter that nobody understood the words – it was just the fact that we had a go.

It wasn't the most comfortable evening sitting on reindeer skins and getting long reindeer hairs all over us, but we managed to pile the skins up well enough into a heap

and lie or sprawl against them. I don't think either of us would be very good at this lack of table and chair business for long.

Today, it is a vile morning outside, cold, wet and windy, but I am lying down on my side cosily still in bed writing this. Nevertheless there is lots of birdsong outside. Last night I saw a common but lovely bright blue and green kingfisher diving into the big river, and a beautiful, brown speckled bird with a long beak, I think perhaps a curlew, which rose from the little stream when I went to wash. There are ravens around all the time.

Getting up and going to bed is awful, even though we don't undress. Scrabbling about on hands and knees, we never seem to be able to find anything. We have sworn yet again not to go camping anymore – will we ever resign ourselves to joining the common herd of OAP tourists and forgoing these wonderful adventures of ours? Breakfast was in Valya's tent; she really is a marvel, and Sergei did do the fire, but it's just too wet outside. Fried bacon and eggs never tasted so wonderful.

Then came the departure of Anatoly the vet, his wife Illiana, his son Alexei, and little daughter Larissa. Stefan, another Swiss who is living with them for some months, was also leaving. Blue-eyed Anatoly is also Even but with mixed Russian blood. He is very intelligent looking and quiet but has a distant "look" about him. When I mentioned this to Valya she said, yes, that he had been lost in an avalanche for four days, facing the very real prospect of death. When he was finally rescued he had sustained some terrible back injuries which give him a lot of trouble, and it seems he gets relief from visiting a shaman.

He is headman of Camp Six, but we were at Camp Four. He has about 1,000 reindeer, so because Kyria Petrovitch has a large herd he allowed Sergei to take one of the butchered reindeer with him. If they make good time they will make it to Esso in two days. Each of the seven ponies carries at least 150 kilos, and there is also a foal. Wee Larissa is the only one riding, perched on top of the pony in her fur hat, surrounded by saddle bags, clutching the two balloons Elise gave her.

It took some time to get everything packed up, and then they were on their way. Valya turned to me, tears streaming down her face and said, "it's always sad when people you meet and like go away". I couldn't even reply. I hardly knew them but what we had all shared yesterday somehow brought us together; anyway, it certainly was very emotional seeing them all walking off into the distance. I could see Elise some yards away on her own and I knew she would be in tears also. We watched the little train until it disappeared in the distance, then decided to follow them for a while, but lost their tracks when we had to cross the river.

We were invited to the yurta for barbecued reindeer, when suddenly the heavens opened and it poured while the wind blew up and raged round the camp. The reindeer tasted great but most of it was pretty tough. The yurta was approximately five metres wide with a framework of branches covered with cotton in summer and hides in winter. There was a central fireplace with a pole over it with chains and hooks for cooking and curing. A bag with knives and tools and some cutlery, skin boots hanging off the walls and piles of reindeer skins for lounging made up the permanent belongings, while, since the reindeer kill, all sorts of pieces of meat and fat, etc, were hanging on hooks over and around the place. Wee Alexei, our horse-riding leader, was absolutely zonked after last night's bash!

7.30pm, back in Esso. We were all sitting around after lunch outside, now in rather spasmodic sunshine, when to our huge surprise we heard the helicopter. No one expected it with the bad weather all around. Everyone was galvanized into action, racing off to strike camp. After swift farewells and many thank yous, we all jumped into the chopper and were away.

Almost immediately we were into better weather. I stood in the doorway of the cockpit and watched the scenery pass. We took quite a different route back to Esso because the pilots had to look for the camp of another group of herders. This was to our benefit as we saw more wonderful scenery, following along a winding river on its route through the mountains. Luba and her son were with us as they will stay now in Esso all winter to enable him to go to school while Kyria and the men stay behind during the long, bitter months.

Back once again to the boiling-hot house in Esso and a shower. Boy, you do appreciate

the hot water after the freezing stream in the camp; mind you, its one great benefit was that it was great for cooling the vodka, and such pure water for drinking with it! Neither Sergei nor Valya drink, so we invited the Italians to share a beer with us – but they don't take alcohol either. I don't think I've ever been on holiday with so many abstainers – thank God Elise enjoys one or two.

In the evening we went to see the ethnic dancing group, Nulgur. They perform in a very Soviet-style "people's house". The performance was very, very enjoyable. A semi-professional group of 11 Even, Koryak and Russian dancers, it included a wee boy of only five. Their costumes would have been their normal clothes, and the dancing was excellent, quite evocative and sensual, almost all of the dances portraying the life of the people, their land and their animals. There was a seal dance, a bear dance, and a seagull dance which incorporates the bird's call in with the music.

They also sang, and one of them was able to perform throat singing, which we had never heard before but which has quite an amazingly deep, echo-like sound, and is apparently quite often performed by northern tribespeople. After the performance the dancers came amongst the audience to talk to us about their dancing and traditions. As Valya translated, it become apparent just how very knowledgeable and proud they were of their traditions, and of their enthusiasm for keeping them alive.

Bear claws are used by a native shaman during a performance in front of a *yurta* fire.

The Indigenous Peoples of Kamchatka

Thanks go to Lisa Strecher for help in the
preparation of this section

Archaeological evidence shows that people have been living in Kamchatka for possibly
as much as 10,000 years. At about the end of the 17th century, when the Russians
first came to Kamchatka, Itelmen and Ainu lived in the south and centre of the
peninsula, enjoying an economy based on hunting and fishing. Small communities
dotted the coast and river valleys, many of them not more than a day's walk from
one another. The Ainu inhabited Sakhalin, the Kuril Islands and the very southern
tip of Kamchatka (they are known to have lived here but left very little archaeological
evidence).

The origins of the Itelmen are something of a mystery. They consider themselves
the original aboriginals of Kamchatka: their mythology and legends make no reference
to any other lands, while their name "Itelmen" means "native inhabitant", and their
language is said by linguists to be quite different from that of the Koryak and Chukchi
to the north. Their language is now almost extinct, the vast majority of ethnic Itelmen
being Russian speakers.

At this time the Itelmen were the most widespread tribe on the peninsula, with
numbers of up to 50,000 natives. Their villages were located along the Kamchatka,
Bistraya, Yelovka, Bolshaya and Avacha rivers on both the Pacific and Okhotsk coasts.

They lived in the winter in dugouts roofed with timber and in the summer in stilt houses, or *balagans*, erected along the banks of the rivers, thus readily available for catching, drying and storing fish. When the first Russians arrived and met the Itelmen people they called them "Kamchadals" because they lived in Kamchatka.

At the beginning of the 18th century, when the Russians forced the local inhabitants to pay a massive fur tribute (*yasak*), violent uprisings were the result with many of the Itelmen being killed. Death from diseases such as measles and syphilis also occurred, and within just two or three decades the indigenous population decreased so significantly that settlements became very scattered. In fact, the yasak became so untenable that the then government of Russia had to reduce the tribute policy.

Now the Itelmen population stabilized at between one and two thousand, but gradually, by the early 20th century, parts of the Itelmen population (the Ainu having already departed) had been assimilated into the Russian population through mixed marriages, all becoming generally known as Kamchadals. There was mutual exchange also in the social sphere, and particularly in economic activities such as gardening and farming. Likewise, the descendants of the Russian settlers learned Itelmen ways of fishing and hunting.

The Kamchadals of today are something like the Creoles of the Caribbean, who are neither Spanish, African nor European – they are Creoles. You therefore have to distinguish what is meant when sources talk about "Kamchadals"; historically Kamchadals are Itelmen, but today Kamchadals are the new ethnic group that evolved from the mutual adaptation and interaction of the first Russians who settled in Kamchatka and parts of the Itelmen population. Today, Kamchadals are considered one of the ethnic groups of Kamchatka along with the Koryak, Even and Itelmen, and mostly live in central Kamchatka around Milkovo.

The Even (Lamut) ancestors came to Kamchatka in the early part of the 19th century from the northern parts of Sakha, east of the Lena River, changing their traditional occupation of hunting for reindeer herding. They speak their own Even language, one of the Tungusic languages. Some of them have managed to preserve different forms of pre-Christian beliefs, such as shamanism.

The later Russians, when they arrived in Kamchatka, discovered the nomadic Even based by the Sea of Okhotsk, called "*lamut*" – meaning "living by the sea", as they mostly fished and hunted marine animals; and the reindeer herdsmen, called "*orochi*" – meaning "reindeer men", living mainly in the central part of Kamchatka, particularly in the Bistraya region. In contrast to the other indigenous peoples of Kamchatka, the Even use reindeer sleds rather than dog sleds. These are works of art, made entirely of birch and fastened together with undressed reindeer hide. This keeps the sled pliable and supple and despite its slenderness, incredibly strong, and, like the dog sleds, they can be mended anywhere out in the forest. These sleds still exist and are in use.

The Even do not wear "blind" clothes – that is their parkas lace up down the front. This is made of reindeer skin and also the trousers and chest apron which are often decorated with beading in beautiful designs. Knee protectors, fur stockings and boots soled with bearded sealskin complete their warm outfits, all sewn together with reindeer sinew.

By the end of the 19th century there were about 500 Even in the Bystrinsky area, with a reindeer herd numbering, in total, approximately 20,000–30,000, each individual herd counting probably around only 200–500 head.

During the Soviet "collectivisation" reindeer were transferred to state farm herds. According to incomplete lists, by 1938 17,000 reindeer had been removed from the

An Even woman collects dried salmon at a summer fishing camp by the Khailino River.

people. At the same time, the administration tried to make the people sedentary and encouraged them to live in villages with only a small proportion engaged in herding; large herds were grazed by up to five herdsmen, with the remainder employed on cattle farms and vegetable growing, with all these non-traditional activities regulated by the increasing non-indigenous administration.

Today, the Even are one of the main indigenous groups living in the villages of Anavgai and Esso in the Bystrinsky region, but they now comprise only 30 percent of the total population of this area. A few families also live in the revived traditional villages of Lauchen, Tvayan and Kekuk. The total population of Even in Russia is somewhere around 20,000.

The Koryak are the main indigenous people of the north of the Kamchatka Peninsula, and perhaps the least known of all the tribes of Siberia. When the explorers Steller and Krasheninnikov came upon the Koryak, they thought their name derived from the Koryak word "*khora*" for "deer", but it appears this was not actually so. The Koryak called the coastal residents of their group "*nimilany*" or "residents of a settled village", while the nomadic reindeer herders called themselves "*chavchuvens*" meaning "reindeer people".

The Koryak are intelligent and self-reliant, and recognize no master. They tenaciously resisted the Russian invaders and in their fights with the Cossacks proved themselves exceptionally brave. Families gather into groups of six or seven, in which the nominal chief has no predominating authority, all being considered equal. In the past Koryak were occasionally polygamous, and it was accepted practice that if a man's brother died he would take the wife of the deceased and vice-versa. Koryak hospitality is proverbial, in fact, they have such large herds that folk from other tribes often come begging for their surplus stock, which the Koryak give in exchange for mere trifles.

At one time they were known to kill off the aged and infirm in the belief that this saved them from unnecessary suffering; it was considered the highest form of affection (they cremate their dead). Their prevailing religion was shamanism; sacrifices were made to all kinds of spirits, the heads of the victims being placed on stones facing east. Animism, the belief that spirits animate everything in the world, is the basis for shamanism. Shamans are specialists, and among other abilities are able to make contact with these spirits. Today there are believed to be some of these shamans still left within family groups.

Intricate beadwork and warm fur combine beautifully on an antique Koryak jacket.

"Big Raven" is looked upon by the Koryak as the founder of the world. All the tales about Big Raven are part of a cycle of myths that are popular on the American as well as the Asiatic side of the North Pacific. Some tribes consider him the creator of the world, but the Big Raven of the Koryak appears more as the transformer of the world, that is, the world existed before he appeared, but his creative activity revealed things previously unknown and sometimes changed one thing into another.

There are many stories about Big Raven, one of which concerns the *Amanita Muscari* (fly agaric), the dramatic red-spotted mushroom that induces an exaggerated influence upon motor control when eaten, and causes death from an overdose. The tale goes that Big Raven was incapable of hauling a large bag of provisions and so summoned help from the deity, Vahiyinin (Existence), who told him to seek out spirits called Wapaq. Vahiyinin met him at the appointed place and spat on the ground; where his spittle fell, small white plants grew and Big Raven was told to eat them. This he did and suddenly found the strength to easily carry his burden. Big

A Chukchi reindeer herder looks to the wellbeing of his animals on a cold winter's morning.

Raven asked the Wapeq to live forever in the earth (as mushrooms) and instructed his children to learn whatever they had to teach them. The *Amanita Muscari* was consequently highly prized among the Koryak and used as a valuable bartering commodity.

Traditionally, for the nimilans the main way to survive was fishing. Fish were generally caught in the rivers using nets made from the stinging nettle; it took around two years to make one net, which was only used for one year. In settled villages around the coast, marine hunting was the other way of surviving, entailing perilous trips out to sea in skin-covered boats called *baydarkas*. Seals and whales were hunted with stone-tipped harpoons. These animals' skins were used for boat covering, footwear, bags and belts. Domestic activities were well developed, with wood and bone carving, metalwork, traditional clothes and carpet making, embroidering with beads and braiding all practised to a high degree of skill.

For the chavchuvens, reindeer herding was the only way of life, giving them everything necessary for survival; meat, skins for clothing and for building their nomadic dwellings, the *yarangas* or yurtas. Bones were used for making tools and household articles, while the fat of the animals provided lighting. There are approximately 8,743 Koryak living in Russia today. They did have their own autonomous *okrug*, or region, with Palana as its capital, but a more or less democratic referendum in 2005 has resulted in this okrug being reunited with the Kamchatka oblast. The reunification will take place in the middle of 2007, when the whole of Kamchatka – north and south – will be called Kamchatski Krai.

North of the Koryak live the Chukchi people, some of whom moved south to Kamchatka from their own land of Chukotka. They speak the Chukchi language and are akin to the Koryak, whom they closely resemble in physique, lifestyle and language. In their religion, also similar to the Koryak, all objects, whether animate or inanimate, contain a spirit that can be either harmful or benign.

Like the Koryak, the Chukchi are also reindeer herders, with a holder of less than 100 reindeer considered poor. As might be expected, through their mutual history these two peoples vied constantly with each other over reindeer herds. Also like the Koryak, many of the Chukchi lived in settled villages and made their living by fishing and hunting for marine animals. Their traditional hunting implements were bows and arrows, spears and harpoons. For catching waterfowl and game they used a bolas. The Chukchi were highly skilled seamen operating open boats, often accommodating up to 20 or 30 men on the wild and frigid sea. It is well documented that they traded with the American Eskimos across the Bering Straight; with a favourable wind they would hoist a square sail made of reindeer suede. There are about 15,000 Chukchi in the world today.

As their name would suggest, the Aleut came originally from the Aleutian Islands. They called themselves "*unangan*", which means "seaside residents". Many of their traditional occupations were naturally to do with the sea, such as hunting for marine animals, fishing and collecting sea birds' eggs to store for the winter. The dwellings of the Aleut were quite similar to traditional dugout houses. Among their household possessions were baskets and bags made from plaited grass. These were used for storing fat, yukola, crowberries and other natural produce.

On Bering Island, dogsleds became a popular means of transport, but for mountain walking the Aleut used broad skis covered with sealskin so that the nap enabled them to slide forward and prevented them from slipping backwards. Many Aleut were resettled in the previously uninhabited Komandorsky Islands around 1825 in order to expand the Russian fur trade. Today, about 446 Aleut people live on these two tiny islands, mostly in the only settlement, Nikolskoye on Bering Island.

As winter gives way to spring, reindeer herders choose the weakest animals in their herd to cull.

Puchinski. Back to the start

Puchinski Hot Springs. 15 September

It was a wet morning but we decided to get on the road as we wanted to go to Puchinski. Whether or not this meant two more nights camping we were not sure, but we'd soon find out. After a search for diesel at the petrol station, Sergei eventually had to pay over the odds for "private" fuel, in fact black market or something that fell off the back of a lorry.

We had a long day driving, but the rain stopped so the road was again terribly dusty and we couldn't see a thing as we bumped along. We had lunch by the Bistraya River that we followed down from Esso, and bought two big salmon from a fisherman. In the five days we have been in Esso and the reindeer herders' camp, the trees have almost all turned colour. They are stunning, the sunshine lighting up the reds, golds, oranges and yellows. In Milkovo once more, we went to the museum and art gallery again to meet Misha the Mystic. I had hoped to buy a lovely painting that I had had my eye on, but it wasn't for sale, only his daughter's work was and I didn't like it particularly. However, Valya bought two of her works and was terribly excited about them.

We took Misha with us as a guide to Puchinski Hot Springs. We had to go some way back along the road to Petropavlovsk and then 15 kilometres up a forest track, just about negotiable by vehicle. We were talking about the possibility of seeing bears, when suddenly one ambled across our path ahead. Very excited we set off in hot pursuit across van-high vegetation to a little lake renowned for bears as the fish hide there during the day. Alas no more bears for us, just that one that gave us a tantalising passing glimpse. Obviously there are bears all over the place, we have seen them and evidence of them, but unless you actually have a hiding place, where you can sit and wait for them to appear, they are much more aware of us than we of them and keep well out of the way.

Autumn paints the land with rich colours as the reindeer herds move to winter grounds.

We arrived in Puchinski at about 8pm, just as dark descended. A big outdoor fire was blazing away and various people were eating round it. There was a log cabin for a dormitory and a roofed eating area. We were shown downstairs in the cabin but it was very hot and stuffy and seemed full of naked men, with two awful looking beds – not a promising combination!

We weren't one bit keen to join in so we were shown the loft above. Sergei was obviously highly amused by our reaction, but Misha was terribly anxious to make us as comfortable as possible. We settled for the loft and dragged our bags and sleeping paraphernalia up the ladder to our chilly eyrie, made up the beds, and then went down to join everyone else for a great dinner of – you've guessed it – fish and spuds.

After dinner and lots of chat, off we went to the thermal pool. Valya was talking about not wearing a costume as it was dark. As we undressed Elise said she was certainly going to wear one. By this time I couldn't care less, we had jumped in and out of so many hot springs and baths with and without clothes. Of course Valya was wearing her bikini, and Misha a sort of g-string, but Sergei was in the buff. In we all went, very gradually, to the roasting hot pool. Then Misha beckoned me to him.

We had been warned that he was a sort of healer and was going to try to find out any illnesses that we might have, so I wasn't too surprised when he started quietly and gently touching my face, then each arm, each leg, my back and front. It was all quite an odd experience and certainly one I had never had before. The sensation of energy in the man was so apparent. He said I had some back trouble and must keep very active. I had had trouble as a child and although I had lost an eye, I now had three eyes, the other two being able to see the past and the future; he would like to be able to help me develop this gift, but of course I couldn't stay in Kamchatka, however I should try and find someone at home to help me. He then went over Elise the same way. He said that she had something to do with animals in her life and of course she has horses at home – quite bizarre.

We had a lot of chat about healing with Valya translating, then he had another go at me. I have to say I found the whole experience delightful; very calming and gentle, and all of course under the warm water. We stayed in the pool quite some time and eventually got out warm and tingling into the cold night air. Tired and feeling very relaxed we all went straight to bed.

PUCHINSKI HOT SPRINGS, 16 SEPTEMBER

In the middle of the night the moonlight coming through the open window woke me, and I realized I needed a piddle. It was freezing cold with bright, bright moonlight. I thought, there is no way I am going down that ladder on my own in the middle of the night, and I have to admit to hunkering on the top rung of the ladder and having such a fit of giggling that I just prayed nobody was about who would hear me. I hurriedly scrambled back into my still warm sleeping bag, but my head felt cold. An awful draught was blowing between the window and the door, so I pulled on the hood of the sleeping bag and was fine.

Elise by this time was awake and in even more of the draught; she was warm enough but conscious of the cold whistling round her. She put on her warm helmet and we stacked both our travel bags between her and the window and hoped she would be OK. When, at about 6am, Misha came in calling "Diana, Lisa, therma," I replied rather ungraciously, "Niet, niet". Absolutely no way were we getting up at that hour, in that cold!

By the morning Elise had a sore throat and a roaring cold, poor thing. Everything, inside and out, was frozen, our bathing things from the previous evening were rigid where we had left them hung inside to dry, our water bottles and even my tube of face cream was frozen stiff! No wonder everyone thought we were mad choosing our loft to sleep in when we could have had the warmth and companionship of down below. Elise decided there and then she'd had enough of roughing it: "From now on," she said, "I'm calling the shots and I'm not camping one more night!" I think we were all pretty tired by this stage and even if we did have two days in Petropavlovsk, so be it. There was no way we could spend another night here, beautiful as it is.

Sergei and Misha left at about 7am to get Misha to the main road for a bus, and of course, typically, on his way back, Sergei saw two bears where yesterday we had seen the one. It was about the only time he has been away without us – sickening.

Elise, Valya and I did, in fact, have another bathe when the sun finally appeared, very late as we were in a deep narrow valley at the start of the headwater of the Kamchatka River. Valya discovered to her annoyance that her second salmon, which she had left in a plastic bag in the river to keep cool, had been eaten overnight by a bear. God save us, they are everywhere *except* when we want to see them! Mind you, she might have guessed it would be taken. I felt perfectly vindicated at not going down the ladder during the night.

Sergei arrived back and we all went for a good walk up the river valley. It was mostly stony and easygoing. We came across two big pieces of glacier left over from last winter, but now it was necessary to cross them. Amazing how they melt with the running water from underneath leaving huge ice caves. This one will not melt much more as it's so cold now at night, and only a matter of time before the first snow arrives. I think we have been incredibly lucky to have had such brilliantly fine weather almost all the time.

We saw a lot of bear tracks all the way up the course of the river, but Elise was not feeling at all well, so we girls turned back and left Sergei to continue on to explore a bit further, telling us later that he came to a beautiful, three-tiered waterfall but it was too difficult to climb above it. There was still a good fire going back at the springs and while Elise lay down for a while and Valya started packing up, I had a go at cooking some sort of dampers on the campfire; they were quite good eaten with jam and quite a luxurious change from salmon.

PETROPAVLOVSK. RUSKI HOTEL. 17 SEPTEMBER

4.30pm. We left Puchinski yesterday about 6pm, arriving back in Petropavlovsk about 10.45pm, all of us tired and Elise with a really horrible dose of the cold. It was a pretty awful drive as again the road is hard core, and as it was so dry it was very dusty every time a car passed. I don't know how Sergei managed to see where he was going, but then the road is dead straight and there was, in fact, very little traffic. However, the sky remained clear and the lowering sun gave wonderful colour and light and shadow on the surrounding mountains as we approached the capital. Finally a huge golden full moon rose as we arrived in the city. Elise was by now feeling awful and went straight to bed. I am feeling grand but assume I shall probably catch her cold. I had to eat all on my own, but the staff were friendly and I enjoyed a good dinner of crab.

This morning Elise stayed in bed. I think she has a temperature and has put herself on antibiotics and has slept all day. I had breakfast late at 10am and Valya called at 11.30 and took me to get/send e-mails, but we had forgotten that today is Sunday and of course all the offices are closed. Funny how even in Soviet times, people still respected Sunday closing.

It's quite suddenly much colder with quite a feel of winter about. It's dull and grey but still Avacha Bay is attractive, although now looking quite mysterious, slightly misty with the mountains shaded in grey.

The spring sun creates dramatic icemelt in the Mutnovsky region.

Valya's Dad picked us up and we went to the market to buy fish. We discovered that the market is closed on a Monday – tomorrow – so I had to guess what Elise wanted. On the way into the market at the bus station, by great chance we bumped into Sasha the hunter from Esso, who had taken us to look for bears. I thought it was such a coincidence, but as Valya says, with such a small population you meet everyone. In the market, Nikolai, Valya's father took over the shopping. As a fisherman himself, he knew all the different fish and the best type of smoking. I bought two different sorts of salmon and two big chunks of a white sea fish, possible turbot and definitely delicious. We had to taste them all to decide the best. I also bought a small pot of caviar and three bottles of Kamchatka vodka, one for Valya's family who have invited us for dinner tonight. Everyone has been so kind and hospitable.

Sunday 11pm. We had a lovely evening at Nikolai and Ilena's apartment. No wonder Valya likes her stepmother, she is delightful and obviously she and Nikolai are very happy; she is his third wife. They, as everyone else, have a really nice apartment in a grotty old building, a terrible staircase with peeling plaster, graffiti, cigarette butts and the smell of pee. We had a lovely meal: fish soup again (but vastly superior to the last time), two kinds of salmon, fresh brioche bread, stewed fruit and copious amounts of vodka. We were given really nice glasses and crockery this time, but again no knife – only a fork, so as usual we had to use fingers for the fish.

They wanted to know about fishing in Ireland and who did the cooking, gardening and cleaning in our homes. They were amazed to hear that we did it all ourselves – they thought we would have an army of servants. Then they wanted to know how we got our vegetables. In Russia almost everyone has a dacha with a vegetable plot, so you don't really buy vegetables in a shop or market. They were surprised to hear that although some people grow vegetables, more or less for pleasure, we mainly buy them in a shop or at a farmer's market.

This couple have also been devastated by perestroika and say that it's the same for most of their friends. Again, brought up to have an ideal of Sovietism – only to be told it's all wrong. It's fine for the young, but for these middle-aged and elderly souls it's awful. People who were about to retire must keep on working as prices are rising so rapidly. Also, even though it's now supposed to be a democracy, there is still no real free speech.

Later on, Zhenya, my hero of the volcanoes, arrived as a surprise which was lovely. We will meet his girlfriend tomorrow evening when we take them all out for dinner.

PETROPAVLOVSK. RUSKI HOTEL. 18 SEPTEMBER

We both had a dreadful night, Elise coughing her head off and me now with a really sore throat, which I'm very fed up about. However, thank goodness Elise was feeling well enough to take part in this, our last day's activities.

It was a perfectly horrible day, pouring rain and zero visibility – just the sort of day to end a great adventure and head for home. We went back to the library, I got an e-mail from Jill and replied, so that was a great achievement. Then we went souvenir hunting. I had bought practically nothing, so what money I had was burning a hole in my pocket. We went to a pleasant little shop where I bought a lovely pair of Art Nouveau silver and quartz earrings and a wonderful little carving in mammoth tusk of an Itelman lounging and smoking a pipe – I'm thrilled with it.

Next we went in search of furs, not that we wanted to buy any but we wondered where all the skins went to. Nobody seemed able to tell us, so we still don't know, as we only saw a few fur coats in one dreary department store. We had lunch in the same cafeteria as we had with Irena Smolina the other day. Then off to look at a new Roman Catholic church built just five years ago. It was very nice, small and unpretentious but full of icons and beautifully painted walls, all done by artists from central Russia. Unbelieving Valya lit a candle – just in case, she said. Isn't the world a crazy place – having had Sovietism thrust down their throats and no churches allowed, now everyone wants religion and is prepared to pay for gold and paintings for its places of worship. I believe the Russian Orthodox

Church is terribly rich – it's all such an anachronism!

This evening we took Valya, Sergei, Zhenya and his girlfriend Olga to a Korean restaurant for dinner. Although Zhenya had said it was the best and most expensive restaurant in town, we thought it was quite inexpensive, and very enjoyable. It was quite posh with tablecloths, napkins and entire place settings of cutlery. The Korean food was delicious, with lots of little dishes, some hot, some cold.

No one drinks alcohol except Elise and me, so the evening went quite quickly, particularly as everyone wolfed down their dinner, being unused to the concept of a drink and a little social intercourse. They all seem, for their ages, so unworldly and naive. As the youngest, Zhenya was the most relaxed and "into it"; Valya, with her usual wonderful smile and lots of chat, still fitted in; but Sergei was really quiet – he is not a party person at all. We made lots of toasts to each other, Elise and me with vodka, the others with the ubiquitous Coca-Cola. The members of this little team have all been terrific – making us do things we never thought possible and constantly looking after our welfare. We happily exchanged photos and addresses with each other; Sergei has taken some really beautiful pictures.

A very bizarre experience followed back at the hotel. There was a knock at the door and when we answered it, a fellow was there looking for a light for a cigarette, or so he said. At this time of night? I think not. We decided this might be a "house of ill repute", as all night there was a lot of noise, doors opening and closing, beds being moved about and generally a lot of "extracurricular activities" going on next door to us. They certainly made the earth move – I thought we were having an earthquake!

We arrived down for breakfast full of curiosity to see if we could make out what had been afoot, but all we found were two chaps still drunk from the night before, and still very interested in chatting us up!

AEROFLOT FLIGHT, PETROPAVLOVSK–MOSCOW. 2PM LOCAL TIME, 19 SEPTEMBER

It is absolutely clear down below. We are somewhere due north of Vladivostok, about 60-70 degrees north, just a little south of the Arctic Circle. Below us is a pristine wilderness of snow-capped hills and mountains with long river valleys, not quite completely covered in snow yet. Quite soon we will cross the Lena River. It is like this on either side of the plane as far as the eye can see, and will be the same for hours and hours as we cross Siberia on our route to Moscow. Maps in atlases are so deceiving; being a flat surface it is impossible to show the enormous distances that are involved. I believe a globe is the only way, and then one can see just how massive Russia is.

At the airport we had fallen in with a group of Norwegian hunters plus their massive trophies of bear and big horn sheep waiting to go through customs. We felt sad and perplexed at how anyone can enjoy such a pastime, particularly as the sheep are an endangered species, but I suppose it takes all sorts, I certainly wasn't going to get into another slanging match about it.

We finally left Petropavlovsk an hour late, having said a very tearful farewell to Valya and Sergei. We were all very emotional. We have had quite the most amazing trip with these two young Russians. We had had no idea, really, about the places and conditions we were letting ourselves in for. We ended up going to quite extraordinary places – in the true sense of the word – and staying either in peoples houses as one of the family, or in ridiculous little tents because there simply was nowhere else to stay.

Sergei has been a wonderful driver and knowledgeable young volcanologist, and Valya a most remarkable guide. I think she is supposed to be just a cook and interpreter, but in fact she has also been a marvellous guide with a deep knowledge of Kamchatka, it's geography, flora and fauna. Her enthusiasm got us to places we would never have gone otherwise, and her rapport with people made her friends wherever we went. The memory of her wide smile, wild hair and, when we were a bit timid about doing something risky, her catchphrase of "Why not?" will remain with me always.

TRADING IN KAMCHATKA

ABOUT IMPORTS, EXPORTS & POTENTIAL TRADE ON KAMCHATKA

Excerpts from *Steller's History of Kamchatka* by Georg Wilhelm Steller, 1709–1746
Translated by Margritt Engel and Karen Wilmore
With permission University of Alaska Press

A VIEW of the TOWN and HARBOUR of

Contrary to other nations, the Itelmen used to trade neither with others nor amongst themselves, but each made do with what the land and his own labour provided. However, in times of need, which frequently occurred, they relied on their friends and received what they needed from them, without having to return anything, which is why they previously knew nothing of borrowing, lending and returning. It wasn't until 150 years ago that they first started to acquire commercial goods from the Japanese, the "needle men", eg iron and copper implements, especially knives and needles, but initially this trade only happened when their ships were brought to Kamchatka accidentally by a storm. It is known, however, that thrice before the arrival

ETER and St. PAUL, in KAMTSCHATKA.

of the Russians, a Japanese vessel lay at anchor in the Bolshaya River and traded goods with the Itelmen.

Since the country was occupied, approximately 50 years ago, trading was the only way of interacting with the Itelmen and in this regard each Cossack is to be viewed in three ways, as a settler, a soldier and a merchant. Everyone coming to Kamchatka brings along goods and trades them to the Cossacks for cash or pelts...

...Trading on Kamchatka is carried out in the following manner. The merchant comes into the Russian villages, selling goods in the public stores to the Cossacks and Cossack children. The Itelmen rarely come into the Russian villages and are not used to buying something more cheaply for cash; rather, even if they have an ample supply of pelts on hand, they borrow the goods from the Cossacks with whom they have made friends and then pay three or four times as much for them later. Therefore, in winter, the Cossacks travel to the Itelmen villages with goods, collect payment for debts incurred the previous year, and give away the newly bought goods again on credit. The merchants, however, receive their pay on the Cossacks' return in pelts, and thus all trade in the villages is done between the merchants and the Cossacks all by means of bills and promissory notes, whereby the Cossacks have a special style, and right of exchange.

In summer, when the Cossacks are short on money and pelts, they trade among themselves with nothing but bills of exchange and documents and sometimes a bill of exchange passes through ten or more hands between the date on which it was set and the day of payment. For some years now, the commanders of Kamchatka have, in defiance of express orders and for fat presents, allowed the merchants to trade (in place) of the Cossacks, without taking into account that the Cossacks, who have to serve the commanders without pay, are thereby deprived of all subsistence. In order not to come to grief altogether, the Cossacks take by force, unjustly, from the Itelmen, what otherwise they would have gotten by trade, and thereby cause rebellions.

The merchants take from the people labourers without any pay, teams, dogs and sleds, trying to regain what they gave away in order to bribe the government employees. The merchants take advantage of the people, eating up the people's and their dogs' provisions without pay or thanks and scolding and beating the people as if the merchants' affairs alone were of the utmost importance, whereby again the people are ruined and infuriated.

The merchants, who are only living a few winters on Kamchatka and do not care if the Itelmen become their friends or enemies or if the whole country is ruined, increase the price of goods in an unchristian fashion, cheat the people outrageously, and, because they do not want to wait until the people can pay, haul the people under arrest from distant places into the Russian village or they sell them, in which action, contrary to their orders, the commanders assist them, and for a piece of silk many an Itelmen with his entire family is ruined and the others scared off from all civilized life...

...There are three kinds of imported goods: (1) Russian or European in general; (2) Asian, Chinese, Bukharan and Kalmuck; (3) Koryak and Anadyrsk...

...The goods exported from Kamchatka consist to date only of furs, ie, sea otter, sable, fox and river otter skins.

If the sea route were to be established and made available to the inhabitants and merchants, the following things lying unused up to now could also be included in the trade: walrus tusks, of which from Cape Chukotskiy to Olyutora 400 to 500 poods [one pood = 36lbs, or 16.4kg] could be obtained annually, and 60 to 80 poods of baleen.

If some day trade with Japan or China were to be established, the whales, frequently found around Kamchatka, could, through an established factory, also become very profitable, especially since the oil is liked in Japan, the Japanese buying it here or there on the islands to take it to their country. The Anadyrsk pelts and tanned skins also sell well with them, as the distant islanders dependably assured me.

On the Sea of Okhotsk, from Opala to Kampakova (Kolpakova), an equally great stockfish and cod fishery could be established as in Iceland or New England in America if it were ever needed, or if one found out that the neighbouring peoples wanted to include it in trade, which I do not reliably know of either the Chinese or the Japanese. But no one thinks of it to date, anyway.

Interestingly, nearly 200 years later, Sten Bergman in his account of the epic journeys he made with his wife, *Through Kamchatka by Dogsled and Skis*, describes Usk Kamchatka, the easterly port on the mouth of the Kamchatka River (now called Ust Kamchatsk), thus:

The canneries, which lie on the north bank of the river, belong to the Russo-Japanese firm of Denbigh & Co. They consist of two blocks, standing at a distance of a mile and a half apart alongside the river. They afford employment to a couple of thousand Japanese workmen in the summer, and they are run on ultra-modern lines. South of the river, at a distance from each other of about ten miles, there are two other canneries, which now belong to the Japanese firm known as 'The Nichiro Company', and which also employ a couple of thousand workmen. During the winter both canneries are idle...

...Close to the Denbigh canneries stands an extremely up-to-date and very powerful Japanese wireless station, which had been erected only a few weeks before out arrival. Its purpose is to enable these Japanese canneries, in case of a threatened attack by Bolsheviks in the winter, to notify the Japanese warships which lie on guard at Petropavlovsk. During the previous winter there had been some looting by the Russians, but now the Japanese were armed to the teeth in case of the recurrence of anything of the kind.

In this connection it may be mentioned that the Japanese, after the Russo-Japanese War, assumed salmon-fishing rights along the coasts of Kamchatka. On the other hand, they do not possess fishing rights on any of the rivers.

His description of the weather in Ust Kamchatka is also noteworthy:

Ust Kamchatka, from the standpoint of climate, is a dreadful place – like Cape Lopatka and the whole of the western coast. From October to April there are almost daily snowstorms – Kamchatka's dreaded "purga". Sometimes the snow comes down in such dense masses that you cannot see more than a yard in front of you, and the storm is so violent that you cannot breathe when facing it, or hold yourself upright. Sometimes the snow is extraordinarily fine and then it works its way in everywhere, sometimes it feels like sharp needles so that one cannot keep one's eyes open. Usually the temperature during a snowstorm is not very low, but the wet "purga" is almost worse, for then the temperature stands at about freezing point. Luckily this does not occur often. Woe to the man who ventures far afield from human habitation during a wet "purga". All his clothes are drenched through with the wet snow – he feels that the damp has penetrated his very bones. When the snowstorm is over the extreme cold returns, and how icy that is cannot be described.

Most of Kamchatka's indigenous people have used dog sleds for centuries (this page), but the Even tribe differ in their use of reindeer for the same purpose (opposite).

A MAN of KAMTSCHATKA, TRAVELLING in WINTER.

KAMCHATKA
IN THE 18TH CENTURY

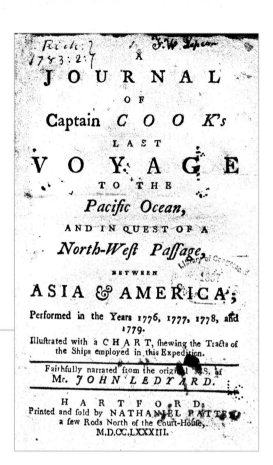

John Ledyard was an American adventurer who found his way onto Captain James Cook's final exploratory expedition in 1776. While a relatively insignificant figure in terms of the expeditionary force as a whole, Ledyard's contribution in historical terms was huge, because upon his return to America his personal account of the voyage was published. The entire manuscript can be found on the website of Meetings of Frontiers (http://memory.loc.gov/intldl/mtfhtml/ mfhome.html), a bilingual, multimedia English-Russian digital library that tells the story of the American exploration and settlement of the West, and the parallel exploration and settlement of Siberia and the Russian Far East.

Following is an excerpt from Ledyard's fascinating work, titled *A Journal of Captain Cook's Last Voyage to the Pacific Ocean, and in Quest of a North-West Passage, between Asia & America*. It tells of the return of the expedition's two ships to Kamchatka after the death of Captain Charles Clerke, the acting commander of the expeditionary force after Captain Cook's death in Hawaii:

Nothing remarkable till the 21st, when early in the morning the man at the mast-head again came in sight of land. It was then at a very great distance, and upon our starboard bow, but before night we were only distant from the mouth of Kamchatka bay, 12 or 13 leagues.

On the 22nd at nine in the morning we had the Resolution's boat on board, to acquaint Capt. Gore with the death of our commodore. We were then within sight of the flag at the mouth of Kamchatka bay, of which mention has already been made, and the wind being favourable, we continued our course for the entrance of the harbour, which then bore from us W.S.W. lat. at noon 52 deg. 54 min.

On the 23rd a little before midnight we came to anchor within the lighthouse.

On the 24th our Capt. Being now Commodore, made the signal to get under way by towing, all the boats were accordingly got out, and the Commodore went on board the Resolution, where it was resolved, for the greater convenience of repairing the ships, and for erecting the tents and forge to go within the upper harbour. And about four in the afternoon both ships came to, and were moored in three fathom and a half water, muddy bottom.

Early next morning the tents were erected, and the sick were got on shore.

From the time we set sail out of this bay in June, till the present day, we had been in no harbour to refit; and had been driven from island to island among the ice, till our ships had in a manner lost their sheathing, and were otherwise in a miserable condition: we were therefore happy in arriving safe.

August 25th, an express was sent to Balchaiareka, to acquaint the governor of our arrival, and of the death of our late commander: at the same time another express was sent to Paratanka, to desire the attendance of the priest, in order to consult with him concerning the interment of Capt. Clerke, whose desire was to be to buried in his church: while we were waiting the issue of these messages, the several promotions took place that followed in consequence of the Commander's death. Mr Gore went on board the Resolution, and Mr King, first Lieut. of the Resolution took command of the Discovery. Other promotions took place, which the reader will remark by the sequel. The first care of the commanders of both ships was to provide for the recovery of the sick, and the repair of the ships; and for that purpose a house was procured for the reception of the former, and a contrivance made for heaving the latter dry.

The weather being now temperate and the country delightful, the officers and gentlemen rather chose to sleep in their Marquees on shore, than in the apartments in the fort, or in the houses in the town. It was however thought expedient to show every mark of respect to the Russian officers, who, though not of the first rank, were notwithstanding the only people with whom we had any concern, or with whom we could have any communication: they were therefore frequently invited to dinner, and they as often attended.

On the 26th the priest arrived, when Capt, Gore acquainted him with the death of our commander, and of his desire to be buried in his church. The good old gentleman seemed much concerned; but started several difficulties: and appeared very unwilling to comply with the dying request of the deceased. He urged several reasons to show the impropriety of it, those of most weight were, that the church was soon to be pulled down; that it was every winter three feet in water; and that in a few years no vestige of it would remain, as the new church was to be erected near the town of A-watch-a upon a drier and more convenient spot. He therefore advised the remains of the Commander to be deposited at the foot of a tree, the site of which was to be included in the body of the new church, where the Captain's bones might probably rest for ages undisturbed. These reasons whether real or fictitious, the officers who had charge of the funeral could not disprove, and therefore people were sent to dig the grave, where the priest should direct.

The 30th was appointed for the interment; and to make the funeral more solemn, every officer was desired to appear in his uniform; the marines to be drawn up under arms, and common men to be dressed as nearly alike as possible, in order to attend the corps from the water-side to the grave. All this was readily acceded to, and the procession began about ten in the morning, when minute guns from the ships were fired, and the drums muffled as usual, beat the dead march. When the corpse arrived at the grave, it was deposited under the triple discharge of the marines, and the grave being covered, it was fenced in by piles driven deep in the ground and the inside afterwards filled up with stones and earth, to preserve the body from being devoured in winter by bears or other wild beasts, who are remarkable for their sagacity in scenting out the bodies of dead passengers, when any happen to perish and are buried near the roads.

This ceremony over, an escutcheon was prepared and neatly painted by Mr. Webber, with the Captain's coat of arms properly emblazoned, and placed in the church of Paratanka, and underneath the following inscription:

There lies interred at the foot of a Tree,
Near the Ostrog of St. Peter and St. Paul
The Body of
CHARLES CLERKE, Esquire,
Commander of His Britannic Majesty's
Ships, the Resolution and Discovery,
To which he succeeded on the Death of
JAMES COOK, Esquire,
Who was killed by the Natives of an Island we
discovered in the South-Sea, after having explored
the Coast of America, from 42 deg.
27 min, to 70 deg. 40 min. 57 sec. N.
in search of a North-West Passage
from EUROPE to the
EAST-INDIES.

The second attempt being made by
CAPTAIN CLERKE, who failed within some few
Leagues of Captain Cook; but was brought
up by a solid Body of Ice, which he found
from the America to the Asia, Shore,
and almost tended due East and
West -------- He Died at Sea,
On his Return to the
Southward on the
22nd Day of
April, 1779,
Aged, 38 Years.

Another inscription was fixed upon the tree under which he was interred. This tree was at some distance from the town and near the hospital, round which several people had already been buried, but none so high upon the hill as the spot pointed out for the grave of Capt Clerke. The inscription placed on this tree was nearly the same as that at Paratanka, and was as follows:

Beneath this Tree lies the Body of
Captain CHARLES CLERKE,
Commander of His Britannic Majesty's Ships,
the Resolution and Discovery.
Which command he succeeded to, on the 14th
of February, 1779, on the Death of
Captain JAMES COOK,
Who was Killed by the Natives of some Islands
he Discovered in the South-Sea,
on the Date above.
CAPTAIN CLERKE Died at Sea,
Of a lingering Illness, on the 22nd Day of
April, 1779,
In the 38th Year of his Age,
And was INTERRED on the 30th following.

On this occasion the inhabitants of both towns, and those of the whole country for many miles round, attended; and the crews of both ships were suffered to continue a shore, and to divert themselves, each as he liked best. It was the Captain's desire that they should have double allowance for three days successively, and all that while to be excused from other duty, than what the ordinary attendance in the ship required, but the season being far advanced, and a long tract of unknown sea to traverse before they could reach China, the officers, representing the hardships and inconveniences that so much lost time might bring upon themselves, they very readily gave up that part of the Captain's request, and returned to their respective employments early the next day.

On 2nd of September the Governor arrived at Paratanka, and with him an officer called by the Russians Proposick, the same as in England is called Collector or Surveyor.

They informed Capt. Gore, that a sloop was daily expected from Janeska, laden with provisions and stores of all sorts for our use; but expressed some apprehensions for her safety, as the boats had been looking out for her several days. This news was of too much importance to be slighted.

T. Fairburn St. Syon M. Cooks.

Accordingly, on the 3rd the pinnacles and boats from both ships were sent to the entrance of the bay, to assist her, in case she should be in sight, in towing her in; but it was the 11th before she arrived. She was a bark of about 100 tons, and had two guns mounted, which she fired as a salute, when she dropt anchor, and was answered by a volley from the garrison, which consisted of a subaltern and 25 soldiers. She was no sooner moored, than the Captain waited on the Governor for instructions, and then came on board the Resolution. He was introduced to the Commodore, to whom he delivered the invoice of his lading; among which was wearing apparel and tobacco, two articles that were above all others acceptable to the ships companies. As soon as the Governor had executed his commission, and delivered up the stores to the Commodore, he took his leave and returned to Bolchaiareka, and the ships being lightened before, and their bows heaved up dry, so that the carpenters could get at the leaks, the Captains and principal officers finding little else to amuse them, made a party to scour the woods for game: but this proved the worse season in the year for hunting. They had been told, that reindeer, wolves, foxes, beavers, and stone-rams every where abounded in the forests of this country and they had promised themselves great sport in pursuing them; but after staying out full two days and nights, during which time they had been exposed to several severe storms, they returned much fatigued, without having been able to kill a single creature. The parties who had been sent out to wood and water had succeeded much better. As soon as the ships were ready to launch, they were ready to complete the hold. In short, the utmost dispatch was made to hasten our departure, so that by the latter end of September we were in readiness to put to sea. The cattle with which we were now supplied, one would have thought, had dropt from another region. It is among the wonders of nature, with what celerity every vegetable and every animal changes its appearance in this climate. On the 12th of June, when we left the harbour of Kamchatka, the spring had but just begun to announce the approach of summer by the budding of the trees, and the sprouting of the grass; but now, on our return, it was matter of surprise to find the fruits ripe, and the harvest in full perfection. The cattle were mere skin and bone, which we were glad to accept at our first coming; but those that were now sent us were fine and fat, and would have made no bad figure in Smithfield market. The grass was in many places as high as our knees, and the corn, where any grew, bore the promising appearance of a fine crop. In short, from the most dreary, barren and desolate aspect, that any habitable country could present, this was become one of the most delightful;

Mr Nelson reaped a rich harvest of rare plants, and had the additional pleasure of gathering them in their most exalted state.

In this interval of idle time, between compleating our repairs, and clearing the harbour, we had leisure to take a view of the town near the shore, where we first moored, and that of Paratanka, where the priest lived, and were the church was situated. These towns have received some improvement, since they became subject to the Russians; but are still most wretched dwellings. The houses are built (if we may call that building, which is half dug out of the earth, and half set upon poles) in two different forms; one for their summer, and the other for their winter residence.

Their winter habitation is made by digging a square hole in the earth, about 5 or 6 feet deep, the length and breadth being proportioned to the number of people that are to live in it. At each corner of this square hole they set up a thick post, and in the intermediate space between these corner posts, they place other posts at certain distances, and over these they lay balks, fastening them together with strong cords, which they make of nettles prepared in the manner of hemp. Across these they place other balks, in the manner of a bridge, then cover the whole with thatch, leaving a square opening in the middle, which serves at once for a door, window, and chimney. On one side of this square is their fireplace, and on the opposite side is ranged their kitchen furniture. On the two other sides are a kind of broad benches made with earth, on which each family lie, and in one of these huts or houses there live several families. To enter these huts by the only opening at top, they use a ladder, not made with rounds between two sides, like ours, but consisting only of narrow slips of wood fastened to a plank. This ladder the women mount with great agility, with children at their backs, and though the smoke would blind and suffocate those who are not used to it, yet the Kamchatkadales find no inconvenience from it.

Their summer huts, called Balagans, are made by fixing up pillows about 14 feet above ground, and laying balks over them as before. On these they make a floor, and then raise a roof, which they thatch with grass. To these balagans, they have two doors, which they ascend by the same kind of ladder.

In the winter they use the balagans for magazines, the thatch secures what they lay up in them from rain, and by taking away the ladder, it becomes inaccessible to wild beasts and vermine.

It being summer, we had no access to their winter dwellings, which were all shut up, and they were not over-fond of exposing their poverty; for though they have little to boast of, they are not without pride. The whole furniture of the commonalty consists of dishes, bowls, troughs and cans; their cans are made of birch bark, their other utensils of wood, which, till the Russians introduced iron among them, they hollowed with instruments made of stone or bone; but with these tools their work was tedious and difficult. In these bowls they dress their food, though being wood, they will not bear fire.

In the winter the men are employed in hunting, making sledges, and fetching wood; and the women in weaving nets, and spinning thread.

In the spring the rivers begin to thaw, and the fish that wintered in them go towards the sea; the men therefore in this season are busied in fishing, and the women in curing what they catch.

In the summer, the men build both their winter and summer huts, train their dogs, and make their household utensils and warlike instruments; but the women make all the cloathing, even to the shoes. Their cloaths for the most part are made of the skins of land and sea-animals, particularly deer, dogs and seals; but sometimes they use the skins of birds, and frequently those of different animals in the same garments. They commonly wear two coats, the under one with the hair inwards, and the upper one with the hair outwards. The women have besides an under garment, not unlike Dutch trowsers, divided and drawn round the knees with a string.

They are filthy beyond imagination; they never wash their hands or faces, nor pair their nails. They eat out of the same dish with their dogs, which they never wash. Both men and women plait their hair in two locks, which they never comb, and those who have short hair, supply the locks with salfe. This is said of the Kamchatkadales who live more to the north; those in the towns which we saw, had learnt of the Russians to be more cleanly.

They are very superstitious; and the women in particular, pretend to avert misfortunes, cure diseases, and foretell future events, by muttering incantations over the fins of fishes, mingled with a certain herb which they gather from the woods in the spring with much labor. They pretend also to judge of good and bad fortune, by the lines of the hands, and by their dreams, which they relate to each other as soon as they wake. They dread going near the burning mountains, least the invisible beings that inhabit them should hurt them, and think it a sin to drink, or to bathe in the hot springs with which their country abounds, because they suppose those springs to be heated by the evil spirits that produce them. They are said never to bury their

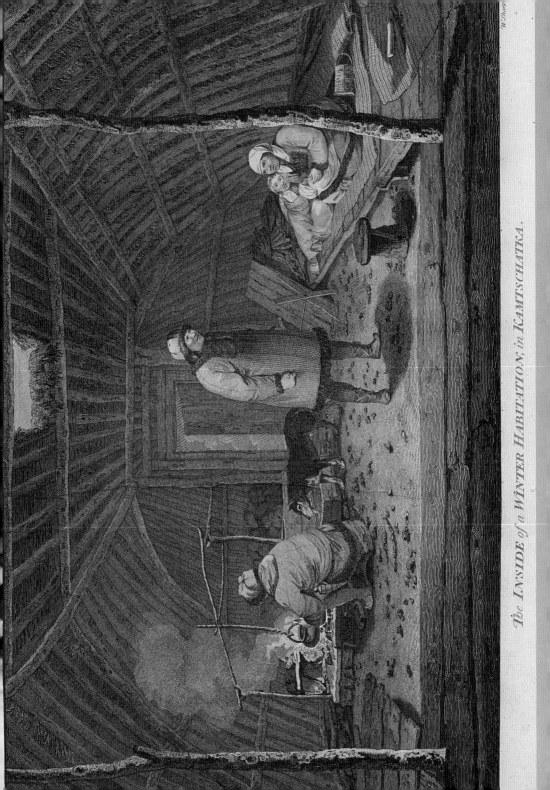

The INSIDE of a WINTER HABITATION, in KAMTSCHATKA.

dead; but, binding a strap round the neck of the corpse, drag it to the next forest where they leave it to be eaten by the bears, wolves or other wild inhabitants. They have a notion, that they, who are eaten by dogs, will drive with fine dogs in another world. They throw away all the cloaths of the deceased, because they believe that they who wear them will die before their time.

The country is said to abound with wild beasts, which are the principal riches of the inhabitants, particularly foxes, sables, stone-foxes and hares, marmots, ermines weasles, bears, wolves, rain-deer and stone-rams; but our gentlemen were much disappointed, who went in pursuit of them. They have a species of weasle, called the glutton, whose fur is so much more esteemed than all others, that they say, the good spirits are cloathed with it. The paws of this animal are as white as snow; but the hair of the body is yellow. Sixty rubles (about 12 guineas nearly) have been given for a skin; and a sea-beaver for a single paw.

Of the bears, the inhabitants make good use; of their skins they make their beds, coverings, caps, collars and gloves; and of their flesh and fat their most delicate food.

The Kamchatkadales, all along the northern coasts, have a particular manner of dressing their food, which is the very reverse of that of the Indians in the south. There they rost or stew with stones made hot and buried, as it were in the earth with their meat, by which its relish is said to be much improved. But here they boil it with hot stones immersed in water, by which its flavour is rendered more insipid. The same necessity, however, seems to have pointed out the same means to the people of the torrid and of the frigid zones; for both being equally unacquainted with iron, and wood being incapable of resisting fire, when brought in contact with it, though the principle was obvious, the application was difficult; those therefore of the torrid zone would naturally be led to call the warmth of the earth to their aid: While those in the frozen climates would think water a more ready assistant; add to this, that the colder regions abound with hot springs; some in Kamchatka, in particular, are so hot, as to approach nearly to the degree of boiling water; but these they think it sinful to use, as we have already observed.

The dogs of this country are like our village curs and are of different colours. They feed chiefly on fish, and their masters use them to draw sledges, instead of horses or reindeer.

The seas and lakes abound with a variety of amphibious animals, of which seals and sea-horses and sea-cows are the most numerous, and the most profitable. Of the skins

A postcard illustration of the Chukchi people of Kamchatka's far north.

of the seal they make their canoes, and on their flesh and fat they feed deliciously. Whales are sometimes cast upon the shores, but very seldom, unless wounded.

With the teeth and bones of the sea-horse and sea-cow they point their arrows, and weapons of war; and of their fat and blubber they make their oil. They have otters in their lakes, but their skins bear a great price. They have birds of various kinds in great abundance. Among the sea-fowl they have the puffin, the sea-crow, the greenland pigeon and the cormorant. They have swans, geese and eleven species of ducks; and they have plovers, snipes and small birds without number. They have likewise four kinds of eagles; the black eagle, with a white head, the white eagle; the spotted eagle, and the brown eagle. They have vultures also, and hawks innumerable.

This country swarms with insects in the summer, which are very troublesome; but they have neither frog, toad nor serpent. Lizards are not rare, but they believe these creatures to be spies sent from the infernal powers to inspect their lives, and foretel their death; and therefore whenever they see one, they kill it, and cut it in small pieces, that it may not carry back any intelligence to their hurt.

But what is most remarkable, and deserves the attention of the curious, is the remarkable conformity between the Kamchatkadales towards the east, and of the Americans, that live on the opposite coast just over against them, in their persons, habits, customs and food; both dress exactly in the same manner, both cut holes in their faces in the same manner already described, in which they put bones like false teeth, and both make their canoes exactly in the same manner. They are about 12 feet long and two broad, sharp at the head and stern and flat at the bottom; they consist of flat pieces of wood, joined at both ends, and kept apart in the middle by a transverse piece, through which there is a hole just big enough for the man to set in his legs, and to seat himself on a bench made on purpose; this skeleton is covered with seal-skin dyed of a kind of purple colour, and the hole is skirted with loose skin, which, when the man is seated, he draws close round him, like the mouth of a purse, and with a coat and cap of the same skin, which covers his whole body, makes the man and his boat appear like one piece; and thus clad, and thus seated and surrounded, he fears neither the roughest sea nor the severest weather.

And now we have had occasion to mention this familiarity between the inhabitants on the opposite shore of Asia and America; we shall embrace this opportunity, to correct a very material error in our account of last year's voyage, where, speaking of the Russian discoveries, we took notice, after examining Bheering's Streights, though the Russians supposed that the lands were parted, here we found the continent to join, by which the reader will no doubt imagine, that we have asserted, that the two continents, of Asia and America join, which they do not; but are separated by a straight between two promontories, which in clear weather, are so near as to be seen in sailing through, with the naked eye. But what is meant is this. When Bheering made his discovery, in coasting along the American shore, he

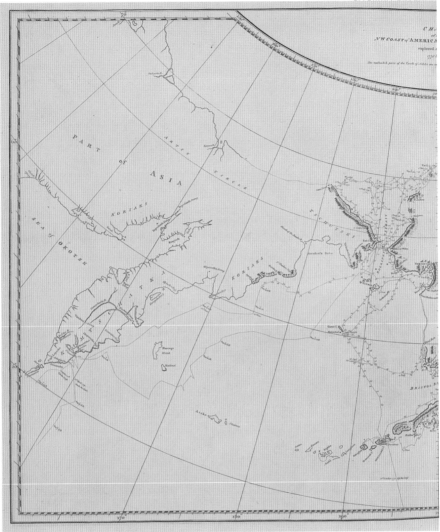

discovered a sound or straight, which having surmounted, he found himself in a great bay, which he imagined was another sea and that the land he had passed was not the American continent but a great island separated from the continent by the sound or straight just mentioned. This sound therefore, and this bay, we examined, and found that what the Russians had mistaken for an island, is actually a part of the American Continent. Hence it appears, that notwithstanding all that was written against it, Bheering is justly entitled to the honour of having discovered all that part of the N.W.

185

continent of America, that has been hitherto marked in our maps as parts unknown.

It remains now only to give a short description of the bay and harbour where we repaired; which at the entrance is between two very high bluff rocks; on the starboard as we enter is the light-house, of which mention has already been made, and at the distance of about 20 miles the volcano, from whence flames and ashes are sometimes emitted to great distance, and to the great terror of the inhabitants. The bay is about 8 leagues deep, and lies from S.E. to N.W. And from N.E. to S.W. it is about 4 leagues. It is inaccessible during the winter, by reason of the ice, but very safe and convenient during the summer.

The harbour where we lay to careen and repair, would contain about 20 ships of the line in perfect safety, being closely surrounded with high hills, except at the entrance. The people are civil, and in their way very obliging; but their manner of living affords nothing very enchanting for sailors.

Our ships being now in as good repair as we had reason to expect from the length of the voyage they had passed, the rigorous weather to which they had been exposed, the boisterous seas they had shipped; and, above all, from the violent concussions of the ice that had shaken their very frame, and had stripped them of their sheathing: And being likewise plentifully provided with provisions and stores, by the generosity of her Imperial Majesty of Russia, and by the care and benevolence of her governor and officers,

On the 9th of October 1779 we weighted and soon were without the light-house, shaping our course to the southward...

This close-up of the detail on an antique Koryak robe clearly illustrates the amazing similarity between Kamchatka's indigenous tribes and the native peoples of North America.

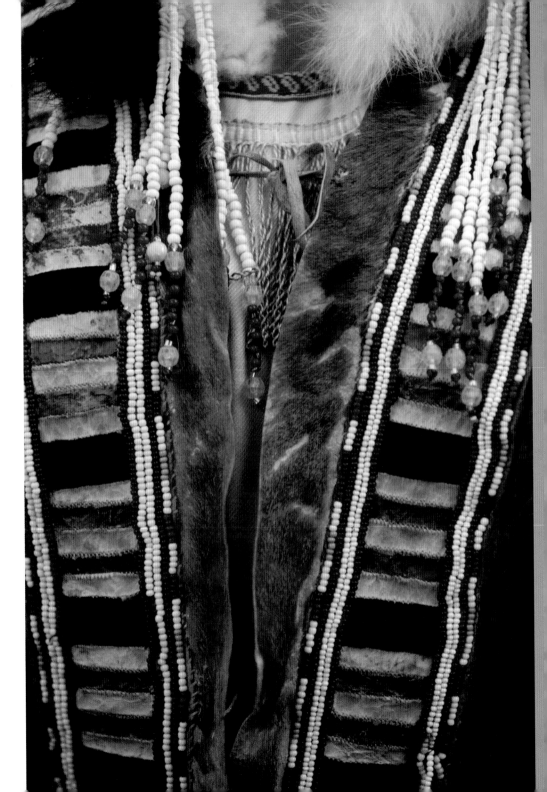

UNFINISHED BUSINESS

BACK TO KAMCHATKA. PAUZETKA. LAKE KURILSKOYE. OZERNOVSKY

PARATUNKA. BLUE LAGOON HOTEL. 16 AUGUST 2006

It is raining here in Paratunka. Not a good, heavy downpour, just thick dreary drizzle without even a whisper of wind. Everything is misty greys and greens. I know there is a dramatic backdrop of mountains and volcanoes but they have been swallowed up by the low cloud. After all the recent hours of stuffy recycled air in planes and airports, it is such a pleasure to be breathing in the warm, damp air, sweetly redolent of flowers and vegetation. Beneath the trees the familiar pink-mauve armies of rosebay willowherb are lying drunkenly at all angles, weighed down by the moisture. This is Kamchatka on a bad day.

Yes, Elise and I are back again in Kamchatka. Back because we have "unfinished business" here. When we came in 2000 we thought we would certainly see the infamous bears that are so plentiful throughout the country. We saw lots of glimpses of them, one bum shot, lots of footprints, droppings, tracks, but never a total, full-face meeting with a bear. Also, I still desperately wanted to go north to Palana in the Koryak Autonomous Okrug to visit the Koryak people, both the coastal and the reindeer herding nomadic peoples.

With this in mind, we are hoping to travel south to Lake Kurilskoye – famous for bears because of the huge quantity of salmon that spawn in the lake, and then fly north to Palana where we are to visit both areas of the Koryak. This has all been arranged, booked and paid for, so we are fairly optimistic about getting to these rather obscure and out-of-the-way places, but we know, through bitter experience, that it can all go belly-up. So, wait and see and hope for the best. I think we are both ready for another adventure in this wild and wilful country.

Our flights here all went pretty smoothly, albeit only a few days after the big airport terrorist scare in London. Security was very tight in Belfast, Gatwick and Moscow. We were

The Palana River lies in Koryak country in the north of the peninsula. It is a coveted destination, but getting there can be an arduous – and often unsuccessful – process.

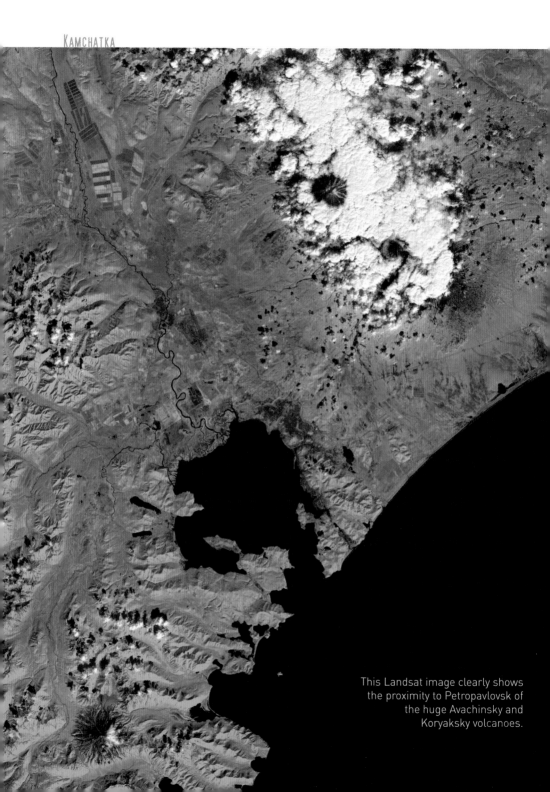

This Landsat image clearly shows
the proximity to Petropavlovsk of
the huge Avachinsky and
Koryaksky volcanoes.

late leaving Gatwick owing to the increased security and we started panicking a bit about our connection in Moscow as we only had just less than two hours, and we knew that there was no flight to Petropavlovsk the following day and the Thursday flight was already full; consequently we *had* to get our flight. So we alerted the cabin staff to our problem. They were great, they asked the pilot to radio ahead and have someone to meet us and rush us through immigration and security. This he did and sure enough, there were three lovely girls waiting for us as soon as we stepped off the airplane. They took us to the baggage collection carousel, fought ahead of the queue for immigration where we picked up two more helpers, whizzed us over to the new check-in area for domestic flights, and saw us as far as they could towards security. Goodness, what a change in attitude. These girls were smiling and helpful, so different from six years ago. The only sourpuss we came across was the girl at security. The airport has had a terrific facelift and is now big, bright and airy.

Sadly, our approach over Avacha Bay was not as beautiful as before. Thick cloud obscured the bay and all we could see were the conical tops of the volcanoes, Avachinsky, Koryaksky and Viljuchinsky. Where previously it had been Valya meeting us, this time it was another lovely girl called Tatiana, or Tanya, who greeted us and helped us pile ourselves and our bags into a taxi. It never ceases to amaze me how well the drivers manage here driving elderly Japanese cars with left-hand drive when they drive on the left-hand-side of the road; it's pretty scary for the novice passenger I can tell you.

It transpired during the drive that both Tanya's father and the taxi driver had been in military service in Kamchatka and had loved the country so much they decided to return and live here. This place gets to some people! We made our way here to the Blue Lagoon Hotel in Paratunka. I remember calling here before for some reason, and I recognized the blue signs. The hotel used to be a children's camp, and it's certainly more like a camp than a hotel; although our room is fine, there are only communal toilets and showers at the end of the corridor, we have to walk two or three hundred metres to a little café for our meals, and there are children playing volleyball and riding "quads" all over the place. We were given tickets for the swimming pool, shown where the café was and left to our own devices for the rest of the day, which suited us well enough.

Having had a snooze, we decided to try out the swimming pool, having so enjoyed the one at the Hotel Helios six years ago. (Apparently the Hotel Helios is now part of a military zone.) Well, it was certainly a bit of a change. The pool here is huge and it was full of people. It is very decorative with murals and even some plants growing in pots. It was wonderfully warm as usual in this area of thermal springs, and we thoroughly enjoyed our swim.

Our evening meal consisted of a starter of mixed shellfish with a cheese sauce followed by fried cod, washed down with local beer. And very, very good it all was – a huge improvement from before.

YELIZOVO. ART HOTEL. 17 AUGUST

It was still lashing down this morning when we woke up. Of course our body clocks are away "up the left", not wanting to allow us to sleep at night and be awake during the day, and thus we both slept badly, eventually resorting to sleeping pills sometime during the night. The consequence of the rain and lack of sleep made me depressed and in bad form.

After breakfast Tanya collected us and we packed our bags and moved on to this little hotel in Yelizovo. It's very nice, small, very modern with lots of pine woodwork, and interestingly decorated with small pictures and little mirrors. It is very near the airport – I just don't understand why we didn't stay here last night when it is so close and convenient, and also much nearer to Petropavlovsk.

We spent the morning and most of the afternoon visiting museums and trying to discover more about Kamchatka's protected wilderness areas, eventually unearthing a map in the Kronotsky Museum showing exactly what I wanted. In the Koryak Museum we were able to "order", I hope, a copy of some old photographs of Kamchatka. The boss lady was not there but will be on the day before we leave, when we will be back from our jaunts, so hopefully I will be able to get them then.

During lunch in an attractive café, we met Hassan, our guide and translator for our trips to both Lake Kurilskoye and Palana. He was in a bit of a rush taking other clients to the airport but wanted to introduce himself before taking us tomorrow to Oznernovsky and Lake Kurilskoye. I'm not at all sure how we are going to get along together. He is half Kazak, unshaven and was rather bizarrely wearing a T-shirt knotted over his head somewhat resembling a turban, which looked a bit odd. However, first impressions are not always right, and I'll reserve judgement until we get to know him a bit better, but I think we will both miss Valya, Sergei and Zhenya – that was such a great little team. We found that Tanya was able to come up with Sergei's telephone number so we phoned him (local calls are free here) and were delighted to find he was at home. He was amazed that we had returned to Kamchatka and we arranged to meet when we returned from the south.

So, here it starts again! We have to sort out our belongings into "wanted on journey" and "not wanted on journey", and I have spent so much time today already bent over maps that my back is really, really sore tonight. God, I could do without this and us about to go on a long, hard trek. We have been told that we are going to walk probably seven kilometres over flat ground into the Southern Reserve. A truck will take us over the Ozernaya River and part way along an old track towards the research station. I wondered to myself, if the track is flat and we are in a truck that can negotiate a river, then why can't it negotiate the entire journey? Well we'll see. I am half excited and half apprehensive.

Pauzetka. Homestay, 18 August

Of course our flight was delayed this morning. At first two and a half hours and finally four hours. And where are our books? Naturally enough, back in Petropavlovsk! Were we going to be reading books on a bear safari? Oh deary-me no, definitely not, silly old us. This morning I tried to buy Brufen for my back as I only have a few with me – stupidly, and was able to get Ibuprofen cream to rub in and an Indian manufactured product of Ibuprofen and paracetamol called Dr Reddy's. I hope they are ready to cure me and won't kill me.

At the airport we had a long, involved chat with Hassan about the political situation here now versus the old Soviet Union. I also learned that the Koryak Autonomous Okrug or Region has been dissolved and the Koryak people have yet again been assimilated into the general Kamchatkan Oblast. This I am sure is not advantageous to the Koryak people, but hopefully we'll be able to find out more about this when we go to Palana. The other thing that became very apparent was Hassan's obvious dislike of Russians, Germans and Japanese – and he is a tour guide? Very interesting and not very promising – at the end of this trip I wonder what his opinion will be of two Irish ladies.

Eventually our airplane landed in Yelizovo and we boarded. This was a tiny twin-prop, Czech-built craft seating 12 people including three children. It was totally overcast until just before landing at Ozernovsky when the clouds parted and we were just able to see in the distance to the south, Cape Lopatka, the southernmost tip of the Kamchatka Peninsula. Below us the Sea of Okhotsk was an angry dark grey, turbulent with white horses tossing around the many fishing boats close in to the coast.

It was obviously very windy outside as our little plane bucked around while we came in to land, but the pilot made a perfect touchdown on a dirt runway tucked in between the coast and the mountainous hinterland.

A car took us in to the town of Ozernovsky, past tiny one-storey houses built of wood with corrugated roofs. A bridge over the Ozernaya River gave us a good view of fishermen casting a huge salmon net using small boats with high bows, rather a pretty shape and a bit like the *curragh* used on the west coast of Ireland. The town is very small, consisting mainly of the usual drab tenement blocks and a large fish-processing factory. We stopped at a little shop where we waited for a car to become available to take us to Pauzetka some 30 kilometres inland. There isn't an actual taxi service here, you just have to wait until a local with a car makes himself available for hire. In the meantime, we asked Hassan if we could buy some vodka. This he did for us, buying it "under the counter" as it is unavailable on the open shelves – it's a real problem here with too much alcohol abuse apparently.

Eventually a pick-up came for us and brought us here to our homestay with Zhenya Themythev. Pauzetka is an even tinier village with a population of only 60 souls. Its *raison d'etre* is a thermal power station which services Ozernovsky and the fish factory. The road here was lined with swathes of mauve rosebay willowherb, yellow *senecio palmatus* and the tall white puchka, amongst myriads of unidentified plants. Elise remarked that there was a lot of land but not an animal in sight; nobody seemed to know why they can't graze cattle or sheep. I actually missed most of the drive as I was asleep – as usual. I slept in the taxi, the plane, even the airport, but not in bed. I don't know if it's my imagination or not but I am convinced that the older I become, the more my body clock is finding it difficult to move forward the 12 hours' difference between here and home. It wants to sleep all the daylight hours and be awake and leaping about during the night. Not at all convenient.

Because we arrived four hours late, our lunch of red Ormul salmon and two fried eggs became supper. We still hoped to set off this evening for Lake Kurilskoye. The huge ex-army truck or "*vakhtovka*" which can negotiate the river was ready and waiting for us and we were restless with anticipation, dying to get going. However, after lengthy discussions between the driver, Zhenya (the owner of the homestay) and Hassan it was decided that it was too late this evening and we would set off early tomorrow. It was by then around seven o'clock and it would take us around an hour and a half to get to and across the river and then we would have a seven- or eight-kilometre trek in big bear country and it would be dark and dangerous long before getting to the station – we could see the logic of waiting until the morning. Very disappointing, but we are learning that delays are the name of the game in this country.

So instead of going on safari, we had a guided tour of Sergei Themythev's garden. This is the son of the house, who speaks quite a bit of English and has an immaculate garden of which he is justly proud. He grows all sorts of vegetables and flowers in neat, tidy beds, and because of the proximity of the power station he has several heated greenhouses in which he grows tomatoes, cucumbers, peppers, grapes and melons. These he sends to Ozernovsky with his mother, who runs a little vegetable shop. Wonderful. The front step of our house is an old radiator on its side making a very good pretence at being a boot scraper. Here we must remove our filthy boots along with everybody else's and leave them in the porch.

After admiring the garden, we decided to go for a walk to the river to see if it was swollen much after the past few days' rain. We were walking along towards the power station where Sergei's father had gone for his night shift when we met two young lads walking towards us. We took absolutely no notice of them but one of them stopped Sergei and spoke to him while we walked on. In a moment, one of them bounded up to us and said, "Do you not remember me?" We looked at him blankly for a moment or two and suddenly together we twigged – it was Zhenya, our lovely helper and friend at the volcanoes in 2000. We looked at each other in astonishment and then we all started talking at once. He had finished his engineering degree and married his girlfriend, Olga and incredibly split shifts with the other Zhenya (Themythev) of the homestay (it's very confusing having two Sergeis and two Zhenyas). It was an extraordinary coincidence. If we had left this evening, or if we hadn't gone for a walk, we would never have known he was working here. If, if, if. He said it was a moment or two after he passed us that he suddenly thought "I know those two ladies". Good for him.

He turned and came back along with us to the power station, chatting about what had happened during the past six years. He hadn't seen Valya or geologist Sergei since we were last here, but had climbed Viljuchinsky and snowboarded down. Hours to ascend and just minutes descending. He looks well and happy but of course misses Olga when he is here. I asked him if he still played the guitar, and he immediately delved into his pocket and whipped out a mouth organ, playing it to show us how proficient he was.

I had been interested in the new power station that we had seen being built in 2000 at Dachne Hot Springs. Zhenya said that it was officially known as the Mutnovsky Power Station and it was finished and all tidied up. The big smart building that was being built when we were there is a big smart hotel for visiting businessmen with a gym, sauna and excellent cuisine. Impressive. I'd often wondered how geothermal power worked and he explained it all to us. The heat from the Earth's core flows outwards. It transfers to the surrounding layers of rock, the mantle. When the temperature and pressures become high enough some of the mantle melts, becoming magma. Then, because it is lighter than the surrounding rock, the magma rises, carrying the heat from below and heating nearby rock and rainwater. Some of this hot geothermal water is trapped in the faults and porous rock. This natural collection of hot water is called a geothermal reservoir. Geologists then drill wells into these reservoirs to bring the hot water to the surface. This hot water and/or steam travels up the wells to the surface, the power of which provides the force that spins the turbine generators and thus produces electricity, now being provided for Petropavlovsk.

It was perhaps somewhat smaller, but interesting nevertheless in the little Pauzetka power station. The original boiler was put in during the mid-1900s, probably during Stalin's time. The "new" boiler was originally in a Russian submarine.

It's very mild and damp here. The southern tip of Kamchatka is renowned for its wet climate; we expected the damp but not for it to be so warm, and we only have thermal clothing with us. The B&B is boiling hot with compulsory central heating and we are both

Viljuchinsky Volcano is a tough, rugged climb, but rewards with spectacular views.

roasting all the time; consequently I have cut the sleeves off my very old micro fleece with a tiny pair of curved nail scissors, giving them a rather trendy, bohemian scalloped appearance which is a great cooling relief.

As we are unexpectedly spending the night now in the homestay and there is a Russian group also staying, we have been offered a single room upstairs and the sofa bed in the sitting room. Neither of us fancies the sitting room as it is indescribably hot, chock full of CD, DVD and video players, and the family and lots of others will be coming back and forth. So we plump for the bedroom and I shall sleep on the floor on a mattress which is fine. Everyone is surprised but they acquiesce to our wishes. We open the window as far as possible and keep the door open as well so there is a little through draft of cooler night air. The house itself is quite big by Russian standards. Two storey with the best-equipped kitchen I've seen so far in Kamchatka and a bathroom with a bath and constant very hot water. Young Sergei, his 18-year-old wife and twin baby daughters live and sleep in one room while the rest of house is used for paying guests. When the lady of the house comes home from time to time, she appears to sleep on the sofa bed in the sitting room. They must be doing quite well as a family as everyone is working and I expect they make quite a bit of profit from their paying guests, which of course is only during the summer.

THE MYTHEV HOMESTAY, 19 AUGUST

Quel surprise, we are still here! It poured all night and morning. Some day, when we have totally overheated our world and water is more valuable than oil, Southern Kamchatka and Northern Ireland will come into their own and reap the benefits! Still unable to sleep, I finally took sleeping pills to try and force my body clock into submission and consequently slept until 9.45am. What with sleeping pills and Dr Reddy's magic mixture I am becoming the complete junkie.

We were supposed to take the big truck across the Ozernaya River this morning at midday, and be met on the far bank by a ranger from the park. We filled in the morning chatting with some of the other guests and watching a very good video about Kamchatka, until around 2pm when we started asking questions as to where the truck was and why were we not on our way. Hassan is really bad at keeping us in the picture. Mealtimes are a nightmare, he pretty well takes over, talking away at the top of his voice to anyone and everyone who will listen – there is no such thing as translating what the general chat is and it's only when we insist on getting some answers that we are noticed and spoken to.

It transpired that a different group had commandeered the truck for a quick crossing of the Pauzetka River to trek up-country to see a waterfall early this morning. The driver thought it would only take 30 or 40 minutes and he would easily be back for us by midday. When there was no sign of him by 2pm we asked if anybody had been to see what had happened. Extraordinary of Hassan not to have started enquiries himself. Finally, by 3pm we were told that the indestructible truck had become stuck in the river which was seriously in spate, and the cab and engine were flooded. Luckily the people on board had been able to scramble on to the bonnet and jump into reasonably shallow water near the bank. They were very lucky. We felt that when the truck didn't turn up as arranged someone should have gone to see what had happened. But then what we think doesn't necessarily mean that other people concur with us.

Still pouring, Hassan went to enquire if there was another vakhtovka which we could

A fissure belches poisonous fumes in Avachinsky crater while Koryaksky looms in the background.

use for our crossing. Sure enough, he ran one to earth – another huge ex-army truck with wheels about four feet high and a very low gear ratio, but the driver was drunk and asleep in bed. Nothing daunted, his neighbour, Igor, said it would be OK for him to drive it but he didn't think he should take it over the river while it was running so fast and suggested we might borrow an inflatable boat in which to cross the river. I have to say I was a tad alarmed by that suggestion but decided to wait and see what transpired.

We had to find waterproof covers for our sleeping bags and clothes as it was so wet. Luckily I already had put mine into plastic bags at home – "Aren't you the smart bitch?" was Elise's inevitable remark, as we stuffed everything into big rucksacks. I was silently wondering how, if the ranger wasn't there, we were going to carry all this equipment when we finally got to the other side of the river. We then looked on as Igor lifted somebody's quite new-looking little inflatable and oars into the back of the truck. Then our gear and finally Hassan got into the back, while Elise and I climbed into the cab with Igor and his new wife, who was coming along for the ride.

Off we went, great fun with the four of us in the cab, lurching along a dirt road through a lush, green valley, again full of wildflowers. After about 20 minutes the radiator boiled and we had to stop. Igor hopped out, found a bucket in the back, scrambled down to the river for water and filled the radiator up and off we went again, another 15 minutes or so through willow and birch trees to the crossing place on the Ozernaya River.

All five of us stood dejectedly on the river's edge gazing across the swift and turbulent water. There was absolutely no way the truck could have crossed this river, which is usually much slower running than the Pauzetka River. There was also, in my mind, absolutely no way we were going to be able to paddle across in an inflatable boat, especially as there was nobody with any experience of boats except me and that did not include wild river crossings. We stood looking across the tumbling water, Hassan whistling and calling the ranger who, naturally enough wasn't there. Waiting in the rain for five hours? I think not.

Elise and I had turned our backs on the river when Hassan actually suggested using the boat to cross, leaving Elise and me on the far side with the tents and gear on the bear-infested riverbank, while he would go on quickly by himself through the bear-infested woods and vegetation, 11 kilometres to the station and get help. Oh no, I don't think so thank you very much. We were appalled at his idea, I don't think he has a clue about what he is doing here. Coming from Kazakhstan he doesn't really seem to understand the conditions in Kamchatka. And then we discovered that he has never been to this area before. Not ideal criteria for a guide. With very little discussion it was unanimously

decided to return to Pauzetka and regroup. Wrong place, wrong time. What is life all about but timing? If the flight yesterday had been on time, if it wasn't raining, etc etc. If everything goes to plan you take it for granted, if not, you realize it's all down to unfortunate timing.

Dismally, we returned to Pauzetka. Later that evening one of the locals arrived at the door and asked if we would like to go to see the drowned vakhtovka. We jumped at the chance and soon arrived at the point on the Pauzetka River where the big, white, indestructible truck was submerged. Wow, and how. The massive vehicle was indeed half drowned, about five feet (1.5 metres) deep, with white-topped waves angrily licking at the lopsided cab. A very big, very expensive job for the owner.

We went to look around other people's gardens during the remains of the evening but it rained harder and harder. Oh bloody hell, how have we managed to time this so badly, if only it would stop raining, if only we had our books… moan, moan. So, another small vodka and I think I'll do my nails – again.

Lake Kurilskoye. Rangers' hut, 20 August

What a day this has been. Here we are now, happily ensconced in the upper room of the rangers' hut at Lake Kurilskoye. Another room with another view – and what a view. It is quite breathtaking. The sun is now low in the sky behind us, bathing the scene with a beautifully soft, pale-golden light. About 25 metres in front of us, beyond an area of mixed grasses and wildflowers, is the lake, looking calm and serene; beyond that, high above the lake, are a pair of Steller's sea eagles coming home to roost. On a spit of land I can see a bear patrolling his patch, while in the distance is the snow-streaked classical cone shape of Illinsky volcano. It's one of those perfect scenes that you want to catch and hold on to and keep among your most precious memories forever – to take out from time to time, dust it off, look at it and remember this day.

It wasn't so wonderful this morning, which broke dull and still raining. We thought "this trip is simply not going to happen" and tried to think of alternate amusements such as going to Ozernovsky to visit the fish factory. However, Hassan seemed to think that the day would fine up as the wind had changed direction, and right enough, it stopped raining and soon there appeared a small patch of blue sky, as my dad used to say, "enough to make a sailor a pair of pants".

Once again we stuffed all our belongings into plastic bags and rucksacks. Hassan had been hoping to find a "boy" who might come along with us and carry one of the big rucksacks with tents and bedding. Elise and I decided we could whittle down some more of our equipment and could manage just the three of us, but Hassan was adamant and certainly when we saw the amount of bedding, cooking pots, food, etc that had to go with us, it became obvious that we needed a fourth body. Funny that Hassan hadn't thought of this weeks ago.

Reliable Igor, the sober driver of the drunk man's truck, was ready to go and at the last minute we pressed into service an 18-year-old lad called Viktor as an extra porter, plus his young Alsatian dog. Off we set in the huge truck, Elise and me in the cab and Hassan, Viktor and dog in the back with the bags.

When we arrived at the river, it still looked very swift although at least a couple of feet lower than yesterday. I heard Elise mumble under her breath as we hit the water "Keep her lit boy, keep her lit," and then, holding hands we entered the swirling water. It's a most peculiar feeling driving in a so-called car into deep water. The truck made absolutely nothing of it – we were across and cruising up the far bank in no time, easy as pie, in fact almost an anticlimax. However, the next bit was no easy drive in the park. There had, in Soviet times, been a proper vehicle track here, but during the past ten or so years it had deteriorated into a barely discernable vestige of a track. Willow and hazel trees smacked into the sides of the truck and saplings grew in the middle of the track, scraping and scratching along the bottom of the vehicle. I kept thinking the windscreen would be sure to break and involuntarily ducked each time the branches hit the glass. In fact, when we could go no further with the truck, we couldn't even get our door open as the very tough mirror guard had been totally bent backwards against the door, effectively locking us in.

Having lurched along for two or three kilometres we finally arrived at a gradient too steep even for our trusty vekhtova. Now I could appreciate why the truck couldn't go the entire distance. I wasn't sorry, I must say. Out we piled, picked up our baggage, said goodbye to Igor, arranging to meet him at the same spot the day after tomorrow evening, and set off the eight or so kilometres to the research station.

By now there wasn't a cloud in the sky and it was really hot. I can see why it would have been dreadful to have tried to do this trek in the wet; not only was the ground still wet, rutted and slippery, but the vegetation would have been wet, soaking us through. As it was, the walk was a four-hour endurance test through, round and over dense, high growths of "stuff", big and small trees, wildflowers, streams and unidentifiable vegetation.

Before long Elise asked Hassan for a drink of water. He had none – only vodka. Well, Elise nearly exploded. Neither of us could believe that we had set out on this long walk on a very hot day without any water. As usual, Hassan took absolutely no notice of Elise – he has a terribly irritating habit of humming the first eight notes of "Pretty Woman" when called to task and has to think up a reply, never an apology.

After about half an hour Elise was very distressed when she tripped over a long creeper, falling heavily – Hassan just walked on, taking no notice whatsoever. He stopped shortly after beside a stream and decided to make tea. Crikey, not really a huge necessity, just water would have been fine. But, he had nothing to collect water in without practically emptying the rucksack to find a container. With great self-sacrifice, I threw away the last of our vodka and orange and used the bottle to collect water. The tea was in fact most refreshing, and we continued on our way now with a water bottle.

We had been told to make some noise all the time to scare away the bears, so Hassan would shout every so often and bang his walking sticks together, while I sang out all the nursery rhymes I could think of – it kept my mind occupied if nothing else. Every so often the dog would disappear barking wildly – obviously at a bear – and one time he came crashing out of the undergrowth right behind me, putting the fear of God through me. The advice on how to handle bears in the wilderness if confronted with one, is don't shout at them or run away; on this occasion I can tell you there was a loud, explosive "Shit!" from me as I shot forward, crashing into Elise. It was really quite scary.

Every so often there were small rushing streams and huge puddles to cross, but as we progressed the trees thinned and we could see to our right sloping land covered with wildflowers. All very beautiful and so, so wild. To our left beyond the river, mountains rose with extraordinary tufa rock formations, looking like upended canoes. The tufa is almost white in colour and is formed by volcanic action. If lava, rising to the surface is oversaturated with water, the steam pushes the water up into the sand, ash and small fragments called "lapilli". In the course of time this is all condensed and becomes a new concreted rock: volcanic tufa.

There is a lovely Itelmen legend about this particular tufa formation. Kutkhu, the Lord and Creator of Kamchatka used to live at Lake Kurilskoye and would go fishing in these boats. When he left Kamchatka, Kutkha left his boats behind, upended against the mountain, and since then the place has been known as Kutkhiny Baty (Kutkha's boats) and is considered a sacred place by the Kamchadals.

We came upon one quite deep, very swiftly running stream down a steep bank. Viktor went first easily as he was wearing waders, then Hassan stumbled across trying to go too fast and fell over into the water and mud on the far bank, getting both wet and dirty. We hesitated, wondering how we would make the crossing, then Elise had the brilliant idea of Viktor coming back and lending us his waders. To his embarrassment when he was taking them off, he had to unwrap newspapers from his feet and legs – they were his Dad's boots and much too big! However, we only needed them simply to cross the river and it worked well. Elise went first then threw the boots back for me then I did the same and threw them back for Viktor.

Bit by bit the view to our left opened up and we were able to scramble up a steep bank

and see the river below, looking for bears. We were lucky, for in front and below us was a large bear busily fishing. We had our binoculars and were able to see him very well. However, as we progressed, we had to pass the place where he was in the water and both Hassan and I shouted and clapped our hands (I think Elise and Viktor had lost their voices for some reason) until we felt we were past him. Anyway, I should think he was perfectly happy doing what he was doing.

Bizarre tufa rock formations — in legend, they represent upturned canoes.

After four or so hours, hot and sticky, and Elise feeling sick and exhausted and not like herself at all, we arrived at the TINRO station – TINRO are the Russian initials for Pacific Ocean Institute of Fishing and Oceanography – where Elise crumpled in a heap on a bench out of the sun, proclaiming she was not going another inch. Oh, for a cold beer, I thought.

This is a research station for Pacific salmon situated at the start of the Ozernaya River as it flows out of Lake Kurilskoye, carrying its vast bounty of fish to Ozernovsky and the sea. There were quite a few souls here, some doing research and others making a documentary with all sorts of fancy-looking cameras on tripods and smaller ones draped round their necks. They were all watching two young bears which had been orphaned earlier in the summer. They were very well habituated and seemed quite unafraid of us humans. They were delightful to watch as they pottered in and out of the water. We were told, sadly, that they would not survive the winter without their mother to provide for them, and would probably be killed by a larger male bear, a tragedy but part of the natural world. We ourselves took lots of photos, as it made such a beautiful picture, the two young bears with Illinsky volcano in the background.

I could see a large bear in the water on the far side of the river. There is a sort of weir across the river here with a facility for counting the fish which pass through on their way downstream, and one can walk across it to the other side. Hassan asked the man in charge if it would be OK for us to look at the bear more closely and to cross the weir (Elise couldn't resist this), and he opened the gate and came with us. This bear was a whopper, and we managed to get very close to him as he stood on all fours, desultorily peering down for fish and gazing up at us, every so often shaking the water off his huge head.

Back at the station, Elise collapsed onto the bench again and refused to move anywhere. It was so unlike her that I was quite worried. Hassan was horrible to us, saying we were not very good walkers, althoough I thought we had done very well, and after all, I hadn't fallen and he had. We had to continue on, only about 100 metres, to the ranger's hut where we hoped to stay the night, so Elise pulled herself together and managed the short walk. Both the TINRO station and the rangers' hut are in small compounds safely enclosed by an electric fence, so once you are inside you are protected from marauding bears.

The two rangers are called Dmitri and Fyodor. Dmitri is the head ranger, a big, tanned young man with a crew cut. He loves his job, which is very poorly paid at US$200 a month. He is married, so has to live apart from his wife for long periods. He has to take exams every so often on both wildlife and legislation. The two guys are here to protect all wildlife, and the bears particular.

The Ozernaya River is the only outlet from Lake Kurilskoye, which is an ancient crater lake with a depth of 360 metres. At least eight reasonably sized rivers flow into the lake. We saw the bears coming right up to the perimeter fence, and ask Dmitri if he would take us for a walk down to the lake. Here we watched salmon leaping and had an exciting encounter with yet another bear coming towards us along the beach. We were very glad Dmitri had his rifle as we cowered behind him, but he stood his ground, facing up to the

bear and it shuffled off into the undergrowth.

Late that same evening a helicopter arrived with a party of 20 or so Russian tourists. They pitched camp and spoiled our privacy. They have been on a finely tuned chopper tour, supposedly visiting different places each day. However, the inclement weather has made endless logistical problems for them, necessitating abandoning some of their venues. We feel vastly superior having made the Great Trek to get here, but I was secretly wishing we had a chopper to take us out.

After a meal in the rangers' hut we enjoyed an amusing, if not very hot sauna, giving each other "the works" with the birch twigs (it always has us in fits of giggles, as we prance around flicking at one another with the wet greenery) until we emerged, pink and relaxed into the warm, calm evening and sat with sundowners outside our room, watching for bears.

KAMCHATKA'S BIG BROWN BEARS

During the autumn the grizzly bear's diet is virtually all salmon. They prefer to feed on the skin of the fish because it is richer in oil, and leave the remains for the seagulls, which flock in their thousands to share in the bounty.

Kamchatka is renowned for its population of brown bears (*Ursos Arctos*), also known as grizzly bears in other parts of the world. These are some of the largest brown bears on Earth – an average bear weighs in at around 700lbs (318kg) for females and 800lbs for males. Occasionally a bear will grow to as much as 1,200lbs, but this is rare. During the summer, cubs may double their weight while mature bears can gain 30–40 percent of their bodyweight gorging on the salmon that is so plentiful in Kamchatka's rivers. Mating takes place from mid-May until the end of June or early July, females mating with several males during the short time of their oestrus. At this time a female will become intolerant of her cubs, who must also avoid the large males pursuing their mother.

From early times, salmon has been the staple diet of the bear and the major source of fat and protein that has enabled them to survive Kamchatka's long and bitterly cold winters. The first European Russians who arrived in Kamchatka during the 18th century were amazed at the number and size of these great animals, which were purported to be at least 7 feet (210cm) in height when standing on their hind legs, and sometimes reaching 10 feet. The people at first were frightened of these large predators, but unlike their Siberian and Alaskan cousins they appear to be relatively mild-mannered. This has been put down to their almost sole diet of fish, except for the first few weeks after they emerge from hibernation, when they live on a vegetarian diet of the early shoots of the shelamannik plant until the fish start running in the rivers in early summer. Until about 200 years ago, the bear had hardly any enemies in Kamchatka. The Cossacks were not interested in it, preferring the more valuable pelt of the sable. The Itelmen hunted the bear in moderation, for food and clothing, using poisoned arrows in summer and in winter sometimes digging them out of their dens.

Nowadays hunters use a variety of methods for hunting bears. Some track the bears with specially trained hounds, the dog running ahead of the hunter and sniffing out the bear. When it locates one the dog harries it, running round and biting at it and annoying it so that the bear does not run away. This is, of course very dangerous for the dog, which has to avoid the bear's sharp claws. The hunter is alerted by the dogs' barking and shoots the bear. Rope traps are also used to hunt bears, the bear getting entangled by the ropes until it is immobilised; when the hunter arrives on the scene he again shoots the bear. One of the main reasons for shooting bears is the extremely profitable market in bear bile used for Asian traditional medicine.

A well-known Canadian scientist, Charlie Russell and photographer, Maureen Enns, have been experimenting over the past years in Kamchatka with the possibility of man living in close contact with bears, and have studied theories that would allow people to share the bears' habitat in a safe and sustainable fashion. However, sadly, deaths have been recorded of people who thought they "understood" bears, including that of Vitaly Nikolaenko, a warden at Kronotsky Reserve who had worked with and protected bears for many years. One is constantly reminded of this with more and more people hiking in bear territory. Bears don't like to be surprised, so it is wise to make a noise, talking or clapping one's hands while in bear territory.

One of the most likely times to come across bears is on a fishing trip – you are in contention with the bear for his source of food so be wary, if bears are fishing where you want to fish, just wait until the bear is replete and goes away. Don't put fish guts in the river unless it is fast-flowing, as gulls will home in and bears recognise gulls circling and calling as a sign of food, and they may come in at the run. Keep your fish with you, bears will even find fish in plastic bags left on the riverbank. If a bear does attack you are advised *not to run!* The professional advice is to fall to the ground on your stomach, protecting your face and neck and trying to stay in this position until the bear, hopefully, goes away. If, however, the attack persists, and the bear continues to bite, it is obviously making a predatory attack, at which point fight back as hard as you can with whatever means you can muster!

During the Soviet era, when Kamchatka was a military zone and strictly out of bounds even for Russians, there was plenty of wildlife, and as many as 20,000 bears roamed this wilderness. Now, with a lack of resources to pay wardens, illegal poaching and trophy hunting have drastically reduced the species to around 12,500.

The grizzlies of Kronotsky National Park are very shy animals. They can smell you 100 metres away and can run at 60kph over short distances. Only 200 people are allowed in the park per year, so a majority of the bears are scared by the unknown scent of humans.

Pauzetka Homestay, 21 August

Dmitri took us on the most lovely boating trip this morning after the Muscovites had struck camp in preparation for their helicopter departure, and Dmitri had sent them off with Fyodor for a nature walk, hopefully to see bears. We motored all around the lake, every now and again a little breeze ruffling the calm surface, and Hassan timidly hanging on, his face grim and fearful. Through some rocky islands with the tiny stone birch managing to cling to the stony surfaces, Dmitri pointed out the Steller's sea eagles' nest complete with chick, dizzyingly high on a rocky pinnacle – what a treat.

We stopped at the mouth of a small river flowing in to the lake, hoping to see bears which come here to fish for the Nerka salmon that come up this river to lay their eggs. There were lots of footprints but no bears appeared. Back in the boat and cruising along watching the shore, we did, indeed come across a bear. So had the nature walk crowd. They were slowly following the bruin and we kept well offshore so as not to disturb him with the sound of our engine. No wonder Lake Kurilskoye is so renowned for its population of bears, they are, indeed, almost everywhere.

We spent a lovely, relaxing couple of hours on the lake. I imagined how wonderful it would be to have a wee sailing boat here. But that would probably mean other touristy recreational equipment. If this were Europe I'm perfectly sure there would be hotels, camping areas, yachts and speedboats with of course the accompanying detritus of plastic bottles, bags and junk. How lucky we are to be here in this absolutely magic wilderness, if only, if only it can be kept like this forever and ever.

Back at the rangers' hut we tried, over lunch, to get some more information from the lads about this area, but Hassan, as usual was holding court. He is very well informed on lots of subjects – particularly history and politics – which he wanted to tell us about, but he would not translate our questions, nor the rangers' responses, so we gave up. He, or they, suggested that we go to see the manager of the TINRO station later in the day and get some answers from him.

And so it was that later in the afternoon, having yet again packed up our belongings in readiness for the walk out of the park, we visited Alexei Masaov, the manager of the research station. He was a delightful man, sitting quietly ready and willing to answer all my questions. With him were two Austrians who were making a wildlife documentary. When I was introduced as writing a book, they were very impressed, asking me should they know my name and was I famous? I had to laugh and replied that no I wasn't famous yet, but after this book I would be! They were interested in listening in to my questions.

From Alexei I learned quite a lot.

Lake Kurilskoye is 360 metres deep – an ancient volcanic crater. The water level doesn't vary much during the year, being a little higher only after the snow-melt in spring. The salmon breeding here are sockeye and since 1940 the count has been several million – the maximum was in 2003 when the lake produced 21,000 tons of red fish with 200,000 crossing the barrier. That is an amazing amount. There are many more fish here than in the Kamchatka River which runs into the Pacific Ocean at Ust Kamchatsk. The main market for fished salmon is Japan. Apart from bears, the only other predator is man, with over-fishing becoming a very real threat. Legislation has been introduced making a ban on fishing for non-Russians inside a 200-mile (320km) coastal limit. On the other hand, global warming and the consequent heating up of the oceans is helping small fish survive, which in turn will help the numbers coming up to the lake to spawn. In 1999 a bear count showed approximately 500 brown bears in the lake watershed, with probably around 1,500 in the zakaznik, but they are being diminished as a result of a disease in the elfin cedar which is affecting the cubs.

I thanked Alexei and wished him well as we humped our bags onto our backs again in readiness for our trek back to Igor, the vakhtovka and Pauzetka. But we had hardly set off when we spied an enormous bear which had come to fish on the lower side of the fish barrier, standing up on his hind legs and pouncing at them, only about 30 metres from where we were. Elise was the quickest to get her camera out and went rushing off to take photos of him.

Off we set again, but before we had gone 200 metres, there, wading across from the far bank to an island midstream, was a mother bear with three disorderly cubs in her wake. We stood entranced as we watched the mother patiently waiting for her offspring while they be-sported themselves gambolling off in another direction or pushing and shoving into each other with no idea of having to actually take to the water and swim behind her. Eventually she had them under control and they all made it to the little island, where we watched them for a minute or two while they shook the water off their bodies, the spray from their long pelts sparkling and dancing in the sunlight. It was a magical few minutes, watching this lovely family who were completely oblivious to our presence, until we lost sight of them as they trundled off into the vegetation.

On this return trip we had the reassuring company of ranger Fyodor, complete with rifle. It was the same hard trek fighting our way through the high grasses, willow and birch saplings. At last we learned the difference between the shelamannik and the puchka plants. Fyodor explained it to us, noting that the puchka was poisonous; although we have fought our way – often – through this type of vegetation, blissfully unaware of its properties, we at least know now to try and avoid it.

As the 18th century Russian explorer and geographer Stepan Krasheninnikov wrote, "Grasses all over Kamchatka are, with no exception, so tall and rich that you can hardly find alike ones wherever in [the] Russian empire. At the rivers and lakes and in the copses they are much taller than a man's height and grow so fast that you can coch [cut] hay in one and the same place three times a year".

Almost as soon as the snow melts the shelamannik, a huge grassy plant along with krestovik and puchka starts to grow. The stems can easily be three metres high and with its broad leaves this makes it impossible to see where you are going. The plant is not dangerous, the leaves and stems are soft and easily moved by hand or stick. The shelamannik's young sprouts are edible and are the first food for bears when they come out from their winter dens. The puchka (*Heracleum dulce*) is an extremely handsome plant with large white flowers which looks, to us, like enormous cow-parsley. It is, however, an insidious plant. Its juice is sweet, but leaves blisters and sores on the skin that ache for months. The Itelmen used to extract a sort of sugar from the plant and the Cossacks distilled a wine that produced a strange, hallucinatory effect.

On our return trek, where we had jumped over or waded through the streams, Fyodor

Finding the trail while hiking through the lowlands of Kamchatka during summer and autumn can be a trial. Huge grassy plants such as shelamannik and puchka can grow three metres high, making progress - and navigation - extremely difficult.

now took us on a short detour of a few metres to find little rickety bridges to negotiate instead of the water. We would never have found them ourselves, hidden away as they were. It was still very hot and both of us were aware of the mosquitoes. Elise had been really badly bitten during the night, but mine weren't quite so bad. We had sprayed ourselves and the room and lit a mosquito coil, but the wee bastards are very tenacious and had made a real meal of Elise's shoulders, and now being hot and sweaty it really exacerbated the very itchy bites. We tried wearing veiled hats, which keep the mossies off your face OK, but the sunlight shone from the side through the netting, making it terribly difficult to see where you were going.

We made just three stops for a rest and one brew-up (we made sure we had water ourselves this time) and amazingly, topping a steep rise, there was wonderful Igor and the Big Truck. It had only taken us three hours this time. We were very pleased with ourselves and, feigning casualness, gave the impression to Hassan of being totally laid-back about the walk and prepared to have gone further had it been necessary. In fact, glad as we were to see the truck, this next part we both hated, bashing through the trees. The mirror bracket still wasn't fixed, so we had to climb in through the driver's door – there were two very big, high steps up into the cab, and as I am very small, I had to haul myself up holding on to whatever came to hand. We said fond farewells and grateful thanks to Fyodor and off we set. Crossing the river was again a doddle, even more so as the water level had dropped quite substantially.

What a trek and a wonderful couple of days we have had and such huge satisfaction and delight at having achieved our goal of seeing, "face to face", the renowned bears of Kamchatka – up the Grannies!

We were pretty whacked this evening when we returned to our homestay, but everyone was delighted that it all went so well. We dived pleasurably into a couple of rather warm beers, and I had a great bath with my undies on and got them and my hair and everything else well washed. Bliss. The old back's a bit stiff tonight so off to bed with two Dr Reddy's and an antihistamine for the bites – this should make me sleep.

HOTEL OZERNOVSKY, 22 AUGUST

Don't get stuck in Ozernovsky! It's not exactly the hub of the universe.

We got up this morning at 8am as arranged to find the entire house covered with sleeping bodies. Every piece of floor space was in use, but where was Hassan? We packed up our own stuff and waited for him to appear, which he eventually did after we had already organized breakfast. We asked him where he had been and said we hoped that it was OK for us to have gone ahead and done our own breakfast. His response was that he was paying plenty for the homestay and it was up to them to prepare our food. Oh dear.

Having said our farewells to the family off we set for the airport for our flight to Petropavlovsk at 1pm. We thought we were very early, but Hassan wanted to go and see the ocean since living as he does in Kazakhstan, he doesn't get to see a beach and the sea very often. That was fine by us, we are game for anything that comes our way, but it would have been nice if he volunteered this sort of information without us having to prise it out of him.

We passed the airport and continued on a further half-mile or so until we came to lots of fishing boats, heavy machinery and all the detritus of the fishing industry. We climbed a sand dune of black sand and slid down the other side onto a beach facing the Sea of Okhotsk. Here, dozens of ancient rusting hulks of vessels whose glory days of fishing were long gone, had been drawn up above high tide mark. What a sad sight, made more dismal by the grey, lowering sky. And then, suddenly, the heavens opened. It tipped down on us as we all ran for shelter, hiding amongst the rusting relics. As the rain lessened a little, we made our way along the beach to where the Ozernaya River emptied into the sea. It was amazingly narrow here, but swift and deep with small overfalls where the rushing river met the incoming tide. We continued on until we had almost arrived back at the car, when once again it lashed rain. This time we sought shelter in somebody's office.

Well, of course, what do you think happened next? Bad weather, so flight delayed until 1.30pm. We sat in the tiny 12 x 14 "departure lounge" in the company of Hassan and three local ladies, one of whom was the lady with the scare gun for frightening off the birds when the flights come and go. They were very friendly and curious, and are the proud possessors of lots of stainless-steel teeth. The gun lady I would think is part Itelmen, with broad, high cheekbones. Suffering from extreme boredom we decided to play "town endings". This is a childish game where you have to think up a town, or whatever, starting with the same letter with which the previous town's name ended. It gave us a laugh, anyway.

Then the flight was cancelled. It was ominous that we were the only "eejits" who turned up for the flight. Did everyone else know something that we didn't? This was definitely not good news. Shit, shit. This will now have a knock-on effect on our flight tomorrow to Palana. Years ago in Peru we swore never to have just one night in out-of-the-way places in case of flight cancellations, and here we were in exactly that situation. It was never intended when we first made our bookings – we should actually have been a day *earlier* coming to Ozernovsky and returning *yesterday* with two nights in Petropavlovsk before going to Palana, but then they cancelled that original flight to Ozernovsky months ago. So here we are, and it doesn't look good.

Hassan was upset too, and made phone calls to Tanya in Petropavlovsk where it is sunny – which didn't improve our mood. He then made enquiries about a hotel here as we had to find somewhere for the night. We arrived at a very unprepossessing tenement block in the long empty street of apartment blocks and mud from the airport to Ozernovsky town and climbed the steps to the hall. Two very pleasant ladies welcomed us in and showed us down a long corridor to a sort of apartment – two bedrooms, both with huge fridges and a room with a sink and lavatory. It's clean and suits us fine. Hassan has his little camping gas stove on which he can make us a meal of sorts.

Elise's bites on her back and shoulders are terrible, massive, angry and very itchy and she got me to put some antihistamine cream on them before we ventured out to do some shopping in the town. Her bites are much worse than mine; maybe Dr Reddy's has hidden virtues.

The road to town was muddy and full of puddles but the rain had stopped and we walked beside the river towards the bridge where the fishermen were hard at work dragging in a huge net full of salmon. About 24 men pulled the net in to a circle, then a crane hauled up the net, emptying the fish into boxes on a lorry. They must have emptied about 7cwt at a time in to eight containers on one lorry, and about another four onto a second lorry. Each salmon looked to us to be about 9–10lbs (4.5kg) in weight – that's a lot of salmon. The men seemed very friendly and tried talking to us, but of course no common language, and as usual Hassan had wandered on and was sitting on an upturned boat minding his own business. One man did ask us "English?" and we replied "Niet, Irish". Another offered

us a salmon. Oh boy, what we could have done with that had we been at home – a fresh wild salmon? Sadly we had to refuse the lovely offer.

We pottered on into town and bought vegetables from gardener Sergei's mother in her little shop. Hassan said he was going to cook us "plov" for dinner, which we love. We then sent him for a replenishment of vodka while we went in search of juice and a lemon. We knew the word for juice was "cok" as we had seen it on cartons previously, but we were a little dubious about two middle-aged ladies asking for a carton of orange cok until Hassan told us it was pronounced "sok". Everyone in the shop was fascinated by us and our lack of Russian as we correctly asked for "sok" and pointed to a lemon. The amount came to R500 and Elise produced our kitty, which of course did not contain small enough change, but a man – another customer – swept it aside and insisted on paying, saying "I present you". What a generous gesture.

There seems so little here in the way of amenities. No cafés or restaurants, of course no pubs, no public transport, dirt roads, two or three tiny shops with so little to buy and anything imported terribly expensive. We are terribly spoiled at home and I wonder just how many people appreciate their lot? Elise and I realize it, and I remind myself so often when I'm at home just how lucky we are, but I don't think for one minute either her or my children are aware of how the other half live and even though I tell people they simply don't seem to take it in – unless you experience it first hand it just goes in one ear and out the other.

Back at the hotel we found that Hassan was already there, somehow having passed us on the road. He said he was not making plov after all, and produced a meal of reconstituted noodles, tinned salmon and pasta. We are passed caring and tired of writing and playing games, and badly want our books. Elise turned to me and said "You know what? We are now going to have to talk scribble |rubbish| to each other".

A Steller's sea eagle on the wing, its mighty talons hidden but its massive bill clearly visible.

Birds of Kamchatka

by Fergus Crystal

The Steller's sea eagle is one of the largest and most magnificent eagle species in the world, and a significant part of the world population breeds in Kamchatka. No visitor to the peninsula can fail to be impressed by the memorable sight of one of these huge but graceful eagles soaring purposefully overhead. The boldly patterned black and white plumage and massive yellow bill and cere are distinctive even from some distance away.

Pairs mate for life and construct their massive stick nests in the upper reaches of the largest trees in mature birch forest. Males attract their mates from afar by perching prominently near choice feeding sites in their massive territories, throwing their heads back and flinging them outwards and upwards, giving a loud staccato series of barking calls. When perched on the upper branches of a birch tree, these eagles can truly be described as stately. A closer look at the massive talons and thick legs gripping impossibly frail-looking birch twigs shows how deceptive the massive profile of these birds can be. Despite their apparent bulk, Steller's sea eagles are deceptively compact, and what looks like a huge raptor at rest is transformed into a streamlined cruiser in flight. The tail is characteristically wedge-shaped and longer than in other sea eagle

species (including the North American bald eagle) and acts as an efficient rudder to enable swift turns in flight.

These eagles are adept at both plunging for fish and quartering cliff tops and boulder slopes in fast pursuit of seabirds singled out from the throng. They also show a liking for carrion and dead fish and are often found near fishing ports after the breeding season. At this time of year, when the sea ice forms and the peninsula is blanketed with snow, the eagles turn coastal and gather in large winter roosts in tall leafless trees that serve as lookout posts over the bays. In winter, the eagles eat mostly fish and are often found in close proximity to fishing ports. As well as fish, sea birds, gulls and wildfowl up to the size of whooper swan are taken as prey. While some of the population migrate south to Sakhalin and Hokkaido (Japan) for winter, the majority remain on the peninsula.

However, it is not just the chance of seeing eagles that keeps the visiting birdwatcher alert. Kamchatka offers a wide range of pristine habitats where breeding populations of songbirds abound. Exploring some of the birch forests and riverine woods in early summer can reveal large communities of some of the most sought-after

Siberian songsters. In the mossy forests, the buzzing song of Arctic warbler and the jingling trill of the unobtrusive rufous-tailed robin are noteworthy. In more open habitats with lower scrubby vegetation, the rustic bunting gives its low, throaty warble while cheery wolf whistles and querying notes come from the ubiquitous common rosefinch. Mealy redpolls jangle overhead and smart, summer-dressed bramblings say "cheese", while the olive-backed pipit gives ecstatic flourishes of notes from shady forest.

At dusk or dawn, a wait by the mirror-calm pools of a marsh will treat the listener to the protracted fishing reel-like song of lanceolated warblers. In open tundra and on *Primula*-studded alpine slopes Lapland buntings give their jaunty, rhythmic song, as pechora pipits pulse. Arctic rosy finches can be found in their smart pink-tinged

A snow bunting rests on volcanic soil.

summer plumage. Perhaps the most beautiful song comes from dense scrub, a complex burst of chatters and pure whistles that often seems to mimic other birds in the vicinity. A patient wait by the bush could reveal the presence of the *chanteur*: a male Siberian rubythroat. With his back turned he may appear to be just a nondescript brown robin trying to attract attention by cocking his tail and flicking his wings, but on turning he will reveal the shimmering ruby patch on his throat and smart black-and-white mask that will finally net him a mate. Other highly coloured denizens include the livid colouration of the daurian redstart with its bold patterning of reddest rust, grey, white and black, and the red-flanked bluetail with its shining cobalt brow and epaulets that glint even in the murkiest patches of forest.

Around the wide, gravel-fringed bays and river mouths of the peninsula,

Harlequin ducks pair by the shore.

birdwatchers have the opportunity to observe some of the world's most stunning species of seabird or waterfowl in smart breeding dress. Early summer, before the mosquitoes hatch, is the best time to observe birds in their full array. Taking a boat around the shores and islands of the peninsula, or exploring up meandering rivers

reveals many different species. The strange honking calls of black scoter with their smart yellow bill shields are never far way, while harlequin ducks, the males with their boldly patterned purple plumage, can be commonly seen. Divers (or loons) are abundant: the red-throated variety are the most common, followed by black-throated, but it is the white-billed divers with their immense size and bizarre banana-like bills and shining monochromatic patterns that command the most attention.

Far eastern curlews, the females often with impossibly long bills, emit desolate piping whistles and the beautiful rusty tones of Mongolian plovers can be glimpsed as they move across short turf at the shore. Glaucous-winged gulls gather on beaches or at the edge of towns, but the more marine Kittiwakes prefer steep coastal cliffs. There are two species: the more abundant black-legged kittiwake line the ledges, but closer to the raging sea surface the diminutive and stubby-billed red-legged kittiwake prefers to nest. Long-billed murrelets are tiny auks that are found on the water of calm bays. Like penguins they busy themselves feeding by diving and pursuing small fish, but they nest in the upper branches of tall conifers, sometimes far from water.

Among the cliff ledges of the many small, steep-sided islands other auks make their nests, sometimes in huge numbers. Horned puffin, with broader and more yellow bills than their Atlantic counterparts, have spiked "horns" above each eye, which give them a dapper expression. Pigeon and Brunnich's guillemots are common and easily seen flying to and from the ledges, but the most eye-catching ledge user is the tufted puffin, with its bizarre cream-coloured headdress, white mask and salmon-red bill. These soot-coloured birds occur in colonies of up to 20,000 individuals on islands, and their antics are best observed from a passing boat. A view of several of these distinctive birds that seem to come from a distant age, peering at you over a bare ledge, encapsulates the otherworldly aspect of a trip to Kamchatka.

The tufted puffin is an eye-catching resident of the peninsula.

CHAPTER 8

PALANA DISAPPOINTMENT

POSTPONEMENTS. CANCELLATIONS. DESPERATE DECISIONS

YELIZOVO. ART HOTEL. 23 AUGUST

Because there was no telephone connection from our hotel to the airport, or else Hassan's mobile didn't work from there, at midmorning he walked to the airport to find out if/when there would be a flight to Petropavlovsk. He returned with the news that there would be one later, so we tried to remain optimistic as we packed up again, keeping a weather eye on the low cloud. We have been here a week now, in which time we have spent two glorious days actually doing what we came here for. Thank goodness we gave ourselves the week to do it.

Our three local ladies with the silver gnashers greeted us like long-lost cousins and made us take their seats. Gradually a heterogeneous collection of people arrived for the flight – which seemed on the face of it, fairly promising. Everyone seemed to know the drill; as they arrived they weighed in their own baggage on a set of ancient scales and labelled each bag. Obviously it is quite unnecessary to bother with a check-in desk.

Before too long a small jet arrived, disgorged its passengers, and we queued up for what we assumed was our security check. Not a bit of it. No security whatsoever. We carried our own luggage to the back of the plane and for a while there was total mayhem as everybody tried to climb the steps up the rear with their own stuff. However, quite quickly Hassan and another man took over and between them carried up and stowed the baggage for the 32 passengers. While this was going on I was looking at the rather old and battered plane, noticing that there wasn't a shred of tread on the its tyres – bald as coots they were. I hesitated drawing Elise's attention to them, but she was already well aware. We all climbed up the steps, squeezed past the bags and found our seats. The interior of the plane was on a par with the outside. Most of the seats were barely connected to the floor and the back of mine wobbled about quite uncontrollably.

Kamchatka's prodigious salmon population provides an essential source of food for all who live on the peninsula.

However, up we went, circling round out over the Sea of Okhotsk and soon heading north into bright, clear weather. With the Pacific on our right-hand side we enjoyed stunning views as we flew over and round volcanoes and mountains for the half-hour it took the little jet this time.

With sunny weather to greet us we returned to the Art Hotel in Yelizovo, hoping against hope that Hassan would be able to get us tickets on a flight to Palana on the morrow. We went off to shop in the local market, ostensibly to buy Elise a mug and a large plastic bag for her sleeping bag, but also to have a nosey around and see what was for sale. It's always good fun poking around in markets. As usual there was lots of smoked fish and salmon "caviar" for sale. We also visited a dear little church which looked like another house from the outside but had all the Orthodox paraphernalia inside.

There is, of course, now a huge problem with our getting to Palana. Having missed our flight today, we now hope to be able to go tomorrow. However, apparently in April there was a very big earthquake in Korf, on the northeast side of the peninsula and most of the flights are full taking officials north to Palana, or refugees south to Petropavlovsk. Now with winter in the offing it is imperative that everyone is safely housed. They say there will be a flight tomorrow and Tanya has incredibly managed to get two tickets, she says through the governor of the Koryak district, for Elise and me. But Hassan does not have one and unless he can wangle a black-market seat, the decision is do we go ahead without him – nice thought – but with nobody in Palana speaking English how would we manage? Hassan is trying to find out if there is a teacher in Palana who might be able to speak a little English. Oh dear, we will just have to wait until the morning and see what transpires.

In the warm, sunny evening we took a walk down to the river and watched children playing in the water and a courting couple lying on the bank. It was beautiful and peaceful with the two huge volcanoes standing sentinel over the scene. This year we are here only two weeks earlier than the last time, and then it was freezing cold weather with all the trees turning colour, this time it is actually hot – when it isn't raining – with not a sign of approaching autumn. We sat on a little bench outside the hotel for our pre-prandial drinks it was such a lovely evening. I retreated into my Paul Theroux book about his travels in Africa – it's really odd, I get so involved with Africa that I have to do a real double-take when I stop reading to realize that I am not in Africa but Russia.

YELIZOVO. ART HOTEL. 24 AUGUST

Today started badly when, at breakfast, we saw on the telly that there had been a fatal plane crash in the Ukraine, 160 dead including 40 children. They say it might have been a lightning strike. A very cheering start to the day – I don't think.

Then Hassan arrived at 10am and asked could he talk to us in our room? Up we went and he talked for three-quarters of an hour, explaining how much money he had spent what with delays and cancellations and so on. He did calculations and addings-up and takings-away till we were totally confused with what he was telling us. It was really, really dreadful. We couldn't get a word in edgeways until finally we shouted at him to stop and be quiet for a minute and let us speak. Elise was apoplectic – I was actually frightened that she was going to get up and hit him – she's not known for taking prisoners! I said that it wasn't our fault that the weather had been bad, that flights had been cancelled and that his business really wasn't our affair.

We felt he should have "built-in" expediency arrangements, and should know from experience what the conditions are like here. "Oh," he said, "I am a very experienced travel guide and have been organizing people coming to Kamchatka since 1990." Eventually we asked him where all this was leading? Was he looking for more money? He denied that and just said he wanted to tell us how much he had spent. Also that he had had to give Tanya the sack as he couldn't afford to pay her anymore. It was all awful, embarrassing and very upsetting.

We got a taxi to the airport, hoping that we would be able to get Hassan a ticket, but the way we felt, we would have liked to be without him for a while. Anyway, what do you know – the flight was delayed until tomorrow at 9am because of bad weather in Palana! Lovely Tanya had turned up at the airport anyway to see us and she said this really wasn't unusual, that sometimes people actually camp out at the airport waiting to get flights to Palana, sometimes waiting three or four days.

We were very browned-off. We had discussed this possibility, knowing that the flights are so unreliable and had decided that if today's flight were cancelled we would just call the whole thing off. Maybe it wouldn't even go tomorrow and we would have lost yet another day. Then there was always the doubt about a return flight and we had to be back for the 29th. So I said that we would cut our losses and forego Palana, in any case, even if we went tomorrow we would not now have time to go to Lake Palanskoye.

I was heartbroken about it. I so wanted to go north, but it was obviously not to be. Driving away from the airport Elise took my hand and I just couldn't stop the tears. That's twice now we have been thwarted in our plans to visit the Koryak people. I felt totally despondent and didn't give a damn what we did next.

Hassan, I felt, was quietly overjoyed at not going to Palana. He has never been there and I had the feeling he was nervous about the whole thing. We repaired to his apartment-cum-office, a dingy place consisting of three rooms smelling of pee and ciggies, in an equally dingy apartment block. He says every time he comes here from Almaty he is shocked by the housing. I don't know why he does business in Russia at all, because housing is like this everywhere, and he goes to such pains to criticise the Russians, the Americans and the Germans. He offered us sleeping space on the floor for the night, but now that we are foregoing Palana we decided no way, we needed to go to some sort of hotel or B&B where we could regroup and just be on our own.

We discussed what the alternatives were in lieu of going to the Koryak and plumped for the idea of taking the regular bus as far as Kozyrevsk, on the road to Ust Kamchatsk, and having a look at the Kluchevskoye Volcanic Group. Kamchatka's tallest and some of its currently most active volcanoes are part of this 60 x 70km area. This group marks the meeting point of the Kuril–Kamchatka volcanic chain which stretches from Japan up through the Kuril Islands and Southern Kamchatka before meeting the Aleutian volcanic chain which is traced by the arc of the Aleutian Islands. The group includes Ostry and Plosky Tolbachik, Novy Tolbachik, Mount Bolshaya Udina, Mount Ovalina Sima, Bezymyany, and Kamen, Kluchevskoy and Ushkovsky volcanoes. There are huts and, I think, a geological station on Plosky Tolbachik where we hope to stay a night or two.

With this in mind and beginning to get over the disappointment of not going to Palana, we left Hassan to book bus tickets and organise the rest of the new trip while we took ourselves off into Petropavlovsk lower town and harbour. The day was hot and sunny, and we wandered down to have a look at the sea and the people enjoying the lovely weather in Lenin Park. There was a little café playing a Beatles number, with people having drinks and snacks outside, and an area full of swings and roundabouts for children to play on. We spent the rest of the afternoon looking for an exhibition on Kamchatka, which we finally found at 5.15pm, just after closing time – typical.

We were to meet Hassan at the Avacha Hotel at 6.30pm, so in plenty of time we climbed the hill to the hotel and sat in the foyer to wait for him, sitting beside a most remarkable looking lady. Forty-five plus, bright-red hair, a very naked pink lacy top, an above-the-knee froufrou skirt, fishnets and cripplingly high heels. She came and went to the door a couple of times, teetering along in her high heels, when the penny dropped as to just what she was about. It made me feel very privileged, extremely prim and quite uncomfortable. We had been aware of very pretty girls all day sauntering around the town, often in the skimpiest and most provocative of clothing and wondered just what they were at. Well, there was certainly a "lady of the night" coming and going from the foyer of the Avacha Hotel.

Hassan arrived, having managed to get everything organized for the next day to go and see the Tolbachik volcanoes. He took us to a small, new B&B in upper Petropavlovsk which belonged to a friend of Tanya's. He warned us that the outside was pretty bad but some rich Muscovites had bought three apartments and had knocked them all together and made it into a little hotel. He was right, the outside was appalling, the usual dirty, drab concrete block, but inside it was lovely, brand new and very attractive. The girl who welcomed us spoke very good English and showed us up to our room.

When we came down again, Hassan had disappeared with no mention of dinner or where to go to get it. I was still feeling terribly depressed and even a bit weepy about not going to Palana, and this childishly seemed to be the last straw. However, Tanya phoned to say that Sergei lived very close and would come round to see us. We were so pleased and decided we would ask him where we could get a meal.

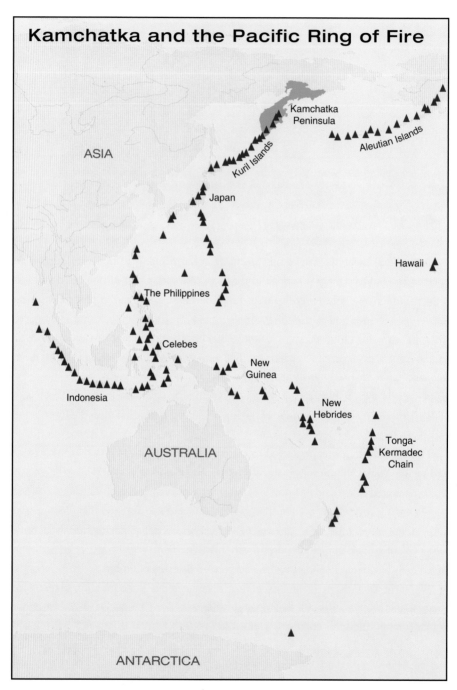

Kamchatka and the Pacific Ring of Fire

ASIA

Kamchatka
Peninsula

Aleutian Islands

Kuril Islands

Japan

Hawaii

The Philippines

Celebes

New
Guinea

Indonesia

New
Hebrides

Tonga-
Kermadec
Chain

AUSTRALIA

ANTARCTICA

Sergei hadn't changed one bit. He was still tall, slim and blond, and had a rather shy stiffness in his movements and a familiar embarrassed giggle when we went to embrace him. It is lovely now to have met up with both Zhenya and Sergei. He brought us to his apartment and having introduced us to his, then, partner, sat us down, gave us a drink and his girlfriend gave us sausage rolls, fried eggs (I have eaten more eggs in the past week than I would eat in a month at home) and delicious cake. He then took us into his sitting room – the apartment is full of photographic material – and showed us his most recent photographs on the computer. There were hundreds, mostly of Mutnovsky, Gorely and Avachinsky. Stunning pictures also of gorgeous naked girls, whether they were his girlfriends or not we didn't like to ask. They were all outside poses taken by rivers, in fields of flowers, draped round trees and even in the snow! I asked him to put on CD about 100 to 150 – without the girls – and I would collect them before we left Kamchatka.

On the way back to our hotel, we mentioned that we needed to stop at a shop and buy both juice and vodka. He said he had very good vodka back home which we could buy from him and we should go ahead and buy the juice, which we now were very good at; with great aplomb we asked for orange "sok", which we were given. We arrived back at the hotel to discover we were locked out, but luckily Sergei turned up with the vodka and knew the code and the right buttons to press, and was able to let us in, promising to meet us after we returned from Kozyrevsk.

I first heard about Lydia Chechoolina from Lisa Strecher, a most interesting young German ethnologist and translator, while we were staying in a hut on Plosky Tolbachik Volcano. I was bemoaning the fact that I hadn't been able to get to Palana to visit the Koryak people and Lisa suggested that her friend, Lydia, might be glad to have her story written in my book. I am delighted to have it here, as it gives a clear idea of the trials and pleasures of the traditional Koryak way of life, and a warning of the diminishing of Kamchatka's cultural wealth.

Life among the Koryak

I, Lidia Innokentyevna Chechoolina, was born on the 13 January 1957 in Anapka village, which is situated in the Karaginski area of Koryak, an autonomous region. My nationality is Nymylanka – from the shores of Koryak. In 1958 the original Anapka village was relocated to the shore. The majority of the population was made up of native Koryak. Our main occupations were fishing and deer herding. The original inhabitants were relocated from their small huts and deer herder's yurtas (a hut made from animal skins) into small houses were two families would share each house. A new future was being built – Communism. At the time of World War II the local people fished on a commercial scale for herring and salmon. Many of the fishermen were awarded medals and commendations for their hard work during the war effort, including my father. Female work teams also operated in the open sea. In winter all the women also tanned deer hide and sewed fur clothes for Russian army soldiers.

A Koryak woman's clothes are warm and functional, but also sport beautiful decorative designs.

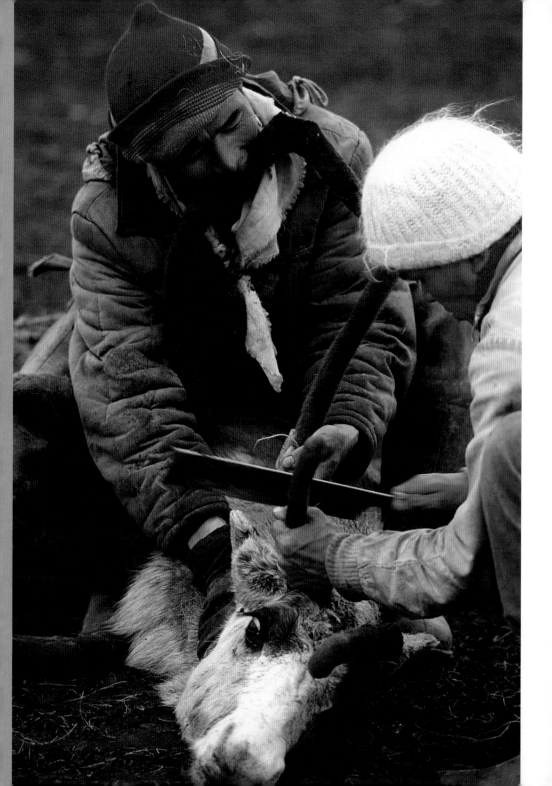

That generation worked in such hard conditions that it took a severe toll on their health, many working themselves close to death.

The population of Kamchatka lived much like their ancestors did until the 1930s. They were aware of Soviet power but it had no impact on their lives. Deer herding Koryaks lived in their yurts, packing up and moving every three days to new pastures during the summer. The herds were moved so often to preserve the tundra, specifically the yagel moss that the deer eat, and moving frequently like this enabled the moss to re-grow. This way the native people instinctively cared for the ecology, helping nature to stay in balance. There were huge numbers of deer in each herd, often 6,000-7,000 head. Each Koryak had his/her own herd within the larger herd, identifiable by unique markings cut into the deers' ears. Each newborn child was given his/her own little herd that grew as the child grew. Little girls were expected to carry out their own chores from the age of four. When a young woman got married her dowry would be made up of deer. The native people were reluctant to give their daughters to any outsiders like the Yakut, Chukchi or Even tribes. It was deemed that outsiders would not care for the deer as well as the Koryak could.

The relationship between the Koryak and their deer was very caring and respectful. Deer were only ever killed for food, never for sport, and deer bones were never thrown away but were always burned in the fire. Boys were taught the ways of their fathers and physical strength was forged from a very young age. They were made to run a lot to build up their stamina and laughed at and despised those who were overweight. Older people were never sympathetic to overweight children; they just forced them to lose weight. Extra weight on a deer herder is an unacceptable burden.

When a young man was getting married he took on the responsibility for his young woman, ensuring that she would always live in his family until her death, especially if she had children. At the same time a woman would never forget her relatives, brothers, sisters, mother and father, despite how well she was doing in her new family.

Deer were used for anything and everything that they could provide. Antlers were used to make tools such as knife handles, buttons, thimbles and other household items. Tendons were used to make thread and deerskin was used to make clothes and yurts, while the neck hair was used to make decorative items for clothes. Everybody, from the youngest to the oldest, was always busy with their chores. They would sit around the fire during the long winter nights and do their work. Women tanned

Reindeer antlers are used for a multitude of purposes by the Koryak.

Bark from alder and larch is used to make dye for clothing.

deerskins and sewed clothes; men made household items and tools. Grandfathers and grandmothers would recount old legends and fairytales, real-life stories and sing songs. They also loved to solve riddles, often not guessing what the answer was for days, and would embroider scenes of animals and birds, in the process passing on invaluable experience to the next generation.

Deer herders celebrated "Kilvey" at the beginning of April to mark the birth of the new deer calves. They also celebrated the return of the herders from the summer pastures. Everyone wore their best clothes and the celebrations would attract visitors from neighbouring settlements. There were deer and sleigh races, Koryak wrestling and everyone played games in the fresh air, children and grown-ups alike. The prizes for the winners would be prepared in advance and would include snow cat furs, deer meat and sealskins. The top prize would be a small herd of deer.

The shore Koryak were fishermen. The catch would be dried in the sun and come autumn it would be frozen. Some of it was buried for winter feed for the dogs. Women gathered berries, roots and nuts in the summer. This was stored in vessels made from sealskins. The skin would be removed from the carcass in one piece, inflated, and then dried in the sun so it would take the required shape. Women also gathered a lot of herbs and seaweed. The seaweed was used to make baskets, rugs, walls and roofs for the summer huts. Shore dwellers also loved to celebrate. "Hololo" was the main celebration, taking place late in the autumn and attracting many visitors. This was in honour of the seal and lots of food would be prepared. The main dish of the day was *Tolkusha*, a mixture of berries, roots, seal fat and dried caviar.

The shore dwellers also performed lots of rituals, such as making little seal toys from tree branches tied with holy grass called *laho'ten*. During the ritual they threw pieces of seal fat into the fire to appease the sea, so that there would be no storms or ice, and so that all the hunters would return home safely. They also made offerings at holy places so that hunts would be successful. All the participants would do the dance of the sea, imitating the waves with their skirts and mimicking seal cries. They then threw the seal toys into the fire, and opened all doors and windows to enable the seal spirit to return to the sea. The whole ceremony would be orchestrated by a host and on his command everyone would turn towards the sea to mark the return of the seal spirit to the sea. They would then turn back towards the land and the celebrations would start in earnest.

Each guest showed his/her skill in dancing and singing. Each dance was very individual, and the singing was filled with personal feelings. There were also competitions of skill, dexterity and bravery. One such competition was called the pulling of *talytal* – a form of tug-of-war using a large wooden disc through which a 5–7 metre length of seal leather would be pulled. If the leather broke on the first evening of the celebration then nuts were showered over the crowd by the hostess. It was a lot of fun and people would catch the nuts in their hands or the folds of their skirts, some falling over and all laughing. They also played tug-of-war through the doorways of houses with branches. Those inside would try and pull over those who were standing outside. Such celebrations continued up until the mid-1960s and took place in each and every village and deer herding community.

During the period of centralisation, when small villages would be closed and people would be moved to larger settlements, the rituals and traditions of the people declined. They even began to forget their own native tongue. It was forbidden to fish in the traditional fishing grounds, and as there was no longer any food for the dog packs they vanished. This was a tragedy, as the dog teams were the means of communication to relatives who lived hundreds of kilometres away. Over time, the people have forgotten how to live in the tundra, despite the fact that for many generations the tundra provided everything the people needed. Nowadays the population of deer is very small, there are no celebrations and there is no work in the winter. There is now a high incidence of alcoholism among local people, many people suffer from tuberculosis and I think that only those with a strong spirit will survive.

Those who are over 70 always try to go to the tundra in the summer to gather berries and do some fishing. And although there are few deerskins they still try and make clothes for themselves or to sell, but their children do not know their native language. Held within the language of the songs and fairytales is a culture and a way of thinking. In some villages they still try and teach the Koryak language, but for children it is simply a foreign language. These are difficult times for the Koryak region. During Perestroika a lot of fishing factories were closed, the deer population diminished and all traditional means of transportation disappeared. Life is hard. All professional people such as doctors or teachers have left the villages. In the 21st century we still need education and stability in everything. I left the village because it did not even have the basics for life such as running water. The water pipes were frozen and damaged and there was no money for repairs. I was eager to study and educate my daughter so I moved to Petropavlovsk-Kamchatskiy. Here in the city we sing and dance for the tourists. I am a primary school teacher teaching native arts and dances of the northern peoples of Kamchatka. I try to save what I still remember and know.

The multiple associations of native peoples, communities and dance groups of Kamchatka also help to save our culture for future generations.

An Even woman in traditional costume dances around the fire inside a *yurta*. Performances for tourists are authentic and help to keep traditional customs alive.

THROUGH MORIBUND REGIONS ALONG THE OKHOTSK SHORE

Excerpted from *Through Kamchatka by Dog Sled and Skis*
by Sten Bergman, D.Sc. (1927)

From Tigil, (some 80 miles south of Palana) we had a journey of about six hundred miles to Petropavlovsk. The greater part of it was over one continuous tundra. On this tundra lie 18 Kamchadal villages situated at distances of from thirteen to fifty miles from each other. A great portion of the tundra is as level as the sea. You can see no end to it. Here and there stretch small birch woods, which are indescribably welcome to travellers in the winter. At other points its uniformity is broken by somewhat rough ground. Low hills and valleys alternate. The rivers which run through the tundra are bordered by a streak of salix (willow) vegetation. The tundra extends some twenty or thirty miles inland from the sea and is bordered on the east by a mountain range.

The people who dwell in this God-forsaken region belong probably to the most pitiable in the whole world, and a journey through it is depressing in the extreme. Here live the last remnants of a race which will soon be wiped off the face of the earth. In all the other parts of Kamchatka the natives have become so intermingled with the Russians that they have forgotten how to talk their own language, whereas in some of the west-coast villages – ten or twelve of them – there has been only a little intermingling, and the Kamchadal language is still in use. But even here civilization has set its mark on what is left of the inhabitants, for every one of them

LAMUT WOMEN IN THEIR FESTAL DRESSES

The dresses are richly ornamented with beads arranged in very beautiful patterns. Variously coloured bits of dressed hide form part of the ornamentation. A row of bells is always hung on the bottom of the dress and tinkles with each step. Note the row of empty cartridge-cases worn by the woman in the middle. Sometimes one sees padlocks worn as ornaments.

– men, women and children – suffer from hereditary syphilis introduced long ago by Russians. This malady has raged appallingly in these wildernesses where no kind of medical assistance is available. In addition, the Japanese and Chinese and Russians vie with each other in drenching the degenerate villagers in spirits, which, in their miserable condition, they value above all else.

The consequences are that the west coast of Kamchatka furnishes a terrible example of what can happen when a civilized nation takes control of a primitive race and sends its worst representatives to rule over it.

This was the tract through which we were now to travel. It was not an agreeable prospect, especially as we were to be absolutely dependent on these villages for our provisions. We decided that as soon as we reached the village of Chairusovo, situated 120 miles south of Tigil, we should leave the Kamchadals for a time and betake us up into the fjells again to continue our studies of the Lamuts and the Koryaks.

With this plan fixed upon we duly set forth from Tigil where we had been most hospitably entertained by Mr. Pimenoff, the agent of the Hudson Bay Co. From him we had directions as to the houses in the various villages in which it would be least unpleasant to spend the night.

The first village on our way was Napana – a cluster of grey-hued, tumble-down huts standing in the midst of the tundra, and looking as though they had been dumped down there by chance. We reached it in the afternoon. Our dogs got scent of its putrid fish from afar, and when we got near it we were greeted as usual by the barking of the village dogs. The inhabitants, clad in garments of skin acquired from the Koryaks, hurried out of their huts to peer at us inquisitively. As soon as we had tied up the dogs, placing one of them by the sled on guard, I sought out the man in whose dwelling we were to spend the night, and he conducted us to it through the ramshackle village, which consisted of about ten huts in all.

When we went in through the door such an appalling stink reached our nostrils that we nearly fell backwards. The hut consisted of only one room. There was no furniture whatever except a table. A couple of boxes did service as seats – on one of them one could read "California Fruits", on another some Japanese words. On the ground, in a corner, lay heaped up together a lot of dirty-looking ragged clothes, reindeer skins and a damaged gramophone. A couple of natives, who were evidently ill and hardly able to rise, lay covered up with rags in another corner. Some half-naked children were playing on the floor with a piece of meat. Near the fireplace lay the entire frozen carcass of a reindeer, ready to be cut up. The woman of the house came forward shyly, greeted us, and then went back to the chimney corner, where she began to busy herself with a samovar. A Kamchatkan hut never lacks a samovar even if it should lack everything else. In these surroundings we accepted the invitation to sit down on a box at the table and drink tea – brick tea, without sugar, and served in dirty mugs. But we let them serve our tea in our own mugs.

While we were at tea all the dogs in the village suddenly began to bark, which meant that another sledge was arriving. We tried from old habit to look out of the window to see what sort of persons were in the sledge, but we found that the window consisted of fish-skins sewed together. It allowed some light to enter, but one could not see through it. One of the neighbours had a window made of bears' entrails sewn together, others had windows made of seals' entrails. But the most common substitute for glass was fish-skins. They serve the purpose not at all badly, but the hut owner has to take the precaution to have the window at such a height that the sledge dogs cannot get at them, otherwise he would run the risk one fine day of having his window eaten up.

I took a stroll among the huts, trying to procure food for the dogs – often a

THE KORYAK JUTTA AND HIS FAMILY BY THEIR BEAR-FAT LAMP IN THEIR SKIN-TENT

This was the most attractive Koryak family we learned to know. Double walls of woolly reindeer hides protect them from the cold outside, and this is done so thoroughly that the men often throw off their own furs and sit naked to the waist.

Photo by the Author

difficult business. The entire village stank of putrid fish. All the huts were alike – everywhere the same disgusting stink, the same filth, the same misery, the same signs of illness. The Kamchadals are so indolent that they do not trouble in the summer to catch as many fish as they require, although it sometimes does not take them more than a week's work to lay in the necessary store.

It was getting dark, so our Kamchadal host lit his "schirnik" (or lamp), which consisted of an iron bowl, filled with bear's grease or seal's grease – a little shred of cloth served as a wick. We sat and talked with him. He talked Russian quite well, but his family could talk only the Kamchadal language. He told us how difficult it was to live in Kamchatka; how one had to toil over the fishing all summer; how little fish there was now, since the coming of the Japanese; and how hard it was to get any sables in the winter. "You have sometimes to travel for two or three days from the village," he said, "before you get on the tracks of a sable. If only the Koryaks would go away there would be plenty of them – the Koryaks frighten off the sables. But it is true, I must go to see the Koryaks again in a few days time as I have no food for my dogs. We have run short of fish, and it is still two months to the spring. We never get any rest. How is one to hunt sables when one has to go to get meat every week?"

MAURA, THE BEAUTIFUL LAMUT WOMAN
She was the prettiest of all the nomads we visited. In addition she was retiring and shy, and showed us the greatest hospitality. She is wearing her "everyday" clothes.

Photo by the Author

The fact is that these west coast Kamchadals would starve to death if the Koryaks did not help them. They are unceasingly going to the Koryaks' "jurtas" and begging for reindeer, and the Koryaks, who are too kind-hearted to see their fellow-mortals die of hunger, supply their needs. The Koryak women make clothes out of reindeer-skins for the Kamchadals, who declare they cannot sew, but are too lazy to do so.

All the other villages were of the same dreadful kind. If the weather had not been bad, and hunger had not forced us, we should not have gone into them at all. In some of them we could not bring ourselves to spend the night, but contented ourselves with getting food for the dogs and for ourselves, finding refuge instead in one of the earth huts, which were generally situated, for the benefit of travellers, about half-way between the villages.

Ice fishing in winter still reaps rewards for the patient angler.

EARLY AMERICAN TRAVELLERS IN KAMCHATKA

GEORGE KENNAN, 1846-1924

George Kennan, an American engineer from Norwalk, Ohio, was great uncle to the diplomat and historian George Frost Kennan, with whom he shared not only a keen interest in Russian politics and culture, but also his birthday (16 February). In 1864, George Kennan senior, who was keenly interested in travel, secured work with the Russian/American Telegraph Company to survey the possibilities of a telegraph line through Russia and Siberia and across the Bering Strait. He thought he was going to Alaska, but instead found himself in the wilds of Kamchatka and Chukotka.

At this time the country was still mostly inhabited by the Koryak and Chukchi people, plus a few Russian traders. In small parties of a few men, they travelled for two years using reindeer and skin canoes and sleeping under canvas, sometimes in temperatures of -60°C. Eventually Kennan returned to Ohio via St Petersburg. Here he both lectured and wrote his book, *Tent Life in Siberia, Adventures Among the Koryaks and Other Tribes in Kamchatka and Northern Asia* (see Recommended Reading on page 302).

He returned to Russia in 1870 when he travelled to Russia's newly acquired Dagestan in the Caucasus mountains. However, rather than being deterred by the hardship of his adventures in Kamchatka, he returned to Siberia in 1885.

When he started out on his travels to Russia, Kennan was an avid supporter of the then Tsar. However, after meeting with many émigrés, he became an ardent campaigner for democracy and spent much of the next 20 years lecturing and promoting the cause of the Russian Revolution.

"A view of the harbour", created by a member of Von Krusenstern's 1803-1806 expedition.

JOHN LEDYARD (1751-1786)

John Ledyard was born in Groton, Connecticut, but when his father, a sea captain, died of malaria in the Caribbean, his family moved to Long Island. Three years later, the young Ledyard went to live with his grandfather in Hartford Connecticut, where he went to school. His grandfather died just before Ledyard's 20th birthday.

He briefly attended Dartmouth College, which was then only 19 years old, but left without permission to lead a camping expedition, finally abandoning the college in 1773. Memorably, he made his own dugout canoe and paddled it downriver to his grandfather's farm. At a loose end, he decided to travel and shipped as a seaman on a voyage to Gibraltar and the Caribbean. On his next voyage he jumped ship in England where he was press-ganged into joining the British Navy.

In 1776, Ledyard joined Captain James Cook's third and final voyage, the expedition lasting until October 1780. During those four years, Cook's two ships stopped at many Pacific islands before venturing to the northwest coast of America, making Ledyard, perhaps, the first US citizen to touch its western coast. They continued along the Aleutian Islands into the Bering Sea and back to Hawaii where Cook was murdered. Under Captain Clerke, who had taken command of Cook's ship and the expedition, the ships continued north again where they landed in Kamchatka.

Returning to England and still a marine in the British Navy, Ledyard was sent to North America to fight in the American Revolution. He deserted, returned to Hartford and wrote his *Journal of Captain Cook's Last Voyage*. The book was eventually published in 1783 and was the first work to be protected by copyright in the US.

WASHINGTON B. VANDERLIP (BORN 1867)

Washington B. Vanderlip Jr was a mining engineer with a wide and varied career that took him not only all over the southwestern part of the United States, but also to Australia, the Far East, Africa and Alaska. Here he became interested in the rich deposits of gold in the Yukon River and later on Cape Nome. This led him to examine the possibilities of gold extending across the Bering Sea to Eastern Asia, where he was employed by a Russian firm to make an extended prospecting tour north of the Sea of Okhotsk and east into Kamchatka. His experiences there during the summers of 1898 and 1899 led him to write the very interesting *In Search of a Siberian Klondike* (see Recommended Reading on page 302).

In the autumn of 1920, Vanderlip, representing the Vanderlip Syndicate, a large American concern, went to Moscow for talks on a concession for fisheries and exploration for extracting oil and coal in Kamchatka. A draft agreement was worked out stating that the syndicate would receive a 60-year concession, after 35 years of which the Soviet Government would have the option of buying out all the concession enterprises. Any equipment would have to be in full running order and would be transferred free of charge. However, the syndicate failed to obtain support from either the government of the US or from any other influential financial groups, and the draft agreement was never signed.

The following is an interesting letter to Washington Vanderlip from Lenin:

Moscow
March 17th 1921

Mr Washington B. Vanderlip

Dear Sir,

I thank you for your kind letter of the 14th, and am very glad to hear of President Harding's favourable views as to our trade with America. You know what value we attach to our future American business relations. We fully recognise the part played in this respect by your syndicate and also the great importance of your personal efforts. Your new proposals are highly interesting and I have asked the Supreme Council of National Economy to report to me at short intervals about the progress of the negotiations. You can be sure that we will treat every reasonable suggestion with the greatest attention and care. It is on production and trade that our efforts are principally concentrated and your help is to us of the greatest value.

If you have to complain of some officials please send your complaint to the respective People's Commissary who will investigate the matter and report if necessary. I have already ordered special investigation concerning the person you mention in your letter.

The Congress of the Communist Party has taken so much of my time and forces that I am very tired and ill. Will you kindly excuse me if I am unable to speak with you shortly.

Wishing you much success I remain

Yours truly,

Wl. Oulianoff (Lenin)

JESUP EXPEDITION 1900–1901

Morris Jesup (1830–1908) rose from humble beginnings to become a millionaire in the railway banking business. He helped found the American Museum of Natural History and, as its president, financed this most ambitious of American ethnological expeditions.

In the early 20th century, the Koryak people of northern Kamchatka remained the least known of all the tribes of Siberia. During the 18th and 19th centuries Georg Steller, Stephan Krasheninnikoff and C. Ditmar had done a considerable amount of research, but by the beginning of the 20th century no one had made a complete study of these people.

In the winter of 1900–1901, Waldemar Jochelson with his wife, Dina Jochelson Brodskaya, as part of the Jesup North Pacific Expedition, left Vladivostok for Kushka, at the mouth of the Gishka River right at the northern tip of the Sea of Okhotsk where the Kamchatka Peninsula joins the mainland of Eastern Russia. From here, they hoped to either cross the tundra or go by boat to Penzhina Bay, where the Maritime Koryak lived. However, they had no suitable boats for such a dangerous journey, so a small party with just 20 horses set out overland.

The trip across the boggy tundra was a nightmare for both horse and rider. The horses got stuck in the bottomless ground and had to be hauled out, while the Jochelsons got lost for two days without food or shelter before being found. Eventually in early October they arrived in Kuel to begin their winter among the Maritime Koryak, where they found conditions very primitive indeed, the people living in underground dwellings.

After several months and in the middle of winter, the Jochelson party left the Maritime Koryak with 20 dog-sleds and started out for Kamenskoye to study the Reindeer Koryak of the interior. Conditions here were hardly any better, and so cold in the native huts that they put up a tent with a small stove and slept at night in bags made of wolfskin.

In May, the party returned to Kushka, where they wrote up and catalogued their findings, considered to be the most significant collection from the peoples of the Russian Far East outside of Russia. It includes tools, weapons, boats, sleds, items of daily use and particularly shaman paraphernalia. Over 11,000 objects from the expedition are available online, and the ethnographies authored by the members of

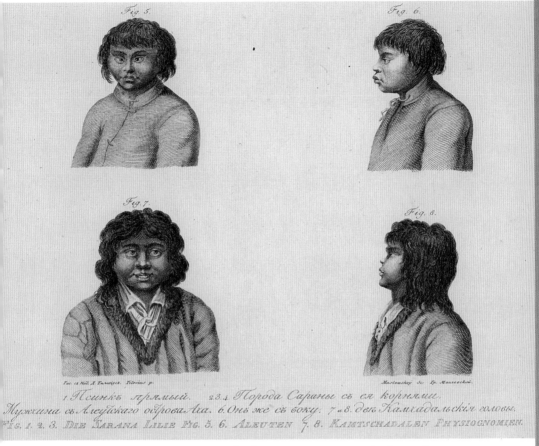

Early renditions of Aleutian islanders (top) and natives of Kamchatka (bottom).

the expedition team are a well-known scholarly resource. Jochelson's book, *The Koryak* (The Jesup North Pacific Expedition, Memoir of the American Museum of Natural History. Vol. V1. Leiden, New York, 1908) contains the results of his experiences.

ONE DOOR CLOSES, ANOTHER DOOR OPENS

North, across the Kamchatka River to Kozyrevsk. Plosky Tolbachik. The burnt forest.
Kamchatka: To go or not to go... that is the question

Kozyrevsk. At Masha's. 25 August

We have done this journey before, and after the first hour or so it is excruciatingly boring.
The road from Petropavlovsk north to Kozyrevsk is paved until Malki and the scenery is
beautiful. After that it becomes a dirt road lined to the edges with birch forest so you can
see nothing.

We were up early to get the bus and found great seats at the front. They have an
interesting system here consisting of a driver and a relief driver. The buses have a wide
shelf over the dashboard beside the driver on which his relief curls up and has a good
sleep. It's a great idea and ascertains that the passengers know they always have a fresh
driver at the wheel. The drivers also load the bus with everybody's luggage, which is
generally pretty bulky. It is crammed in at the back of the bus behind the last row of seats,
piled up in a very hazardous looking way, looking like it could all come tumbling down on
the passengers at any moment.

We stopped for a snack at a wayside stall about an hour into our journey, then at
lunchtime we stopped at Milkovo for a bite to eat in the bus station café. I wondered if
Alexei and Nina were still doing their B&B and if Misha was still around.

The highlight of the trip was the crossing of the Kamchatka River. This is without a
doubt the peninsula's predominant river. Its 720-kilometre length is not particularly
noteworthy by Russian standards, but in a country where most of the other rivers – and
there are plenty of them – are less than 100 kilometres long, it is a giant. Rising near the
village of Puchino, the river drainage basin is the geographical heart of the peninsula, the
headwaters originate in both the eastern and central mountain ranges which, with the
snowmelt of 420 tributaries, combine to eventually produce a river more than a kilometre
wide where it enters the Pacific Ocean. The millions of salmon that spawn in the

The "Eruption of the Century".

Kamchatka River once supported the native Itelmen that lived alongside it. Russians also found the river valley a good place to live; most early expeditions travelled by river, and two fortifications were built near it, one close to Milkovo and the other near Klyuchi. Although the water is terribly cold, it is said that during Soviet times, locals from Kozyrevsk, with the help of a little "Russian Courage" used to swim across it! It might, in fact, be a surer way to cross than looking for a bridge. There is only one along the river's entire length, and it is located south of Milkovo. Further downriver there are four ferry crossings, this one being the first.

Every time I use a ferry it reminds me of a little poem my younger sister learned at school. We used to adopt a very posh English accent for the girl and a broad Belfast accent for the ferryman, and fall about in kinks of laughter:

> "Ferry me across the water, do boatman do."
> "If you've a penny in your purse I'll ferry you."
> "I have a penny in my purse and my eyes are blue,
> So ferry me across the water, do boatman do."
> "Step into my ferry boat, be they black or blue,
> And for that penny in your purse I'll ferry you."

I didn't have to produce a penny here as the ferry is free, being government-run. A timetable is placed on a stand at the edge of the river, stating departure times that are strictly adhered to. It is just a stony, muddy landing site and as it had been raining slightly it was very mucky. I stood there and looked across the rushing river and beyond to where we could see the Kluchevskoye group of volcanoes beautifully silhouetted against the bright evening sky. I could feel my despondency evaporate and a new feeling of excitement and expectation take its place. I still felt defeated at not having been able to go to Palana, but, as they say, one door shuts and another door opens and I was keen to start this new volcanic experience.

Everyone stood around waiting and watching as the vehicles were loaded and the rain started again. There were six small buses, a lorry and a minibus for the crossing, and we all walked onto the ferry after the vehicles had been loaded. The ferry departed on the dot. It is just a very old floating platform with no engine, but an equally ancient tug of indeterminate years is lashed to the side of the platform with heavy, frayed cables; rusty and leaking oil, this propels the ferry across the wide and swiftly flowing river.

Back on the bus, everyone now soaking, and half an hour later we were in Kozyrevsk

in a grand little wooden "tent". An enterprising local lady has opened her home as a B&B and in the garden they have built five or six little wooden houses like tents with no sides. Each one has two single beds, a table and electric light. It is new and clean and just the job for us. There is a washbasin in an open area used for dining, however the "long-drop" is about 20 metres from the tents across the vegetable patch. We enjoyed a very good, very hot sauna and as there seemed to be quite a lot of mosquitoes here we sprayed ourselves liberally and lit a mossie coil to have at our feet while we enjoyed our pre-prandial drink. Sitting outside our "tent" in the last of the sun with our books, I returned to Theroux's *Dark Star Safari*. Hassan is a changed man, pleasant and helpful; he admitted he is much happier here than in Pauzetka – he is now on familiar ground – which is interesting. He is very friendly with Masha who owns the B&B, and we were fed in the house whereas mostly it is self-catering for others. Our supper was grand and we retired happily to bed, looking forward to the next day's adventure.

AT MASHA'S. MORNING. 26 AUGUST

After breakfast this morning, before we left, I was chatting with some Swedes who had arrived here last night in such good form we almost threatened to join their party. They, of course, all spoke good English and we exchanged tales of the amazing experiences we had had. They asked us where we came from and when we said Ireland they told us they had an Irishman with them. We were amazed and presumed he would be from the south of Ireland, but when he eventually appeared it transpired he was from Derry, right up in the north of Ireland. We fell on each other like long-lost friends, it seemed so amazing to

meet someone from near home so very far from home.

I asked him how he came to be with the party of Swedes. It appeared that Joe, who is an avid fly fisherman and has fished all round the world, had seen an article in a fishing magazine by a man who was hoping to get a party together to fish some of the rivers in Kamchatka. Joe lost no time in adding his name to the list and in due course it was arranged for August 2006. They flew to Petropavlovsk, came north, like us, by bus/truck and were finally helicoptered in to a river which had apparently never been fished before. The fish were finished on this first river so they moved on, again by chopper, to a different one. Here, not only did they find an abundance of fish, but also of bears which, naturally enough, were of great interest and delight, but also of terror. His account was hilarious of the one girl among the party, having been told all the rules about not running away when confronted by a bear, immediately taking to her heels and running full tilt back to the camp.

PLOSKY TOLBACHIK. AFTERNOON CAMP. 26 AUGUST

"Great God, this is an awful place." Captain Scott's words when he arrived at the South Pole struck me as we alighted from the truck at the camp on Plosky Tolbachik. His "awful place" was a white desert of snow – ours was a black one of ash. I stood and looked around me, peering through the bitterly cold, swirling mist, seeing, as the visibility came and went, a featureless landscape of black ash and cinders.

Ostry (sharp) and Plosky (flat) Tolbachik form, together, the Tolbachik massif that is aligned parallel to the east-west border fault in the northern part of the Tolbachik tectonic depression. The Tolbachik "Eruption of the Century" was called the Big Cleft eruption, and is considered one of the largest basalt eruptions ever known. It lasted for one and a half years (July 1975–December 1976) and is included in the list of six of the most powerful cleft eruptions ever. And now, here we are, standing, more or less, in the middle of it. Crikey.

We arrived here in the early afternoon by another vakhtovka, again an enormous 6WD behemoth with wheels over a metre high which can cross rivers up to 1.5 metres deep. It is equipped for 18 to 20 people and we had it to ourselves, but we needed it for, yet again, crossing rivers and driving through the very difficult terrain. The journey started easily enough along a forest road that quite soon brought us to a river crossing. We got out of the truck in order to see the black volcanic debris over which we were driving and through which the fast, shallow river was pouring, turning the water coal-black. We could see where other vehicles had driven, and footprints in the soft ash showed the marks of man, bear and moose. The track from here on gradually worsened as we ascended, with branches whipping the sides of the truck. We stopped a couple of times to stretch our legs and our driver, Dima showed us loads of berries to pick and eat; as well as bilberries there were black, elongated berries of the honeysuckle plant. Ours at home are red and I've never tried eating them – maybe I will now as these ones were delicious.

Eventually the vegetation diminished and dwindled out altogether and the intermittent patches of mist, which had started in the woods, became almost total, obscuring our view. We drove up and up through absolute whiteout, Dima finding the way by experience because we could see no distinguishing features at all until, after a four-hour drive we arrived here.

We saw that there were four little wooden huts, some of which are used as a seismic station and were to be our home for the next one or two nights. We quickly went into the first hut which was the dining room, and where three or four girls were preparing lunch for a group of German geology students. They offered to let us join them in return for Hassan and Dima bringing water from a spring some distance away.

We hoped against hope that we wouldn't have to spend the night in a tent, as all the bunkhouses were full. However, a very kind interpreter and her boyfriend offered to sleep in with some of the students and let us have their two bunks for the night. And wouldn't you know, here we are again in the upper floor of the hut. To get here you have to "walk the plank" up from the ground, over the roof below and in through our door. The room is rough wood with two rough wooden bunks to sleep on – thank goodness I bring my wee foam mattress everywhere. There is a metal chimney running from a fire below, up through our room and out the roof, so apparently it gets lovely and warm at night when the fire is

lit. We hurriedly put on the clothes that we'd brought for just this sort of weather, and felt the immediate warmth and comfort of our thermals and fleeces. We are at about 2,000 metres here, so no wonder it's cold.

After an excellent late lunch we put on even more clothes and went out for a walk and to find the loo. When we arrived we couldn't see it for the mist, but during lunch the fog and clouds had lifted and the sun had come out. The loo is at least 100 metres away, a tiny little wooden hut, sticking out like a sore thumb – not very private, and at that distance I hope I won't need to pay a visit during the night.

We now had a breathtaking view of the older, dormant Ostry Tolbachik, looking very close and dramatic with its 3,682-metre conical peak towering high over us. We climbed a nearby hill of ash, from where we had the most fabulous view of this extraordinary lunar landscape where Soviet lunar vehicles had been tested some years previously.

All afternoon we wandered around this extraordinary place, climbing shallow ridges and sliding down the other side, laughing as we did so. Great ridges of ice poked up now and again from under the ash, never having melted all summer, and it would be winter again soon. Here and there tiny young plants were struggling to maintain a roothold; how they do is amazing as there would seem to be a total lack of nutrition, and yet tiny yellow poppies, some grasses and mosses were valiantly hanging on to life, their sparse splashes of colour making a surprising and welcome change to the black surroundings. This is after 30 years; I wonder how long it would take for vegetation to really re-establish itself – but they say Tolbachik erupts every 30 years or so.

The volcanic events of 1975 began in the middle of a wood some 18 kilometres from here. The eruption was accurately forecast by P.I. Tokarov of the Institute of Volcanology of the Far Eastern Scientific Centre of the AN SSSR. It is hard to imagine the cataclysmic events that followed the first spate of earthquakes, which signalled the eruptions to come. Ash rose 1,500 metres above Tolbachik, at night reflecting red from the molten core below. Within days, the magma, reacting to the high pressure below, was forced to the surface with the gases in the magma expanding and exploding, firing molten rocks, steam and gas up to the incredible height of 11 kilometres.

From time to time new fissures opened up with more and more violent eruptions, often more violent at night, changing day into night and night into a firework display like no other, often accompanied by lightning and thunder. Lava flows, the front of which stretched several kilometres wide and moved at 300 metres an hour, incinerated trees

The immense power of Plosky Tolbachik's eruption in 1975-76 changed the face of the surrounding landscape.

and plants and destroyed a reservoir in moments. Ash and cinders rained down, levelling hills and hollows. By December 1976 a crater measuring 350–400 metres across and 150–200 metres deep had been formed, and lava flows and hundreds of thousands of tons of ash, cinders and rocks had completely changed the geography of the entire area.

A great party ensued in the evening with all the students back from field trips doing tests, taking samples and measurements and learning all about the volcano. Elise and I were the oldest by a very long way – not including Hassan. It didn't actually make me feel old, just somewhat out of place. But nobody seemed to take the slightest notice of our advanced years and we had lots of chat with anyone who could speak English. The meal was great and everyone was drinking vodka or beer. As the sun slipped towards the western horizon Elise went out and photographed Ostry in the setting sun.

A young guy from Lost World Tours came bouncing up to me and in very good English said, "I hear you are a writer and you are writing a book about Kamchatka – what exactly is it about?" I felt very silly and mumbled something about it being a very personal journal of my thoughts and experiences in Kamchatka. He quite quickly lost interest in me as there was quite a considerable amount of talent about. I had a long and very interesting chat with a German girl, Lisa Strecher, who is an ethnologist and also has a degree in biology and Slavonic Studies. She is here as interpreter for the German students as she speaks fluent Russian – and although she denied it, her English is also first rate.

Lisa was a mine of information. She had been to Palana several times and said you simply need plenty of time and patience. I asked her if she would write a book about her experiences and she said she didn't know, that the more she learns the more she realizes how little she knows. She has been here several times for three months at a time – guess how little I know in comparison. I then met one of the premier mountaineers in Kamchatka, a weathered, lean man of few words, but Lisa translated between us so I discovered he had climbed most of the mountains and volcanoes in Kamchatka, both dormant and active.

Later a young 17-year-old who is working here appeared, sat beside me and told me her life story, all about her father, who has had three wives (she is the daughter of the middle wife) but doesn't bother with them even though he is a politician and quite wealthy. She has one older and three younger half-sisters and would love to know them; the older one is keen to meet up, but I wasn't sure where she lived, it could have been the other side of Russia, which would not make it too easy. She is a bright student and hopes to do an exchange visit with an American student, but she needs money and better English in order to qualify. She seemed a sad little thing and I felt terribly sorry for her, but everyone is hard up here. She, at least, has youth on her side, I am more sorry for her mother, I wonder how she copes and how she will feel when her one daughter goes off to the States.

Before going to bed we made our way by torchlight to the "long-drop". The silence and blackness around us was absolute, but above us, another reminder of how insignificant we all are, a billion stars sparkled with the brilliance only seen in air as unpolluted and frosty as this night. Up in our loft, it was toasting, the chimney red hot. Beyond our room there were six youngsters all in bed with the door open between us so that they could get some of the warmth from our chimney. We spent no time undressing and snuggled into our sleeping bags for the night.

AT MASHA'S. 27 AUGUST

This has been a hard night's day! Our stay in the hut was toasting warm but pretty sleepless all the same. I woke early, before dawn, and of course what was the first thing that came into my mind? I told myself to go back to sleep – that it was pure imagination, and that I did not need to go to the "long drop" – but to no avail. I didn't go back to sleep

and my back was sore – well, that was hardly surprising. Oh God, I am getting too old for this sort of thing! I lay there, listening enviously to the deep breathing of others having a sound night's sleep, until a reasonable hour for getting up and venturing out.

It was a gorgeous morning, and we set off in our huge truck to explore some lava caves and the burnt forest. As we left the little huts and drove off into the black wilderness, to our surprise a big hare jumped up almost from under our wheels and bounded off to some boulders. It was a very light colour, not the rich brown of the Irish hare, and had huge hairy feet. What an extraordinary thing to see in these desert-like conditions. I can't think there would be much sustenance for a hare here.

We arrived at the first of the lava caves, and proceeded to climb up and over rocks and hardened lava flows until we arrived at the mouth of the cave. In we went, torches in hand, being careful not to bang our heads on the rough entrance. This was just a short tunnel but the next cave was much more exciting. We had to climb up and down into a small crater and found on the opposite wall the small entrance to a much larger cave full of stalagmites and stalactites. We continued on as far as we could go until the roof became too low for us to continue.

Lava caves – or tubes – are formed when hot, fluid lava flows down the sides of the volcano. The upper layer begins to cool but the lava beneath continues to flow in tubular conduits beneath the surface. Due to the insulating effects of the hardened lava above, the molten lava can continue to travel some distance. In Hawaii, lava tubes have

continued for 80 or more kilometres from their source. Tubes may also form when lava follows gulleys on the surface, which then roof over as lava accumulates along the top edges. The hot, molten lava can behave very much like limestone, slowly dripping and hardening to produce stalagmites and stalactites inside the caves.

We climbed back out of the little crater, noticing a young rowan tree clinging to its edge – an unexpected splash of green foliage and bright orange berries. Again we wondered how and indeed, why, it has managed to germinate and flourish in this inhospitable place.

As we journeyed on, very gradually more and more small islands of vegetation appeared, and some of the curvaceous hills were covered in a red-coloured ash. Then we entered the burnt forest. My word, what a sight. Thousands of larch trees, buried about halfway up in deep ash. Obviously, during the eruption the hot ash burned the tops of the trees while building up a 3–5 metre layer of ash and cinders underneath. The effect of the skeletal trees was to portray a spectral landscape almost as far as the eye could see, with beyond, in the distance, more mountains and volcanoes. We walked for quite a while in this ruined forest taking photographs and just standing, awestruck at the massive quantity of ash that had fallen and the ensuing devastation of such an enormous area. Yet again, Kamchatka amazes us.

Our picnic lunch was, rather surprisingly, at a table with benches in the middle of nowhere. Well, not exactly nowhere, it was at the base of a volcanic cone which Elise and

Hassan climbed after lunch and where they saw small fumaroles where they could burn a piece of wood, and unusual coloured rocks. I was tired and my back was a bit stiff, so I decided to go and examine some of the small plants which were beginning to colonise the area. There was quite a lot of the creeping elfin cedar, again some of the tiny yellow poppies, some grasses and mosses.

Our journey back to Kozyrevsk was uneventful except for the sighting of a bear just after crossing the river and entering back into the forest. These bears are much smaller than the Kurilskoye bears. They don't have anything like the quantity of protein available from the massive amount of fish there, and must survive to a great extent on vegetation. Still, it was really good to see another bear.

With adequate time before supper back at Masha's, we went to have a look at Kozyrevsk, a village with a population of just 2,000 souls. The village, which is 500 kilometres from Petropavlovsk, is about 100 years old; all the houses are timber and most of the population who are in work are involved in the timber business. They also live from the countryside with hunting, fishing and foraging making important contributions to the larder. As we turned to go back we encountered some ponies loose in the street. We were about to go up to them when a youngster, who was in fact with them, came up to us and said "Hallo". We replied likewise and he invited us into his house nearby, leaving the ponies to wander off. He spoke a little English but neither of his parents did. It was all a bit embarrassing, but it is just so pleasant to be invited into local homes. We were brought tea and made to sit down as we struggled with very broken English. Eventually we looked at our watches and made our excuses.

During supper our hostess, Masha, told us that she works in a hospice or home for the old and unwell, but is making much more money in the summer season from her B&B. She also told us that there is primary and secondary education available for the children in the village.

PARATUNKA. BLUE LAGOON HOTEL. 28 AUGUST

After crossing the Kamchatka River on the way back south, and in pouring rain, we settled down for the nine-hour journey back to Petropavlovsk. This time we were not in a bona-fide bus, but instead another vakhtovka with 25 people and no opening windows. Within half an hour of leaving the river, what with a combination of hot breath and steaming clothes, the windows were streaming moisture and the air was hot and stale. I couldn't bear this for nine hours and asked Hassan if he would ask the driver to open one of the

roof vents. No one seemed to notice or mind the awful fug, and certainly no one else asked for air. Anyway, the driver was quite amenable to my request and what a difference it made. I'm sure we must have looked like a little train from the outside, with steam billowing out from the roof.

We arrived in Petropavlovsk and uncurled our limbs the better for jumping down from the height of the truck. Hassan had been trying to contact Mikhail Mashkovtsev, the governor of Kamchatka who had said he would "receive" me, but we only had the next day and unfortunately he was too busy, so that was that. He also said he couldn't contact our representative who had our onward tickets for Vladivostok, saying the number we had given him was no longer in use. He seemed really put out by this and I suggested trying the number again just in case there had been a mistake. Of course the number did exist and it was Hassan who had made the mistake, and we were able to make contact OK and collect the tickets.

PARATUNKA. BLUE LAGOON HOTEL. 29 AUGUST

We spent our final day in Petropavlovsk with a new guide who we met in the Avacha Bay Hotel. He was born in the Ukraine, is called Oleg and is about 50, fair, blue-eyed, tall and painfully thin, in fact so thin he looks ill. However, he was a delightful man, quiet spoken and anxious to take us everywhere we wanted. We collected two CDs of photos from Sergei, which was wonderful. Then we went to visit the museums again and try to obtain photographs of old maps of Kamchatka. We also went to see an art exhibition of indigenous people by a local artist, which looked very interesting except we weren't allowed to stay as the exhibition doesn't open for another four days. So we went to the Koryak Museum, which opens every day except Tuesday… and of course this is Tuesday! Is someone trying to tell me something?

However, we met up with Zhenya and Olga and had lunch with them, Zhenya being home on leave from Pauzetka. Now that was good timing. They had photos of their wedding and were full of chat, which was lovely. We were comparing the cost of living here to UK. Milk is about the same price – it is all imported – but bread is half the price. They have been fortunate enough to scrape together the money to be able to buy their own apartment overlooking Avacha Bay, and it has increased threefold in value since they bought it four years ago. They are now saving up to buy a car. A bit of a difference to home where newlyweds expect to have everything from scratch.

To finish our day we went for a walk up Nikolskaya Hill to have a last look across Avacha Bay and towards Viljuchinskaya volcano. Some fishing boats lay quietly at anchor on a blue sea under a blue sky. It was quite, quite beautiful.

Our final meal was again at the Korea House. Elise and Hassan's meals were alright, but for once I had chosen well and was brought an enormous plateful, piled high with fried crumbed prawns. It was simply delicious.

Well, here we are, the two of us, coming to the end of another experience and learning curve in Kamchatka. Of course many others have travelled further and seen more but this journal is a reflection of *my* reactions to, and thoughts about, this extraordinary land. Do I hear you say "Why on Earth would anyone go there, it's all so difficult?" Certainly, there are no really luxurious hotels or cosy pubs, and although there is a plethora of fish the best we tasted was over a campfire. The roads are poor and the weather "changeable", so much so that very, very often flights around the country are delayed or even abandoned. No, this country is certainly not for the impatient or the faint-hearted.

But, it does have some of the most stunning and dramatic scenery in the world and an inordinate amount of wildlife. To sit on a berry-covered hill and watch reindeer come floating down the valley against a backdrop of volcanoes; to go fly-fishing on the Kamchatka River or sit in a boat on Lake Kurilskoye and discover a brown bear only metres away; to climb a volcano and peer down into its fiery depths are all great privileges. But perhaps the greatest privilege of all has been the kindness of strangers – being invited into someone's home to join their family for dinner and most particularly, meeting up with three young Russians who have given unstintingly of their time in helping me with this book and have not asked for a penny in payment. So should you go to Kamchatka? Maybe it should become a closed country again and remain a wild and wonderful place reserved for the indigenous people who have always lived there with their reindeer herds. A place in which the brown bears and bighorn sheep can roam without fear of being shot. But then why should it become again, at my behest, a wilderness, when everybody who lives there is entitled to a bite of the financial cherry, and tourism, at present being the ripening cherry, will bring its own huge pressures on the people and their environment.

So yes, go to Kamchatka, now, while you still can – why on Earth not?

KAMCHATKA:
A SUSTAINABLE FUTURE?

by Josh Newell

It was the summer of 1996 and I had arranged for staff from the Moscow bureau of NBC News and a Russian television station to film a documentary of Kamchatka. How could I pass up such a trip? So along with my father, my brother, a professor from the University of Montana, and a researcher studying NASA's aerial photography, we spent two unforgettable weeks visiting some of Kamchatka's most beautiful and remote wilderness. That was my first taste of Kamchatka and to this day, after 15 years of travel throughout the world's largest country, it remains at the very top of my list as the premier eco-tourist destination in the Russian Federation.

Sadly, irrational resource development threatens this magnificent peninsula. Apart from fishermen from local communities, who poach to augment meagre incomes, each salmon spawning season organized poaching teams set up huge nets across river mouths and in a matter of weeks can deplete an entire year's salmon run. Helicopters also allow well-financed fishing brigades of foreign workers to reach remote headwaters. The product has to be transported by helicopter so it is only cost effective to harvest the salmon roe. Huge piles of perfectly good salmon are left to rot along the riverbanks.

Salmon roe is one of Kamchatka's most valuable resources.

Kamchatka is recognized as a border zone by the federal government, so helicopters must receive state authorization for each flight. The ability to control the Kamchatka poaching epidemic does therefore exist. However, in most cases, bribes ensure that these flights take off and land without incident. The federal government enforces regulations sporadically, perhaps when someone does not get paid properly. In autumn of 2006, authorities in Moscow boarded two commercial airplanes at a Moscow airport and seized two shipments (20 tons and 10 tons) of this prized red Kamchatka roe. Yet these seizures are just the tip of the iceberg, with illegal caviar exports from Kamchatka estimated in the hundreds of millions of dollars. Fisheries specialist Sergei Vakhrin estimates that poachers in Kamchatka today catch as much fish as licensed fisherman catch legally.

Enterprising smugglers enlist villagers to do their dirty work. With the fall of the Soviet Union, government support for the thousands of towns and villages that dot the northern landscape dried up. Energy and transport costs skyrocketed and industries folded, leaving many without work and even fuel to heat their homes. A plane ticket from Petropavlovsk to Tilichiki in Koryakia reportedly costs more than a flight from Petropavlovsk to Moscow, even though Tilichiki is ten times closer than Moscow. Villagers have resorted to poaching to survive. Journalist Ekaterina Glikman, who spent time with the Koryak people in the northern part of the peninsula, found that "virtually the entire population of Koryakia, except for the very old and nursing babes, spends every summer on the river, in order to harvest roe illegally and sell it to the first carpet-bagging middleman that comes through town."

The plundering has not been limited to salmon. The great reindeer herds that once roamed Koryakia have been essentially eradicated. Brown bears are poached for gall bladders, which can be sold for a high price in Asian markets. Kamchatka king crab, which many consider the tastiest crab on the planet and which is potentially the peninsula's most lucrative natural resource, has been so thoroughly fleeced that prominent regional government leaders are calling upon the Kremlin to declare a moratorium on harvesting, to allow the species to replenish itself.

In an ideal world, mining, oil and gas development could co-exist with fishing, and in some places perhaps they do. But in Russia there is a vast gulf between what is written on paper and what actually happens in practice. Environmentalists working to protect Kamchatka are experienced in the ways of industrial development in Russia. Despite assurances to the contrary, they fear the past will once again repeat itself. Roads built to service mines and oil pipelines will be built across spawning rivers, opening up pristine wilderness to poaching, while oil and cyanide from mining will find its way into river systems.

The Kamchatka Peninsula is blessed, or cursed depending how you look at it, with a great wealth of mineral resources. In Koryakia, near the town of Korf, lies Russia's second-largest deposit of platinum, which now fetches two times the price of gold per ounce on the world's stock exchanges. Amidst the rubble and dilapidated buildings that make up present-day Korf stand the new, well-maintained offices of Koryakgeoldobycha (KGD), which mines platinum. One would think that with all this mineral wealth the region would be fairly well off, but it is one of the poorest in all of Russia. Reportedly, Koryakia has the highest tuberculosis infection rate per 1,000 people in the entire world. Like so many places in Russia, the wealth has not trickled down to local communities.

Due to the peninsula's remoteness and the presence of hundreds of rich, readily accessible deposits on the mainland, gold mining is just beginning in Kamchatka. A mining operation recently began in the central region around the headwaters of the Icha and Kirganik Rivers. Sadly, toxic spills have already occurred during the development phase of the Aginskoye gold mine, resulting in fish kills in local spawning rivers. Foreign corporations have long seen Kamchatka as an untapped treasure chest, and there are ambitious projects under way. UK-based gold producer Trans-Siberian Gold managed to secure rights to some of the peninsula's largest deposits: Asacha and Rodnikova. Gold production at Asacha, some 150 kilometres to the south of Petropavlovsk, is expected to be 30,000 ounces in 2008, with annual production rising to 100,000 ounces for the subsequent five years, by which time the resource will be essentially exhausted.

Meanwhile, exploration for oil and gas continues off the western Kamchatka shelf, home to the region's richest crab beds and vital for salmon fisheries. Covering over 62,000 square kilometres, the Rosneft and Korean National Oil Company project is the largest exploratory licence area in Russia, with drilling planned for 2007. Onshore, Canadian firm CEP International and its joint-venture partner the Korean National Oil Company are slated to begin drilling for oil in June 2007.

Local and international environmental groups have long cautioned against opening up the region to gold mining and oil and gas extraction. They point out that public involvement has been inadequate. They cite history when claiming that gold mining will benefit a select few and question whether six or seven years of tax revenue from the Aginskoe gold mine warrants threatening the long-term benefits gained from the salmon industry. A coalition of environmentalists is forming to oppose oil and gas development in sensitive wildlife habitat. One primary concern is that onshore drilling will damage two watersheds proposed to be protected as salmon conservation refuges, the Utkholok and Sopochnaya. In addition to being crucial for healthy salmon runs, these areas are prime habitat for the globally endangered Steller's sea eagle. Russian indigenous organizations are concerned that drilling will harm local indigenous peoples' traditional use areas, especially needed for hunting and fishing.

Long a watchdog of foreign multinationals operating in the energy and mining sectors on Kamchatka, San Francisco-based NGO Pacific Environment is branching out by devoting more staff time and financial resources to developing local communities' capacity to respond to immediate threats in the region. They are providing financial and technical assistance to local environmental NGOs such as the League of Kamchatka Independent Experts, working to create protected territories in key habitat areas and watchdog development projects. They also support a network of indigenous organizations, including the Union of Kamchadals, which has mobilized over 200 volunteers in the village of Tigil to set up anti-poaching posts, or "hot spots", along the rivers.

Meanwhile, more scientifically minded organizations such as the Portland, Oregon-based Wild Salmon Center are working to create nature reserves for salmon; the Center and has set up biological stations to monitor the health of salmon and other species. It has also been instrumental in helping the United Nations Development Programme (UNDP) establish a multi-year effort to sustain wild salmon biodiversity on Kamchatka. Let's hope that the precious funds from this UNDP project are used more wisely than the previous project, "Demonstrating Sustainable Biodiversity Conservation in Four Protected Areas of Russia's Kamchatka Oblast", which local environmental organizations complained spent too much on international consultants, data-gathering and report writing, and not enough on actual conservation activities.

Kamchatka is one of those places where the interconnectedness between poverty and biodiversity conservation is stark and easily visible to those who witness it. Yet it is not simply a question of sacrificing this or that watershed to gold mining, or trading off long-term economic benefits from renewable fisheries resources to oil and gas development in the interest of desperately needed jobs and tax revenue, for that is a false trade-off, and simply puts off the inevitable. The underlying causes of why the crushing poverty exists need to be addressed and that, first and foremost, hinges on transforming a corrupt and terribly wasteful salmon industry. As Sibyl Diver of Pacific Environment points out, "There are very real opportunities to increase economic benefits to local people through the existing fisheries industry." There are only a few companies in Kamchatka that process their fish and sell added-value products. In addition, current laws and regulations make it extremely difficult for local residents to obtain fishing rights, says Diver. "If we can change this, we can provide jobs, bring revenue to local communities, and greatly increase the incentive for decisions makers to protect Kamchatka's valuable fisheries, instead of opening the wilderness up to gold mining and oil and gas development."

To transform an industry reliant on raw product (e.g. roe) to one that produces processed products for local and international markets, NGOs point to the successes of the Copper River Salmon industry in Alaska, whose first spring salmon fillets often sell for over US$20 per pound. Pacific Environment has brought Kamchatka community-based fishermen and indigenous leaders to the US to gain an understanding of local fisheries management tools, added-value processing, and niche and direct marketing, as these may prove to be an effective approach to marketing sustainably harvested wild Kamchatka salmon to wealthy Russians in Moscow and St Petersburg, as well as to environmentally sensitive international markets. After taking part in such a trip to the US, Kamchatka fisherman and processor Petr Petrik marvelled: "We don't know how you catch so little fish and live so well."

Clearly, of course, a vast gulf separates the conditions under which the Russian industry works from that of the American model. Widespread poaching, high taxes and low prices for fish, lack of transportation infrastructure and lack of capital are just a few examples of this gulf. International NGOs and development agencies can assist, but addressing these shortcomings ultimately rest in the hands of the regional and federal governments. It requires long-term vision and commitment; something the Russian government has shown precious little of in other parts of the country.

Yet there are signs of hope. In fall 2006, the Kamchatka regional government announced plans to designate five enormous tracts of wilderness as salmon-protected areas, after lobbying from the Wild Salmon Center. This proposal would encompass nine entire rivers and more than six million acres (2.4 million hectares) – an area larger than Yellowstone National Park. The purpose of these reserves would be to protect and produce wild salmon. Commercial and recreational fishing will be allowed, but other industrial activities prohibited. This initiative comes none too soon. Poaching has already depleted salmon runs of a number of the peninsula's rivers. Whether the government can reign in poaching, particularly in these salmon-protected areas, remains to be seen, but it is clearly a step in the right direction.

Addendum: Visitors to Kamchatka can also play their part. Adventure tourism has become a lucrative business on the peninsula. Just how these revenues are being distributed remains terribly unclear. Ask your tour operator for a breakdown on how the money will be allocated and if taxes will be paid. Whether the industry emerges as a positive force for sustainability depends, like all industries, in large part upon whether it is properly taxed and regulated, and if the revenues are equitably distributed. Finally, there a number of wonderful and deeply committed organizations on Kamchatka, such as the Union of Kamchadals (www.pacificenvironment.org) and the Kamchatka League of Independent Experts (http://klie.ru/Engl/eliga.htm), that could use your financial support.

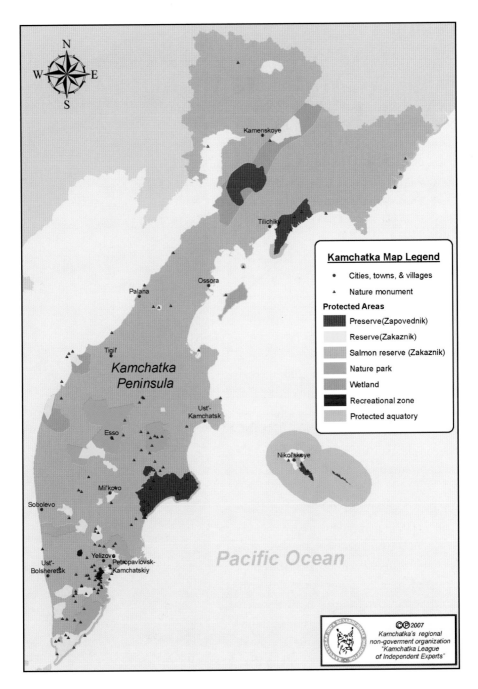

Kamchatka Highlights

People often ask me where they should go and what they should see when visiting Kamchatka. The peninsula is large and to get to some of the best places, you have to travel by helicopter, which is expensive, so you have to choose your spots carefully. Here are some of my favourite places:

Kronotsky Biosphere Reserve

The pride of the Kamchatka nature reserve system, Kronotsky Biosphere Reserve (1,308,854 hectares) has some of the peninsula's most famous tourist attractions. Located in the heart of the reserve, a visit to the famed Valley of the Geysers – which has 20 large geysers and over 200 thermal springs – is a must. Although a boardwalk trail is maintained to minimize impact, the fragile soil and flora can easily be damaged. Stay on the trail and go with a responsible tour operator if you decide to visit.

Another highlight is the massive Uzon Caldera (108 square kilometres), a painter's delight in late summer when the vegetation is a riot of colour. There are fascinating mud pots and numerous hot springs. Warm, underground watercourses create a variety of highly specialized biological communities. You should also make time to visit the Valley of Death at the foot of Kikhpinych

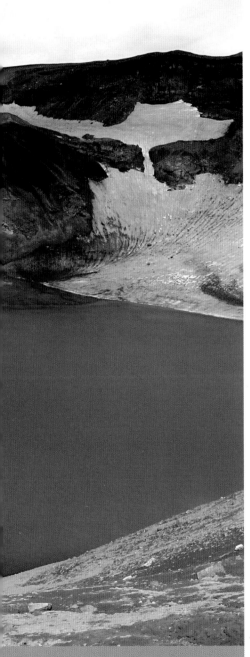

A close-up view of Gorely Volcano's acid lake.

Volcano, where a high concentration of volcanic gases (carbon monoxide, hydrogen sulphide and carbon dioxide), a lack of wind and an abundance of naturally occurring heavy metals in the upper layers of the soil cause birds and mammals to perish when they enter the vicinity. You are likely to see carcasses in the valley, but be sure not to get too close or you may be joining them. If possible have the helicopter pilot fly over Tolbaskoe Lake on your way north to Kronotsky, so you can photograph this gorgeous high-altitude lake, which is an unworldly glacial blue.

Lake Kurilskoye

The gem of the Southern Kamchatka Wildlife Refuge is Lake Kurilskoye. Surrounded by an active group of volcanoes, the lake's shores and the rivers that flow into it have massive salmon runs. Steller's sea eagles nest within the lake watershed, as do hundreds of whooper swans and ducks. In the late summer and fall, you are virtually guaranteed to see Kamchatka's massive brown bears– which can reach three metres in height and can weigh more than 700 kilograms – gorging themselves on salmon along the lakeshores and the rivers, or snacking on wild berries in the meadows just above the lake. There are no facilities to speak of, except for the small cabin where rangers live year-round to stave off poachers or do biological research. There is a nice post-and-beam lookout at a river mouth about a kilometre from the ranger station where you can often see brown bears at close range while they fish for salmon.

KAMCHATKA'S SALMON RIVERS

The entire peninsula acts as a giant incubator, where millions of salmon hatch and grow each year. Up to one-quarter of the world's Pacific salmon population spawns in Kamchatka's pristine rivers. Spending a couple of days rafting down or fishing one of these rivers during salmon season is time well spent. A number of rivers are accessible by vehicle from Petropavlovsk including the Bistraya, which serves as the headwaters for a number of important spawning rivers on the western side of the peninsula, including the Tikhaya, Icha, Tigil and Sopochnaya. In 1995, the Kamchatka government created Bystrinsky Nature Park to protect these rivers and the surrounding wilderness. Two indigenous settlements, Esso and Anavgai, can be found inside the park and can be accessed via road from Petropavlovsk.

AVACHA BAY

If you can get your hands on a boat, then be sure to motor around Avacha Bay, on the shores of which Petropavlovsk sits. Keep your eyes out for rusting nuclear submarines that are still stationed in the

bay. If you motor on outside of the bay, head north or south along the coast and you are likely to spot migrating whales and killer whales; since more than 50 percent of the world's Steller's sea eagles (*Haliaeetus pelagicus*) nest on the peninsula, you are also likely to see some of these great creatures circling overhead.

MUTNOVSKY VOLCANO

Avachinsky Volcano (2,751m) is closer to Petropavlovsk and well worth a day trip, but hiking up Mutnovsky Volcano, one of Kamchatka's most active volcanoes with its boiling mud pits and cauldrons, can also be done in a day, and is a must if you only have time to hike one volcano. Mutnovsky is part of Yuzhno-Kamchatsky Park (980,000 hectares), which protects snow sheep, brown bear, sea otter, and one of the largest populations of peregrine falcons on the peninsula. If you do visit, try to stop by the marvellous Khodutka hot springs, and for renewable energy enthusiasts, the recently completed Mutnovsky Geothermal Power Plant.

Josh Newell

The hike up Gorely provides stunning views across to Viljuchinsky Volcano.

FACTS FOR THE TRAVELLER

(Many thanks go to Tatiana Boyko, Associate Professor, Chair of Translating and Interpreting, Herzen State Pedagogical University of Russia (kambojko@mail.ru) for help in compiling this section.)

GETTING THERE The one really easy thing about travelling to Kamchatka is the lack of choice of transport for getting there. There are no decisions to be made as regards road or rail versus air transport because they don't exist. There is, of course, the possibility of arriving by sea – Kamchatka being almost an island – but there are no regular passenger ferries and stowing away is illegal and definitely not recommended. However, some north Pacific cruises call at Kamchatka which is a comfortable way of seeing a little of the country (see International Cruise Operators below).

There is quite a choice of flights to Petropavlovsk-Kamchatskiy (PKC). Most of the following flights operate during the summer only, although there is a limited but generally reliable schedule from Moscow to PKC in the winter. Of course flight schedules change from one year to the next, but as a guide, as of this book's printing, flights were as follows:

ANCHORAGE, ALASKA TO PKC (THE ONLY INTERNATIONAL FLIGHT) Magadan Airlines flies on Fridays. However, the airline has been known to cancel its flights; the result for one group who were scheduled to fly to Anchorage, was an enforced rerouting of Petropavlovsk–Vladivostok–Seoul–Los Angeles–Anchorage. This is a very long way round, so be sure to verify any flights with Magadan Airlines.

MOSCOW TO PKC Aeroflot flies every day except Tuesday. Transaero flies Tuesdays and Sundays. Domodedovo Airlines flies every day except Tuesdays and Fridays.

ST PETERSBURG TO PKC Pulkovo Aviation flies Mondays and Fridays.

VLADIVOSTOK TO PKC Siberia Airlines flies Wednesdays and Saturdays. Vladivostok Air flies on Tuesdays, Thursdays, Fridays and Sundays.

IRKUTSK TO PKC Dalavia flies on Wednesdays.

NOVOSIBIRSK TO PKC Pulkovo Aviation flies on Saturdays.

VISAS & RED TAPE This is the same as going anywhere in the Russian Federation. All foreign nationals are required to have entry visas to travel to the Russian Federation. Russian entry visas can be obtained at local Russian embassies or consulates. Proper authorisation (invitation) from the passport and visa department of the Ministry of Internal Affairs or specially authorized travel agents is required.

There are many online visa services if you don't want to "do it yourself". These provide all the information and costs of getting a visa, and are recommended, given that the process at the embassies is time-consuming, and should you fail to provide everything in exact order it will be rejected and you must start again from the beginning. Of course making use of a visa service costs rather more than going yourself to your nearest embassy, but the fee of upwards of £70 (approx US$140) for a single entry visa includes the cost of all necessary visa support documents and letters of invitation, registration of the visa in Moscow, Russian Ministry processing charges, local taxes, consular tariffs, delivery, collection and management of the visa application at the consulate. Passports should be valid at least six months longer than your planned exit date and with at least one blank visa page.

As of September 2006, Kamchatka again became a military zone. This will not involve any more red tape than above, but processing data will probably take longer and consequently early booking for visits is very much advised.

PERMITS FOR TREKKING These are certainly required. Before tourists come to Kamchatka, the firm accepting them has to submit an application form to the main office of the Federal Security Service (Federalnaya Sluzhba Bezopasnosti (FSB) – the former KGB). The application should include the following information: the name of the firm accepting the tourists; the period during which the tourists are staying in Kamchatka; a list of places they are going to visit and the exact date for each visit; a list of the tourists' names and their passport data; and the name of the local Russian guide and his passport data as well. This application is submitted before the arrival of the group and on the arrival day, the translator meeting the tourists must have it with him/her, as it may be demanded by the military officers at the airport.

In the case of tourists visiting special military zones (eg Ozernovskiy settlement, Mutnovskiy area, Zhirovaya bay area, etc) one more permit must be obtained. This is a special frontier guard service permit. Permission is obtained at the headquarters of the frontier troops in Petropavlosk by the local travel company before the tourists' arrival.

If your route includes trekking in the territory of the Nature Parks and two National Preserves, special permission is also required from their managing offices (e-mail: park@mail.kamchatka.ru). There are five Nature Parks – Bystrinsky, Nalychevo, Yuzhno-Kamchatsky, Kluchevskoy and Golubye Ozera (Blue Lakes); and two preserves – Kronotsky State Nature Biosphere Preserve and Komandorsky State Nature Biosphere Preserve. For the Nature Parks, tour companies get one permit for the whole year. For the Preserves, permission is given for each group of tourists separately, and is expensive – a group of 10-12 tourists and staff will be charged more than US$2,000 (payable in rubles) for 3-5 days.

In reality, the permit system is only really mandatory for the preserves (which are very serious about control of access) and Nalychevo Nature Park (as it is guarded by the WWF). The other nature parks can be visited without the special permission of the nature parks management, as they are not monitored at all. The last kind of permit required, having been introduced quite recently – is the permission to cut wood and make fires. This is given by the local Forest Departments – each region of Kamchatka has its own one – on payment of a fee, but it is also ignored and the law violated by many firms.

EXPORTING SOUVENIRS Regulations relating to the export of antiques and handicrafts are rather unclear and there doesn't seem to be any formal list of prohibited items. There is no antique trade, because the city is relatively young and the majority of the population arrived here in the second half of the 20th century – Kamchatka is not the place to discover ancient objects for sale. However, the situation with handicrafts is entirely different. Souvenir shops are cluttered with all kinds of interesting items. Local handicrafts are usually made of wood, reindeer fur, whale bone, seal bone, walrus tusks, mammoth bone, bear teeth and fangs. If you buy a handicraft or any other souvenir made from natural materials at a relatively high price (more than US$100), you will be given a special cheque with the price, origin of the object, address of the shop and its seal on it. This cheque should be shown at the customs desk on departure, but there seems to be no problem in buying as many items as you like.

ORGANIZED TOURS & INDEPENDENT TRAVEL Travel in Kamchatka is becoming ever more accessible and pleasurable. There are increasing numbers of tour operators and tourist facilities in Petropavlovsk and one is able to customize one's own trip according to requirements, ie, time, budget, degree of comfort and predictability. It is possible to book as little or as much of your trip as you choose, whether you need a constant guide/translator/driver or want to go it alone – although the latter is difficult as it is not possible to hire a car in Kamchatka, so it boils down to local buses or bicycles.

Kamchatka is there for everyone. While some folk are happy to visit the more accessible places on a daily basis, returning to their hotel in Petropavlovsk, Paratunka or Yelizovo, Kamchatka is a real paradise for the fisherman, trekker and mountaineer. You don't have to be super fit to scale the heights of the likes of Gorely and Mutnovsky volcanoes, and even the rivers near the capital have abundant quantities of salmon and trout. For the hardy, there is superb trekking and mountaineering in the wild and unexplored regions of the country, but for this it is necessary to have a guide.

On the whole, group travel for the reserves is difficult and expensive (unbookable in some places). Backpacking groups are fine depending on where you want to go, while individual travel is much more flexible but on the other hand always more expensive than for a group.

Each year sees more community-based facilities for travellers making independent travel more accessible. For instance there are now homestays in many of the villages.

PETROPAVLOVSK TOUR OPERATORS

Many websites now offer tours to Kamchatka; below is a selection:

GENERAL

Dunkan-Travel, www.dunkan-travel.ru
Travers-Tour, www.kamchatkatravel.netfirms.com
Vision of Kamchatka, www.kamchatka.org.ru
Lost World Tours, www.travelkamchatka.com
Discover the Wonders of Kamchatka, www.kamchatkapeninsula.com
Primorsky Aviation and Travel Agency, www.airagency.ru
Kamchatka Wild Nature, www.kamchatka-wildnature.ru
Pelican Tour Company, pelican@mail.kamchatka.ru
Alpika Plus, www.alpikaplus.ru
Vostok Tour, www.vostok-tour.ru
Kamchatintour, www.kamchatintour.ru
Bel-cam-tour, www.kamchatkatourbel.com;
Travel department "VT" LLC, www.vtechnika.ru/tours
Kamchatka Travel Group Limited, www.kamchatkatracks.com
Travel agency by the Hotel "Petropavlovsk": www.petropavlovsk-hotel.ru

WINTER SPORTS

Kamchatka Dream Tour, e-mail: kamchatkadreamtour@yandex.ru
Diligans, www.kamchatka-trip.com
Russian Heliboarding Club, www.heliboarding.ru

RAFTING, KAYAKING & SPORT FISHING

Club Globus, e-mail: clubglobus@yandex.ru

Kayak Kamchatka, www.kayak.kamchatka.ru
Iaynin Kutkh & Steelhead, www.iksteelhead.com
Stream Fishing, www.explorekamchatka.com

Climbing
THE CLIMB Adventure Centre, www.kamchatkaclimb.ru

Helicopter Flights
Krechet helicopter company, www.krechet.com
Helicopter company "Belkamtur", www.kamchatkatourbel.com

Diving Clubs
ALAID, www.alaid.ru
Deep club, www.deep-club.ru

International Tour & Cruising Operators
MIR Travel, www.mircorp.com
Geographic Expeditions, www.geoex.com
Expedition Cruising, www.expeditioncruising.co.uk
Wild Russia Adventures, www.wildrussia.spb.ru
Top Sport Travel, www.slope.ru
Go Russia, www.justgorussia.co.uk
Adventure and Cultural Travel Services, www.geographicbureau.com
Dersu Uzala, www.ecotours.ru/english
Sokol Tours, www.sokoltours.com
Travel Russia, www.travelrussia.net
Kamchatka's Vision, www.kamchatka.org.ru
Explore Worldwide, www.explore.co.uk
Steppes Travel, www.steppestravel.co.uk/kamchatka-page660.aspx
Wildlife Worldwide, www.wildlifeworldwide.com
Arcturus Expeditions, www.arcturusexpeditions.co.uk
Society Expeditions, www.pacificislandtravel.com/specials/cruises/societyexpeditions.htm
Zegrahm Expeditions, www.zeco.com
Cruise West, www.cruisewest.com

Transport There is no rail network in Kamchatka, and the road network is very poor. The roads are metalled in and around the capital, 32 kilometres south to Paratunka, about 72 kilometres to the north, and about 80 kilometres to the western coast, but that is about all. The road north through Elizovo and 12 kilometres from Malki, via Malki to Kluchi and in the western direction from Apacha settlement to Oktyabrskiy settlement on the shore of the Okhotsk Sea are dirt roads – dusty in dry weather and muddy in wet weather. There are, however, good and regular bus services from the bus stations in Petropavlovsk and Yelizovo.

Air transport is far and away the most practical and used form of transport in the country. Internal flights go to Ozernovsky, Palana, Sobolevo, Ossora and Ust-Kamchatsk. Helicopters are widely used for short hops to the more inaccessible places in the mountains and volcanic regions. There are helicopter platforms in Ivashka, Esso and Anavgai. Many of the tour companies automatically use helicopters for quick and easy access to tourist sites.

There is no facility at present for hiring cars or bicycles, but durable, Chinese-made multi-geared mountains bikes can be bought at a reasonable cost, providing an excellent way to travel through some of the most scenic mountain and volcanic terrain in Russia, if not the world. You need to be aware of the necessity of spare parts for damage caused negotiating the pot-holed roads, and waterproof clothing against the unreliability of the weather is a must, no matter what time of year. Biking alone is not recommended.

Good maps are difficult to find outside of Kamchatka, but The Avacha Bay Company (www.avachabay.com) has an excellent map and guide, scale 1:1,000,000. This map is also available in the shops in Petropavlovsk.

Activities Kamchatka is certainly not a destination associated with either a "toes-up" beach resort holiday, or indeed a "culture-vulture" round of museums, art galleries and theatres. But it is a trekker's and mountaineer's paradise. The country's natural scenery of mountains and valleys filled with lakes, rivers and a kaleidoscope of wildflowers can be enjoyed either from the comfort of a car combined with a short day walk, right through to serious mountain climbing. Kluchevskoy, Kamen and Koryaksky volcanoes provide mountaineering challenges while Gorely, Mutnovsky and Avachinsky are quite scaleable for the not-so-tough. For any of these activities, it is essential to have a reliable and experienced guide. All the local travel companies offer trekking and mountaineering.

In recent years, the hugely exciting sports of heliskiing and heliboarding have become very popular in wintertime on Viljuchinsky, Avachinsky, Mutnovsky and Koryaksky. These areas are not far from Petropavlovsk and easily accessible. Because of the temperamental weather conditions, clients are usually warned that during a ten-day trip there may only be four days when heliskiing is possible. It is an expensive sport with prices over £2,000 (approx US$4,000) for a ten-day inclusive trip – but not including flights to Kamchatka. Some downhill skiing has been available since soviet times near Petropavlovsk.

Kamchatka is a mecca for anyone with even the slightest interest in geology. In fact, just being there provides the most wonderful opportunity for learning, first hand, what goes on beneath the Earth's crust. Live volcanoes, spouting geysers, boiling mud, hot springs, lava flows, it is all there to be wondered at and learned about. A trip to Kamchatka would never be complete without a helicopter flight to the Valley of the Geysers or a dip in a hot thermal pool.

For ethnographers, there is the opportunity of meeting the indigenous people of the north. Visiting the Even reindeer herders by helicopter from the town of Esso is a wonderful experience. For the more adventurous and those with plenty of time, there are the Koryak people who live much farther north. Visiting these people involves a flight to Palana on the west coast, from where you can meet both the coastal people who live off the sea, and the reindeer-herding nomads. Christine Dodwell's book *Beyond Siberia* gives wonderful descriptions of these people.

Horse riding is available with day tours around Petropavlovsk lasting 7–8 hours, and longer trips to the hot springs at Timonovskie, about 80 kilometres from Petropavlovsk.

Rafting and canoeing possibilities abound in Kamchatka, although this isn't the Himalaya so don't expect raging Class V rapids. Each river has its range of difficulty according to the international rafting scale; the Avacha and Bistraya rivers near Petropavlovsk are the quickest to get to, while whitewater rafting is available on the Schapina River and the Opala River north of Tolbachik Volcano and in Kronotsky Reserve.

On a rafting trip you will be accompanied by experienced guides, using standard, durable inflatable rafts, some remaining from Soviet times. All rafters are given safety vests and when the water is calm you will be allowed to row, but the rest of the time you simply enjoy the natural beauty around you, or try some fishing. Encounters with bears are frequent, but not dangerous, as they scare easily and run away. Special fish soup called *Ukha* is guaranteed for one of the dinners during a rafting trip. It is cooked over a fire using salmon, potato, spices, water, vodka, and some coals from the fire, the latter added a few minutes before the fish soup is ready.

Hunting, which used to be the lifeblood of the indigenous people as well as the early Russians who peopled the country, is now very difficult because of declining numbers of game species. Spring hunting of bears is now prohibited in order to try and retain the species, but autumn hunting is still possible, both of bears and bighorn sheep, but at prohibitive prices – US$60,000 and upwards. Nevertheless, wealthy foreign hunters consistently flout the regulations devised to protect biodiversity and offer bribes to local firms willing to poach.

Fishing has to be one of the most popular activities in Kamchatka. The abundance of clean, fresh water, regardless of rainfall, and the endless supply of insects hatching all season makes the peninsula one of the world's greatest fishing grounds. Here one may find six species of salmon – Humpy, Dog, Sockeye, King, Silver and Sima, as well as the world's greatest numbers of rainbow trout and char – Rainbow, Stone, Steelhead, Sea Run and Brown. Dry fly fishing is offered on many rivers on both the east and west coasts. Go fly fishing in Kamchatka and you will find yourself in real wilderness; you will most likely see bears as they compete for the fish, and find trout populations in pristine conditions. This is where rainbows developed and where they are perfectly suited to their environment.

WEATHER Kamchatka's climate is hugely variable, with 20 definite climatic zones divided between alpine, coastal and geothermal areas. The greatest variations occur in these latter zones where whole regions may be warmed by geothermal activity.

Northern Kamchatka, which reaches to about 63 degrees North, a few degrees below the Arctic Circle, has recorded winter temperatures as low as -74°C. The Central Valley of the peninsula, sandwiched between two mountain ranges, is much warmer in summer and colder in winter, being snow-covered between October and May with temperatures falling below -30°C. West coast temperatures are always lower than the mean, kept down by the cold Sea of Okhotsk. It is often windy or foggy and subject to heavy snowstorms.

At sea level the mean temperature in July is 12°C but it can reach 20°C. The mean temperature in January is -4°C to -10°C. Rainfall in the Central Valley is less than 400mm, nearly 1,000mm along the west coast, and nearly 2,500mm in the southeast, which is in the path of monsoonal rains. Petropavlovsk has mainly warm summers and cool winters.

The best time to go to Kamchatka is the second part of August and into the middle of September. The weather is mostly fine at this time, it doesn't rain too much and it is not too cold to sleep in tents at night. The trees start turning colour and the cooler conditions keep the mosquitoes at bay. In addition, salmon and caviar are the cheapest at this time, but the down side is the tours are most expensive during this period. However, the growing trend in winter travel keeps tourism ticking over all year.

SAFETY On the whole, Kamchatka is a tolerant, friendly and safe country to visit. Although the crime rate is low, sensible precautions need to be taken. Drunkenness is common at all times of the day, particularly in Petropavlovsk. I do not know of any begging in the streets. Women travellers do not appear to face any particular danger with harassment seeming to be very rare. Nevertheless, one should be careful in crowded places, such as buses and markets. In the resthouses with thermal water swimming pools (in Paratunka and Esso) it's better not to leave valuables at the edge of the pool or in the changing rooms.

HEALTH It is imperative to have travel health insurance for all your stay in Kamchatka. The Health Service is free for locals. For visitors, a trip to a doctor might cost around US$5, and ambulance services are free. However, for more serious illnesses, normally one would pay cash and get a receipt to present to the insurance company. No immunisations are mandatory, but polio, tetanus and hepatitus A are recommended.

Water throughout Kamchatka is pure and can be drunk from taps or streams. Altitude sickness can affect anybody above 2,500 metres. The symptoms are breathlessness, headache, nausea, loss of appetite and quickened heartbeat. Ascend slowly if possible, around 500 metres per day, and drink plenty of fluids (not alcohol). If symptoms persist get down fast – it may become fatal.

Mosquito and insect bites are almost inevitable. They vary from mildly itchy to seriously irritating. The best solution is to avoid being bitten if possible, by using anti-mosquito sprays (DEET), burning mosquito coils at night and covering up. Using a hat with a net provides excellent protection for the head, face and neck. If you cannot avoid being bitten then antihistamine cream and pills are a must.

A small medical kit is advisable: it should contain disposable needles, painkillers, diarrhoea pills, antiseptic spray or wipes and cream, plasters, dressing pads, bandages, tweezers, scissors, insect repellent and antihistamine. All of these items are available in Kamchatka, but foreigners tend not to trust Russian doctors and medicines, so take it all to be on the safe side.

ACCOMMODATION Accommodation in Kamchatka is very variable. There are no good hotels beyond Petropavlovsk, Paratunka and Yelizovo. Even in the capital, what you see is not always what you get. For instance, the Avacha Hotel looks good and is very central, but smoking is allowed in the bedrooms, which makes it almost unbearable for non-smokers. On the other hand, the Peleken B&B, also in Petropavlovsk and situated in a run-down tenement block, looks terrible from the outside but is absolutely lovely inside; the old apartment has been gutted and it is now very attractive within. The Art Hotel in Yelizovo is a small, attractive, medium-priced hotel, serves all meals and is very convenient to the airport and bus station. The most expensive hotel is the Belkamtour in Paratunka at US$500 per night. Other hotels in and around Petropavlovsk vary from US$60–$130 for a double room.

Following is a list of hotels in Petropavlovsk-Kamchatskiy:

Hotel "Idelveis", Pobedy Av., 27, tel: 5-33-24, www.idelveis.ru
Hotel "Avacha", Leningradskaya Str. 61, tel: 11-08-08,
    e-mail: info@avacha-hotel.ru, www.avacha-hotel.ru
Hotel "Petropavlovsk", Karl Marx Av., 31,
    e-mail: travel@petropavlovsk-hotel.ru, www.petropavlovsk-hotel.ru
Hotel "Albatross", Kutuzova Str., 18, tel: 7-68-06
Hotel "Oktyabrskaya", Sovetskaya Str., 51, tel: 11-26-84
Hotel "Rus", Zvezdnaya Str., 11/2, tel: 7-55-15

Homestays are a good alternative to hotels in small settlements of Kamchatka such as Ozernaya, Milkovo, Esso, Kozyrewsk and Palana. Prices vary, but in general they are less expensive than regular hotels. Usually the homestays are called "At Masha's", "At Alina's" and so on, as they are run mostly by women. Some homestays work legally, tourists (or group guides) are given cheques, and taxes are paid from the received money. But mostly homestays are simply the houses of good acquaintances of people working in the tourism industry. Local people usually let tourists stay in one or more rooms of their private house. You can usually count on finding a good homestay just by asking people in the street where it's possible to stay. In the settlements the locals always know exactly where the best homestays are. Some former homestays have gone on to become private hotels (ie the "Paramushir" and "At Alyona's" in Esso).

MEDIA There are three local television channels, one state and two private, and a special time is allocated on the national channel for Kamchatka. There is one state radio channel and three FM radio stations. Local papers and all national papers are available and English language and foreign papers and periodicals are available by subscription.

MONEY As Kamchatka is part of Russia, naturally the rouble is the local currency. The preferred foreign currency is the US dollar, although euros are increasingly popular. Cash can be exchanged only in banks, not in hotels. Travellers' cheques are not accepted anywhere. ATMs are located throughout the capital. They give roubles at the current exchange rate and instructions are given in English, German and French.

A market stall in Petropavlovsk sells everything from tea to rice to tissues.

It is recommended to notify your credit card company before leaving home if you expect to make cash withdrawals. Banks will only allow withdrawals with Visa or Mastercard, not American Express. For cash withdrawals you will need to show your passport. North of Yelizovo you will not find ATMs so you will find it easier to carry most of your cash in notes (well concealed in a money belt).

One can sometimes use credit cards in hotels, but this isn't very reliable. There is always some reason why the system "doesn't work today". (Actually it may not work every other day). Shops take only cash or credit cards of the local banks. Some tourists take credit cards and try to withdraw money in the banks. This works with some but not all European credit cards. The best option is to bring cash in dollars.

ELECTRICITY In common with elsewhere in Russia, Kamchatka uses European-style two-pin plugs for 220v, 50Hz.

COMMUNICATIONS & POST Kamchatka's country code is 007 415. Local phone calls are free from people's homes, but to use a phone booth you will need a card. These cards can be used internationally as well as locally.

Mobile phones work around the capital and in all the settlements in the south of Kamchatka, as well as in Esso, Kozyrewsk, Klyuchi and Palana. Connection is very good in the settlements and within a few kilometres, but the further one walks or drives, the worse the connection becomes and it gradually disappears, to appear again not far from the next settlement.

Internet services are found in most towns of any size, either in cafés, libraries or tour operators' offices. The postal service is very reliable, but it takes from ten days to two weeks to reach Moscow. As for Europe – it could take from two weeks to one month.

TIME & OPENING HOURS Kamchatka is 12 hours ahead of GMT and nine hours ahead of Moscow time. Regular retail opening hours are 9am–5.30pm, Monday to Saturday.

MUSEUMS, SHOPPING & THEATRE   During the past five or six years the museums, supermarkets and tourist shops have improved greatly. There are two museums in Petropavlovsk – the Kamchatka Unified Museum with two branches in Milkovo and Ust-Kamchatsk, and the Museum of Regional Studies. In Yelizovo you will find the Kronotsky Museum. There is also a delightful little ethnic museum in Esso. Most exhibits represent the traditional way of life of the Evens as they are native inhabitants of this area.

Food and supermarkets are widely distributed in both upper and lower Petropavlovsk, stocking most items of food and drink, and some imported items at a price. The local markets in Petropavlovsk and Yelizovo are excellent, stocking most daily necessities including vast stalls of smoked fish and salmon caviar.

The tourist shops are now well stocked with ethnic and other interesting wares. "Kamchatskiy suvenir" (Petropavlovsk-Kamchatskiy, Leninskaya Str. 54 – on the first floor of the Central shopping mall, www.kamchatkayts.ru/09localattractions/02suvenirshop/02.htm) is a good place to start. It has a few branches: "Art saloon" in Elizowo – Zavoiko Str. Market (near the central entrance) and in the Airport Elizowo (near the registration stand).

The Local Museum of Regional studies also houses a good choice of souvenirs and oil paintings for sale. It also has a few branches: Leninskaya Str. 62 (on the first floor of the Central exhibition Centre); Leninskaya Str. 36 (in one of the exhibition halls); Leningradskaya Str. 74 (a small souvenir shop); and Leninskaya Str. 20 (the museum building).

FOOD & DRINK   The food in Petropavlovsk has improved by leaps and bounds in the past five or six years. Mostly the food is Russian or more or less "International" as there is no national Kamchatkan dish, but although fish of all sorts is readily available, oddly enough there is no culture of gourmet fish cooking. In fact, the place is crying out for a really, really good fish restaurant. Beyond Petropavlovsk and environs, the staple diet is still mainly salmon – which sounds good but often is not. Fresh fruit and vegetables are expensive, most of which are imported. Wild mushrooms and berries are available in the outdoor markets in season and almost everyone grows their own soft fruit – raspberries, strawberries, redcurrants, blackcurrants, gooseberries – and vegetables – cabbage, carrots, onions, beetroot, dill, garlic, potatoes – in their dachas during the short summer months.

The drink situation is of course good – or bad – Russian vodka. There are many brands of vodka and advice should be taken when purchasing a bottle as to its quality. Beer, both local and imported, is widely available, but the local beer is very good and very much cheaper than the imported varieties. Georgian wines very seldom reached Kamchatka even in the Soviet times. Mostly wine is brought from Moscow where Moldova wine is bottled. Good wine is also produced and brought to Kamchatka from the southern regions of Russia (Krasnodarskiy krai) and Bulgaria.

RELIGION With the breakdown of Communism, many people have returned to the Russian Orthodox Church. There are two Orthodox churches in Petropavlovsk, and a Women's Monastery has also opened in recent years. A small Orthodox church can be found in every Kamchatka settlement. In Petropavlovsk there is also a Muslim community and they pray not in the mosque, but in the building adjacent to it.

Festivals & Holidays

1 January, New Year's Day
7 January, Russian Orthodox Christmas
14 January, Old New Year's Day (pre-Soviet), but not a public holiday
23 February, Men's Day (formerly Soviet Armed Forces Day)
8 March, Women's Day
1 May, Labour Day
9 May, Victory Day (World War II)
12 June, Independence Day
1 September, First Day of School – Day of Knowledge – but not a public holiday
5 October, Teachers' Day, but not a public holiday
4 November, Day of National Unity or Russia's Day
12 December, Day of the Russian Constitution
25 December, Christmas Day

Recommended Reading

Annenkov, George (aka Yuri or Georges), *People and Portraits: A Tragic Cycle*
(Interlanguage Literary Associates/Raussen/ NY, 1966)
The author was born in Petropavlovsk in 1889. He was a painter, theatre designer and
critic. Lived in exile in Paris until his death in 1970.

Bergman, Sten, *Through Kamchatka by Dog Sled and Skis*
(Curzon Press, 2000, ISBN: 0700711120)
An account by the author, accompanied by his wife, of travel in Kamchatka and their
experiences of local hospitality – an excellent read.

Burnham, John B., *The Rim of Mystery: A Hunter's Wanderings in Unknown Siberian
Asia* (GB Putnams, 1929) A hunter's trip after bighorn sheep in Kamchatka.

Chilton, Johnny, *A Bullet Well Placed: One Hunter's Adventures Around the World*
(Long Beach California Safari Press, 2004, ISBN: 1571573224)
Includes safaris in West Africa, Mongolia, Kamchatka, Alaska and Australia.

Chubb, Oliver E., *KAL Flight 007: The Hidden Story*
(Permanent Press, NY, c.1985, ISBN: 0932966594)
The author pieces together the evidence surrounding an unexplained Korean airliner's
flight and subsequent shooting down over Kamchatka.

Cochrane, John Dundas, *A Pedestrian Journey: Through Russia and Siberian Tartary to
the Frontiers of China, the Frozen Sea and Kamchatka* (London Folio Society)

Crowley, Gordon and Deacon, Les, *In the Wake of Captain Cook – The Life and Times
of Captain Charles Clerke RN 1741–1779* (Richard Kay Publications)

de Lesseps, Jean, *Travels in Kamchatka during the years 1787 and 1788*
(Russia Observed Series 1, Ayer and Co Publishers, 1970, ISBN: 0405030436)

Dodwell, Christina, *Beyond Siberia* (Hodder and Stauton, 1993, ISBN: 0340562730)
Christina Dodwell's immediately post-perestroika, three-month sojourn living with the
reindeer herders and exploring north and south Kamchatka.

J.Webber del.

W.Sharp sc

A WOMAN of KAMTSCHATKA.

Forbes, Natalie, *Reaching Home: Pacific Salmon, Pacific People*
(Alaska Northwest Books, 1994)

Gifford, Bill, *In Search of the First American Explorer* (Harcourt, 2007, ISBN:
0151012180)
A personal approach to the life and exploits of John Ledyard.

Golovnin, Vasilii, *Round the World on the Kamchatka, 1817–1819*, translated by
Ella Lury Wiswell (University Press of Hawaii, 1979, ISBN: 082480640)
The author sails around the world on the sloop Kamchatka partly to report on the
Russia/American Company in the North Pacific.

Grippenreiter, Vadim, *Kamchatka: Land of Fire and Ice* (1992, introduction by Robert
Perkins, published by Laurence King, ISBN: 1856690202)
Wonderful photography, mainly of volcanoes. A very informative introduction.

Grippenreiter, Vadim, *On the Way to Kamchatka's Volcanoes*
(Planeta Publishing House, Moscow) Development in Russia's Far East.

Gyekis, Kerry D., *Trophies* (Authorhouse, 2002, ISBN: 0759689687)

Hulten, Eric, *The Flora of Kamchatka* (Norwegian Academy of Science)

Irimoto, Takashi, *The Eternal Cycle. (Ecology: Worldview and Ritual of the Reindeer
Herders of Northern Kamchatka)*
(National Museum of Ethnology, Osaka, 2004, ISBN: 4901906232)
Explores today's reality for the Koryak people, incorporating a year in their life; their
general lifestyle, death rituals, spiritualism, etc.

Kamchatka Map and Guide (Order through Avacha Bay Co, ISBN: 0906627747)
An excellent large physical map of Kamchatka plus some guiding.

Kendal, Laurel and Bloch, Alexia, *The Museum at the End of the World: Travels in the
Post Soviet Russian Far East*
(Philadelphia: University of Pennsylvania Press, 2004, ISBN: 0-8122-1878-7)
Covers the Jesup Expedition with related material at the back.

Kennan, George, *Tent Life in Siberia*
(first published 1870, Ayer Co. Publications, 1970, ISBN: 0405030371)
A new account of an old undertaking; adventures among the Koryaks and other tribes.

Kirby, Stuart, *The Soviet Far East* (Macmillan, 1971)
An account of one of the most secret, unknown and strategically important regions of
the old Soviet Union.

Krashenninkikov, Stepan, *Explorations of Kamchatka* (Oregon Historical Society, 1972)
The author became Russia's first native botanist, travelling to Kamchatka with Bering
in 1738 and collating valuable information on plants, minerals, mammals, birds and
people.

Krupnik, Igor, *Arctic Adaptations: Native Whalers and Reindeer Herders of Northern
Eurasia*, translated by Marcia Levinson (Hanover/London Dartmouth College, c.1993)
Kamchatka and Chukotka's aboriginal hunters of maritime mammals and reindeer.

Kushnarev, Evgenii, *Bering's Search for the Strait: The first Kamchatka Expedition,
1725–1730* (Oregon Historical Society, 1990, ISBN: 0875952240)
This was the first important scientific naval expedition in Russia. Bering claimed the
existence of a strait between the continents, which was met with doubt in
St Petersburg.

Kushner, Howard I., *Conflict on the Northwest Coast: American/Russian Rivalry in the
Pacific Northwest, 1790–1867* (Greenwood Press, Conn., USA)

Lensen, George Alexander, *Russia's Westward Expansion* (Prentice-Hall, 1964)
Accounts of the Kamchatka rebellion, Bering and Christov's expeditions, and Russian
attempts to industrialize Siberia.

Litvinov, Boris, *Kamchatkski Razboyinik (The Bandit of Kamchatka)*
(Iceni Books, 2002, ISBN: 1587361205)
An attempt to assess the moral and economic chaos of Kamchatka.

Lodyguin, A., Artukhin, Y. and Bykasov, V., *Kamchatka: World of Wild Nature*
(Russian/English, Knigalyub, Avacha Bay Co, 2005, ISBN: 5990030614)

Majors, Harry M. and McCollum, Richard C., *Northwest Discovery (Early Explorations of Kamchatka, Alaska and the Bering Voyages)* (Northwest Press, Seattle, 1983)

Markham, Yevgeni, *Pluto's Chain: Explorations of the Kamchatka-Kuril Volcanic Belt* (University Press of the Pacific, 2005, ISBN: 1410223078)
An exploration of the Kamchatka/Kuril volcanic system with fold-out maps.

McConkey, James, *To a Distant Island* (1984, www.longitudebooks.com)
A transporting tale, noteworthy for its language, of Chekhov's remarkable journey in 1890 from Moscow to Sakhalin Island in Russia's Far East.

McKinney, Robert, *The Kamchatka Incident*
(New York: Dembrer Books, 1985, ISBN: 0934878536)

Moiseev, R.S. and Tokranov, A.M., *Catalogue of Vertebrates of the Kamchatka Peninsula* (text in Russian)

Montague, Fen, *Reeling in Russia*
(New York, St Martin's Press, 1998, ISBN: 0312185952)
An account of the author's 100-day, 7,000-mile journey across Russia with his fly rod, starting at the Solovetsky Islands to Kamchatka for steelhead trout.

Murphy, Robert, *The Haunted Journey: An Account of Vitus Bering's Voyages of Discovery* (Cassell, 1962)
Bering was commissioned by Tsar Peter the Great to explore Eastern Russia. The expedition faced an overland journey of over 6,000 miles (9,600 kilometres) in cold and savage conditions.

National Geographic Magazine, April 1994, Vol 185, No 4, *"Kamchatka: Russia's Land of Fire and Ice"*. Excellent photos and text of up-to-date Kamchatka, including information on the Koryak people.

National Geographic Magazine, August 2001, Vol 200, No 2, *"Russia's Frozen Inferno"*.
A hardy team reveals the explosive peaks and steam-packed glaciers of Kamchatka, land of volcanoes.

A postcard illustration shows a group of Itelmen, of southern Kamchatka, reaping a fine harvest of salmon.

National Geographic Magazine, Feb 2006, Vol 209, No 2, *"Russia's Giant Bears".* After the Soviet Union collapsed, so did the brown bear population of the Kamchatka Peninsula. In this untamed frontier, poaching keeps the bears at risk.

Nechayev, Andrei, *Kamchatka: Hot Land at the Cold Sea* (Logata Press, ISBN: 5900858286)

Newell, Josh, *The Russian Far East* (Daniel and Daniel, ISBN: 1880284758) A highly detailed and scholarly reference guide for conservation and development in Russia's Far East.

Niedieck, Paul, *Cruises in the Bering Sea* (Rowland Ward, 1901) Big game hunting and travel to Kamchatka, bagging bear, bighorn sheep, walrus and sealion.

Russell, Charlie, *Grizzly Heart: Living Without Fear Among the Brown Bears of Kamchatka* (Random House, Canada, ISBN: 0679311955) An account of how the author lived for seven years among the grizzlies of the Kamchatka Peninsula. The book provides reasons for altering our ideas about bears.

Russell, Charlie and Enns, Maureen, *Grizzly Seasons: Life With the Brown Bears of Kamchatka* (Firefly Books, 2003, ISBN: 1552978567) The authors lived in a cabin among the bears for several summers, in an attempt to reintroduce three brown bears found in a Moscow zoo.

Russell, Charlie and Enns, Maureen, *Learning to be Wild* (Arrow, a division of Random House, 2003, ISBN: 0091799821) Raising orphan grizzlies.

Russell, Charles with Enns, Maureen, *Kamchatka* (Trail of the Great Bear Society, Waterton, Canada, 1997) Grizzlies of Kamchatka as seen through the eyes of naturalist, Russell and artist, Enns.

Russia's Far East: A Region at Risk, edited by Judith Thornton and Charles Zeigler (2005, www.longitudebooks.com) Eighteen articles by leading scholars offering a detailed analysis of economic and political conditions since the collapse of the Soviet Union, focusing on the strategic importance of Russia's Far East.

Russia/Kamchatka Business Guide (Business Information Agency, ISBN: 1418721522) Headed "A Land of Beauty, Contrast and Opportunity"! The guide includes all principle sectors, industries, tourism, agriculture, fisheries, etc.

Sautenella, Chris, *Fifty Places to Fly Fish Before You Die!* (ISBN: 1584793562) Meccas of fly fishing from Florida, Cuba and Brazil to the Zhupanova River in Kamchatka.

Steller, Georg, *Steller's History of Kamchatka,* translated by Margritt Engel and Karen Willmore (Originally published 1755, University of Alaska Press, 2003) Detailed descriptions of flora, fauna, geology, geography and peoples of Kamchatka in the 1700s.

Taplin, Mark, *Open Lands: Travels Through Russia's Once Forbidden Places* (1998, www.longitudebooks.com) An information officer in Moscow in 1992, Taplin jumped at the chance to visit regions of Russia previously closed to the West. Includes gulags, Siberia, Vladivostok and Kamchatka.

Turk, Jon, *In the Wake of the Jomun – Stone Age Mariners Voyage Across the North Pacific from Japan to Alaska* (International Marine/McGraw-Hill, 2005, ASBN: 0071449026) Includes the Pacific coast of Kamchatka.

Under Vitus Bering's Command: New Perspectives of the Russian Kamchatka Expeditions, edited by Peter Ulf Moller and Natasha Okhotina Lind (Aarhus University Press, 2003, ISBN: 8772889322)

Vanderlip, Washington and Hulbert, H., *In Search of a Siberian Klondyke: Prospecting in Kamchatka at the Turn of the Century* (Century Co. NY)

Index

Make the most of your journey with ODYSSEY books, guides and maps

The Odyssey imprint ISBN prefix is **978-962-217**

Moscow & St Petersburg, Masha Nordbye, paperback, 3rd ed, -771-0, © 2007

Afghanistan, Bijan Omrani & Matthew Leeming, paperback, Revised 1st ed, -746-8, © 2007

Land of the High Flags, Rosanne Klass, paperback, 1st ed, -786-4, © 2007

Tajikistan, Robert Middleton & Huw Thomas, paperback, 1st ed, -773-4, © 2007

Georgia, Roger Rosen, paperback, 3rd ed, -748-2, © 2004

Silk Road—Xi'an to Kashgar, Judy Bonavia, paperback, 8th ed, -761-1, © 2007

Russia and Asia, Edgar Knobloch, paperback, 1st ed, -785-7, © 2007

Silk Road—Monks, Warriors & Merchants, Luce Boulnois, paperback, Revised 1st ed, -721-5, © 2005

Silk Road Map, Tucker, Stroud & Tozer, 1st ed, -788-8 © 2006

Distributed in the United Kingdom and Europe by:
Cordee Books & Maps
3a De Montfort Street, Leicester, UK, LE1 7HD
Tel: 0116-254-3579   Fax: 0116-247-1176
www.cordee.co.uk

Distributed in the United States of America by:
W.W. Norton & Company, Inc.
500 Fifth Avenue, New York, NY 10110
Tel: 800-233-4830   Fax: 800-458-6515
www.wwnorton.com

For more information, please visit: www.odysseypublications.com

J.Webber del.

The INSIDE of a WINTER H